THE RUSSIAN MIND

THE
RUSSIAN
MIND

Ronald Hingley

THE BODLEY HEAD
LONDON SYDNEY
TORONTO

British Library Cataloguing
in Publication Data
Hingley, Ronald
The Russian mind.
1. Ethnopsychology 2. Social psychology
I. Title
301.1'0947   BF755.R/
ISBN 0-370-10467-6

© Ronald Hingley 1977
Printed in Great Britain for
The Bodley Head Ltd
9 Bow Street London WC2E 7AL
by Redwood Burn Ltd, Trowbridge
set in Monotype Imprint 101
by Gloucester Typesetting Co. Ltd
First published in Great Britain 1978

CONTENTS

PREFACE

It has been a great pleasure to revise, for British publication, a text which is of special concern to me since it draws on nearly four decades of involvement in Russian studies.

The Russian Mind was first published in New York in the autumn of 1977. Since then I have seized the opportunity, while preparing the text for London publication, to undertake a vigorous reappraisal. Although much of this has been stylistic, leaving the sense unchanged, I have eliminated anomalies and inconsistencies that arose at the previous editorial stage. Bibliographers, librarians and interested scholars, if any, may therefore care to note that this present (1978) text is the canonical version.

I am most grateful to the editors of *Soviet Analyst* (London) for kind permission to use, in Chapter Two, certain (considerably modified) material from my article *Kremlinological Inexactitudes*, as published in their vol. I, 12–14, on 3, 17 and 31 August 1972. That publication was in turn by kind permission of *Problems of Communism* (Washington, D.C.), which had brought out the article in its original form in vol. II, no. 2 (March–April 1962) under a title which is not the author's: *That's No Lie, Comrade*.

For much useful help and advice I am also grateful to my colleagues Paul Foote, Jane Grayson, Max Hayward, David Howells, Valerie Jensen, Mary Kendall, Harvey Pitcher and Harry Willetts; to Geoffrey Henny, and to my sons Martin and Andrew; as also for particularly close and skilled editorial help to Jeremy Newton and to my wife.

Transliteration, dating and certain other conventions adopted in the text are as laid down in my *A New Life of Anton Chekhov* (London and New York, 1976), pp. xvii–xix. Consequently authors' names may appear in a different form in the Bibliography (where the title page must be paramount) from that which they have in the text. Hence, for example, 'Tourguéneff' (Bibliography) but 'Turgenev' (text).

RONALD HINGLEY
Frilford,
Abingdon.
1978.

I
Foreground and Background

LIFE-ENHANCERS OR LIFE-DENIERS?

How has Russia most impressed, provoked and fascinated Western Europeans throughout the ages? Partly as a combination of the familiar and the unfamiliar which has been bemusing visitors since they began to discover the country in the sixteenth century.

Early travellers did not know how to interpret so mysterious a people: Muscovites, as they were then commonly known. On the one hand they were European in their complexions, in their general physical type. They were also devout Christians. For such reasons visitors from the West could not easily regard them as orientals or Asians. But were they indeed fellow occidentals? Hardly, for their notables wore flowing Eastern robes; inferiors prostrated themselves bofore superiors in the kowtow; upper-class women were kept in a form of purdah. Then again, there was the vast power—absolute and yet, impossibly, seeming to be constantly on the increase—wielded by the Russian supreme ruler, the autocratic Tsar of Muscovy. That remote, revered, unpredictable potentate treated all his subjects, high and low, as his slaves, disposing of their persons and property as his own. Surrounded by self-abasing minions, he generated an 'off-with-their-heads' atmosphere at once frightening, comic, inscrutable and devious; and could thus easily be confused in the alien mind with a Caliph, Sultan or Grand Cham. Greeks of the classical period had once looked eastward at the Persian Great King in much the same way: awe mingled with amusement at the barbarian's expense, as may be seen in Aristophanes.

To leap from Muscovy across half a millennium to the present-day USSR is to find Russia's authoritarian politics a continued object of fascination to the West. Now organised on principles termed Marxist-Leninist, and constituting the largest ethnic element in a union termed Soviet, the Russians have—according to their official spokesmen—spent the last sixty years pioneering a new, freer, more democratic way of life than that of any other society: one allegedly bound, by a happy dispensation, sooner or later to spread itself over the entire globe in accordance with certain inexorable and scientific laws of historical development. This thesis has found many devoted disciples in the West, though by no means all Western Marxists have accepted it in its most russocentric form. Moreover, a sharply opposed view has also found favour outside the Kremlin's orbit: that Russian totalitarian controls represent a form of slavery more sophisticated and far-reaching than any previously known in history. The obligation placed on USSR-domiciled Russians, together with other Kremlinised and Kremlin-dominated citizens, to affirm enthusiastically from time to time that they are free, happy and fulfilled, is (in this view) a supreme insult added to many injuries—an indignity which even the slaves of Periclean Athens were spared.

Despite the admitted importance of Russian politics, medieval as well as modern, the country's fascination for many Western addicts has derived less from its system of government than from the lure of the quaint, the bizarre, the incongruous. It is in Russian literature that many foreigners have first encountered such features. A policeman is thrown into a river tied to a bear. A civil servant looks in his mirror one morning and discovers that his nose has mysteriously disappeared from his face in the course of the night. A dog solemnly lectures his owner on citizens' rights. A young man takes a general's ear between his teeth, and holds on for several paragraphs while the author of the tale discourses at leisure on the possible causes and implications of this event.

For drawing these first tentative samples of the Russian ethos from literature rather than life no apology is offered, since the activities of the imagination as expressed in belles-lettres can be the most potent illustration possible of a collective national mind. The above samples happen to come from the works of Leo Tolstoy, Gogol, Michael Bulgakov and Dostoyevsky respectively. If one seeks to add further instances of such casual incongruity from life, history and legend, there will be no need to look far. A sixteenth-century Tsar, Ivan the Terrible, is presented with an elephant, and orders the slaughter of the beast for failing to bow to him; yet the same dread monarch is too frightened, too superstitious, to quell the lunatic naked monk who publicly denounces his sovereign as a limb of Satan.[1] Two centuries later the giant Potemkin, favourite of Catherine the Great, takes as his concubine the wife of Prince Dolgoruky, his subordinate general in the Turkish campaign of 1791, and responds to the titled cuckold's protests by hoisting him aloft in the presence of his brother officers, holding him in the air by the sashes of his decorations and giving tongue. 'You bastard!' yells the gargantuan fornicator. 'It was I who gave you and the others these honours. You don't deserve them. You're all a load of crap and I have every right to do what I like with you and yours.'[2] More recently the Tsar-Emperor Nicholas I amiably settles the route of Russia's first major railway, linking St Petersburg and Moscow, by taking a ruler and drawing a line between the two cities on a map: a line which the engineers faithfully follow, down to minor detours accidentally caused at points where the Emperor's fingers had chanced to protrude.[3]

Nor has the twentieth century been immune from similar absurdities, in which obscenity and cruelty have often been prominent. The drunken Rasputin—a major architect of the Empire's downfall, the absurdly rumoured lover of the last reigning Empress—indecently exposes himself in a Moscow restaurant while introducing the company to the only true and legitimate ruler of Russia: his erect penis.[4] A post-revolutionary tyrant, Stalin, rocks with laughter as one of his police chiefs, K. V. Pauker, enlivens a social occasion by imitating the last minutes on earth of Zinovyev: the political rival recently sentenced to death, and thus to judicial assassination, by the dictator himself through the first major Moscow show trial. The doomed Zinovyev is mimicked as calling in vain—even while he is dragged off to be shot—on the name of Jehovah, and as thereby cravenly apostatising with his final breath from his atheist Marxist creed. After nearly choking with laughter at this sally, Stalin soon ensures that its author, the malign Pauker, shall be liquidated in turn.[5] Pauker and Zinovyev were both Jewish, while Stalin was a Georgian; still, where else but on Russian soil would this grotesque pantomime have seemed so much in place?

It must be hastily added that not one of these stories is fully authenticated, while those first invoked come from avowed works of fiction. But of all it may be suggested that, even if they are not true, it would have been necessary to invent them. All convey an

atmosphere which may be provisionally called, in however superficial a sense, Russian; and which, however much the conception
of things Russian may be modified and expanded on later pages,
may at least serve as the starting point for an investigation. For
good or ill, it was the special atmosphere conjured up by such
episodes, true or imaginary, which seized so violently on my youthful imagination as to divert me many years ago from the study of
the Greek and Latin classics to that of Russia, her language, literature and history. What, compared with these intriguing monstrosities, was a mere Gorgon's head or robe of Nessus? And
where, to my adolescent brain, was the attraction of a long-
vanished people dedicated at least in theory to a policy of μηδεν
αγαν ('nothing in excess'), compared to the fascination exercised
by those live heirs of the Scythians who seemed so gloriously to
proclaim and act out the slogan 'everything in excess'?

Having provisionally identified, however superficially, certain
incidents as characteristically Russian, one may now ask what common features they present. Violence at once stands out as a typical
element. Still, many other peoples have been no less violent than
the Russians, and one may seek other ingredients. Suddenness and
unpredictability are among them, as may be further illustrated from
the methods of nineteenth-century criminals in the Siberian city of
Irkutsk. A rich merchant, capped and swaddled in furs, is staggering drunkenly out of some hostelry into the sub-zero temperature
of the main thoroughfare, when he is suddenly lassoed from a
careering troika manned by whooping highwaymen, and towed
helplessly over the ice at high speed to a remote alley where he is
plundered and stripped, and has his throat cut.[6] The victim could
no doubt have been 'mugged' in some more static, less theatrical
style. But that would have spoiled the fun. The dynamism, the
excess of zeal—as typical a feature of the Russian as a total absence
of zeal—are characteristic. How dull and conventional the procedures of a mere Dick Turpin or Procrustes seem by comparison.

Then again, there is that pervasive episode in Russian history:
the mock execution as meted out, for example, to the high-placed
embezzler Baron Shafirov by Peter the Great. Condemned to beheading, the Baron is solemnly led out to die, dutifully lays his
head on the block, and hears the headsman's axe whistle through
the air: to strike the block, not the suddenly pardoned victim.[7]

Similarly, in 1742, under Peter's daughter Elizabeth, the gouty elder statesman Ostermann is first sentenced to be broken on the wheel, then has his penalty commuted to beheading; he too places his head on the block as one executioner clutches him by the hair and another takes a grip on the axe—whereupon the presiding official suddenly flourishes a piece of paper and proclaims that 'God and the Empress have spared your life.'[8] Need one be surprised to find the youthful novelist Dostoyevsky sentenced, a century later, to execution by firing squad at the behest of the Emperor Nicholas I? Here is another carefully stage-managed scene culminating in a preordained last-minute commutation whereby the young man learns, within minutes of expected death by shooting, that he is to suffer Siberian imprisonment and exile in its place: all (another characteristic feature) for the crime of participating in a private political discussion group.[9]

Though these are all examples of mock executions which ended well for the victims, the contrary switch has by no means been excluded. One thinks of those minor NKVD officials who were ordered to confess to invented crimes, thus implicating Zinovyev, Kamenev and their co-defendants in the first great Moscow political show trial. The understanding was that the lives of these false witnesses would be spared. But once sentence of death had been pronounced they had no way of compelling Stalin to keep his side of the bargain, and they were of course duly shot with the others.[10] This too represents a long-standing national tradition: witness, for example, the fate of the seventeenth-century General Shein, as recounted by the German scholar and traveller Olearius. Defeated at Smolensk by the Poles and accused of treachery by his own troops, the general was solemnly requested—by the Patriarch of Moscow among others—to take part in a form of pageant whereby he would first be led out to the chopping block *pour encourager les autres*, but then pardoned at the last moment. In the event, though, everything went according to a second, yet more secret, plan into which Shein had not been initiated: before he could raise his head to protest it was already rolling on the ground.[11]

A similar style has sometimes been cultivated on a collective level, and by no one more than the arch-Russifier Stalin. His defeat of Finland in the Winter War of 1939–40 having led to the release from Finnish custody of numerous Red Army prisoners of war, the dictator paraded these returning warriors in a victory march through Leningrad under banners ('The Fatherland Greets Its Heroes')—straight through the city to railway sidings. Here cattle trucks were ready to transport them to the concentration camps which were the common fate of those Soviet troops who, for whatever reason, had allowed themselves to be captured by the enemy.[12] Similarly, in 1944, an entire small Soviet Caucasian nation—that of the Chechens—was invited to join local troops in celebrating Red Army Day on 23 February: whereupon, at a given signal, these carousing hillsmen—men, women, children, Party members and all—were rounded up at gunpoint and conveyed in Lend-Lease Studebaker trucks to the nearest railhead: a prelude to concentration camp or exile.[13]

Such examples of the sudden switch, the volte-face, figure frequently in Russian myth and folklore, as when the seventeenth-century rebel chief Stenka Razin suddenly decides, in the popular folk song, to hurl his favourite concubine—a captured Persian princess—to drown in the turbulent waves of the Volga. Nor are these folklore examples of the volte-face inevitably in the direction from benevolence to cruelty. In another song the ataman Kudeyar, robber baron and terror of peaceful villagers, is suddenly transformed into Brother Pyaterim, a saintly monk. How like the KGB 'hit man' Captain Nicholas Khokhlov. Sent to Germany in 1954 to murder a prominent *émigré* Russian politician, he laid aside his weapon, resembling a cigarette case and specially designed to fire poisoned bullets, and confronted his prospective victim with something only a shade less daunting: a confession, *à la* Dostoyevsky, of his mission and of his decision not to go through with it.[14] Russian life, lore, art and myth abound in these conversions of plus into minus and vice versa. They are not of course a Russian monopoly, as the biblical transformation of Saul into Paul illustrates; but they seem more prominent and typical in a Russian context than elsewhere.

To seek further clues to the 'Russianness' of such episodes is to be struck by the frequency with which authority is invoked. Where sudden humiliation, cruelty or death are concerned, authority's most natural role is that of dispenser rather than recipient. Ivan the Terrible, Potemkin, Stalin—these figures are not easily seen as victims. But other Russian potentates have been less fortunate. They have included several crowned victims of assassination: Peter III in 1762, Paul I in 1801, Alexander II in 1881, the ex-Emperor Nicholas II in 1918. Another Tsar, Ivan VI, spent over twenty years in solitary confinement from infancy before being stabbed to death on the Empress Catherine's instructions when an abortive attempt was made to free him. And though the supreme dictators of the Soviet period have remained immune, despite an unsuccessful attempt on Lenin's life, their nearest henchmen have not escaped unscathed. Judicially murdered (Zinovyev, Kamenev and so many others), assassinated in emigration (Trotsky) or peacefully—but how suddenly!—deposed (Khrushchev), they have often figured in the kind of volte-face which seems so characteristic of Russian life and fiction.

The religious world, too, seems to provoke certain characteristic responses directed towards deflating or overthrowing divine or clerical authority. Long before the post-1917 revolutionary government began to attack religion systematically, the Russian land-owner had been apt to duck his local priest in the pond to amuse his guests, or even to coop the poor man in a barrel and roll him downhill. Nor were the very symbols of religion immune. There is Dostoyevsky's story, in his *Diary of a Writer* of 1873, of the peasant who privily removed from church his edible pellet, symbolising the Host and issued to him during Communion, placed it on a post and then proceeded to aim a rifle at the Body and Blood of Christ. There are also the same writer's sacrilegious scenes, especially notable in his novel *Devils*. Here a live mouse is surreptitiously introduced into the case containing a holy icon; an aged Bible-seller has pornographic literature inserted in her stock in trade; and a holy man pelts pilgrims with boiled potatoes.

In seeking to understand such episodes rather than to add further examples such as could be supplied indefinitely, one seems to find their essence less and less in factors discussed above: the obsession with authority, the element of volte-face, the suddenness, the violence, the cruelty. None of these, especially the last, can fairly be claimed as a Russian monopoly. No, for the secret surely lies more in the motive, or rather lack of motive, underlying such manifestations. There seems to be no proper proportion between cause and effect in these sudden acts of violence or absurdity. A rational stimulus may be detected when one scans a given episode;

but it seems nothing beside the element of maniac self-assertion expressed in the reaction, whether one thinks of the lassoers of Irkutsk, the princess-drowning Razin, the elephant-slaughtering Tsar or Stalin's acts against the Chechens and his own soldiers. In all these cases there seems to be an intelligible initial impulse: personal gain, bolstering of prestige, maintenance of military discipline and so on. Yet the motive, no sooner discerned, at once seems to disappear owing to the disproportionately exuberant action to which it gives rise.

In other cases the link between stimulus and reaction is even more remote. Why should a young man, piqued to learn that his mother has become the mistress of an abbot, react by taking a tame canary, tying it to a tree and discharging a double-barrelled shotgun at it, as in Dostoyevsky's novel *A Raw Youth*? There is perhaps no point in asking, and in a parallel episode from Dostoyevsky the history of the text shows that its author explicitly desired to mystify the reader, and that any search for a rational explanation is therefore doomed. This is the episode in *Devils* describing Stavrogin's astonishing treatment, in a country town's respectable local club, of a harmless, middle-aged member who is in the habit of remarking in the course of conversation, 'No, sir, you cannot lead *me* by the nose.' Stavrogin suddenly, apropos of nothing, goes up to the man, seizes him by the nose and pulls him a few paces across the floor. This scandal leads to a second and greater scandal, mentioned above, as Stavrogin, called to account by the provincial governor for his nose-pulling prank, makes as if to whisper an explanation in that worthy's ear, but seizes it firmly between his teeth. Why? The author never gives any authoritative explanation, and in any case it is known from his preliminary work on the novel that Stavrogin was explicitly intended to be an enigma. All Dostoyevsky will concede is a teasing comment: 'People said afterwards that, at the actual moment of carrying out the [nose-pulling] operation, he looked rather thoughtful.'[15]

Such actions, inexplicable or disproportionate, exemplify a phenomenon which Russians term *proizvol*, of which no closer translation than 'arbitrariness' suggests itself. Viewed from a safe distance, *proizvol*, as liberally attested in Russian life and letters, helps to explain the special fascination which the Russian mentality has always exercised over the foreigner. He feels plunged into a world more vivid and dramatic than his own: a moral 'no-go area' where normal restraints and conventions do not apply. Here is a people—the relatively hidebound Briton, German or American may be tempted to feel—more vital, more spontaneous, more dynamic than his own, a people liberated from customary taboos. Yet this very consideration raises one of the major paradoxes with which a study of the Russian mentality is beset. Despite all claims to have pioneered new and exciting areas of human behaviour, no feature of the country is more commonly attested by the united witness of its memoir-writers, poets, critics and novelists, and of foreign witnesses too, than boredom.

A succession of identical villages and towns set in an endless featureless plain: such is the picture which witness after witness paints. Fleeing through Russia from Napoleon in 1812, Madame de Staël complains that the houses in the sparse villages are all built to the same model. No less depressed is a visitor of 1839, the Marquis de Custine: depressed by the monotony and gloom of the villages through which he has passed, 'two lines of log cabins placed along a road which seems unnaturally wide'. Every twenty or thirty leagues along the route Custine comes to a town, but he complains that it is always, in effect, the same one. Nor did the Scottish journalist Mackenzie Wallace fare better during his prolonged visit of 1870–5. To him all Russian towns were villages in disguise, with their straight, wide, unpaved or pot-holed surfaces. He speaks of 'an air of solitude and languor', no street lighting, few or no shops. From these criticisms he exempts two cities only, St Petersburg and Odessa—both major ports, and diversified by a large variety of foreign visitors and residents. As for Moscow, the Empire's second city, Mackenzie Wallace was not the only nineteenth-century visitor to disparage that metropolis as a sprawling Russian village writ large. Native witnesses give a similar picture. Chekhov, one of the most reliable, considered all Russian provincial towns to be interchangeable. 'Yekaterinburg is just like Perm or Tula. It's also like Sumy and Gadyach.'[16]

Recent developments have tended to replace one form of monotony with another. Moscow is now anything but an overgrown village. The replacement of mouldering log cabins, there and in the provinces, with rectilinear concrete-and-glass tenements has improved the amenities and raised the level of the skyline—but has also imported a new and not necessarily more pleasing brand of uniformity. It is still the ancient churches rather than the extravagances (most common in Moscow) of wedding-cake architecture from the Stalin period which succeed most effectively in providing visual relief. The same function of diversifying and lending magic to the immense spaciousness of Russia's plains has long been performed by the onion domes of village churches, often visible from afar, often flashing gold in the sunlight. Nor, even when lacking a domed skyline, does the rural scene present the spectacle of monotony unrelieved. There is the variety of central Russia's hills, woods and streams; there are the great prairies in the south; there are Siberia's majestic mountain ranges, lakes and taiga.

That Russia's monotony has never been confined to matters architectural seems the almost united witness of its nineteenth-century novelists, who have collectively exploited picturesque tedium as a fictional theme. One thinks of the 'superfluous men' immortalised by Pushkin and lesser scribes. There is his blasé Eugene Onegin who, tiring of city life, moves to the country only to discover that rural solitude also palls, and after a mere two days. There is Lermontov's Pechorin in *A Hero of Our Time*—a more energetic and enterprising figure than Onegin, but an experimenter with other people's emotions whose boredom and disillusionment can only be relieved by creating synthetic crises in the lives of his mistresses and other associates. Above all there is Oblomov, that supreme emblem of listlessness, hero of the novel of the same name by Goncharov, and renowned as the only, or at least the first, character in fiction to spend roughly a hundred pages getting out of bed. There are also Chekhov's depictions of frustration, of spiritual unease, of inability to come to terms with life.

That these traits by no means disappeared, but rather increased, with the advent of the twentieth century may be shown from a variety of witnesses who include Maurice Paléologue, French ambassador to Russia during the First World War. No society was more prone to ennui than the Russian, he declared. He speaks of indolence, lassitude, torpor, bewilderment; weary gestures; yawns; an extraordinary facility for easily tiring of everything; a horror of solitude; the perpetual exchange of purposeless visits and pointless telephone calls; fantastic immoderation in religious fervour and good works; facile indulgence in morbid imaginings and gloomy presentiments.[17]

To Paléologue's catalogue of depressive attributes may be added the intense gloom which Russian literature has often seemed to generate even in the titles of some well-known works: *Dead Souls*, *Memoirs from the House of the Dead*, and so on. This aspect of the national literary ethos has been caricatured in Stephen Leacock's parody *The Russian Drama: New Style*. Here, in a dimly lit underground lodging in Pinsk with water oozing through the walls, a thief, an imbecile, a homicidal maniac, an 'immoral woman' and a murderer proceed to kill each other or expire by slow stages between gulps of vodka out of dirty glasses, the action terminating with the imbecile giggling over the corpses. 'In other words it's a regular Russian scene.'[18] Leacock's main target is Gorky's doss-house drama *The Lower Depths*, but there are echoes of Dostoyevsky and other authors too. These aspects of Russian literature, its squalor and exotic melancholy, appealed to Western readers of the early twentieth century and were taken to reflect a comparable degree of squalor and melancholy in Russian life. Nor need such an impression be misleading provided that one does not lose sight of Russian life as a complex affair. To concentrate unduly on any specific aspect of it is to distort it.

The same may be said of the allegedly transformed post-revolutionary era when, by contrast, intense optimism ('saying yes to life') has become an article of officially imposed faith for the happy milkmaids and lathe-operators, all wreathed in smiles, who figure in such illustrated magazines as the Moscow-published *Ogonyok*. Do these reflect a genuine collective euphoria? Or is the obligation to pretend that all is for the best in the best of all possible worlds merely another form of regimentation—and not even a modern one, for the milkmaids of Russian eighteenth-century fiction were often depicted in similar idyllic style? One suspects that neither tedium unrelieved nor euphoria unalloyed constitutes the true state of Russian affairs, but an atmosphere in which individuals are still prone to embrace the one or the other more whole-heartedly at any given moment than are the representatives of many other ethnic groups.

So far, then, this argument seems to have contradicted itself. Here, it began, is a people supremely alive, exciting and stimulating because of its penchant for incongruity, its neglect of conventional taboos, its flair for the spectacular unprovoked sally: a race, in other words, of life-enhancers. But here, it added in the next breath, is a nation supremely dull and drab, sunk in torpor, apathy, boredom and gloom: a breed, rather, of life-deniers. Manics? Or depressives? Perhaps this very contradiction between total inactivity and excess of activity may provide the first clue to the Russian mind. The second element may less contradict the first than complement it. These slaughtered elephants, bitten ears, massacred canaries—may they not be, in essence, a protest against a background of ineffable tedium? If so, it might be correct to invoke, as an explanation of the Russian mind, the immortal words of Herzen: 'The stifling emptiness and dumbness of Russian life, curiously combined with its vitality and rumbustious character, provoke all sorts of crackpot outbursts in our midst.'[19]

Herzen's formula has the advantage of seeming to explain all the problems so far propounded: of seeming to explain rather than of fully explaining. The present investigation is only just beginning, and it is too early to announce, at the end of the first chapter, any triumphant solution to a problem of such complexity. Crackpot outbursts punctuating periods of trancelike torpor—these may seem typical of the Russian, but are only one facet of the problem. Other very different, no less typical-seeming phenomena will be encountered, such as the following, in which the elements of sudden violence are wholly absent. 'A man falls in love with a married woman, and they part and meet, and in the end are left talking about their position and by what means they can be free from "this intolerable bondage". "How? How?" he asked, clutching his head.' Such is Virginia Woolf's account of Chekhov's story *A Lady with a Dog*, of which she speaks as arousing her bewilderment. 'What is the point of it, and why does he make a story out of it?'[20] Perhaps the very pointlessness *is* the point. The story has one factor in common with the 'crackpot outbursts' invoked above: an element of seeming irrationality. But might it not be unwise to make too much of the irrationality and of the tendency towards apparent mental imbalance which can so easily be read into Russians by non-Russians, especially if interpretations are based too exclusively on literary sources?

There are times when it may be salutary to remember the words of an English reviewer, Gerald Gould, writing in the *New States-man* of 8 April 1916. 'My Russian friends are without exception perfectly sane; yet almost all the Russians I read about in books are mad as hatters.'[21]

PROBLEMS OF PERSPECTIVE

The present study is the latest in a long series of attempts by non-Russians to investigate the Russian mentality. They go back to the early sixteenth century and to the first systematic account of the country by a visitor from Central or Western Europe, Baron Sigismund von Herberstein.

After twice serving, in 1517 and 1526, as the Holy Roman Emperor's ambassador to Muscovy, the usual name for Russia at the time, Herberstein returned home to publish his description of this realm not long emerged from the quarantine of Mongol-Tatar overlordship. Since then literally thousands of accounts of Russia, brief or voluminous, have been contributed by European, American and other travellers, explorers, diplomats, businessmen, doctors, spies, soldiers, journalists, scholars and others, among whom many a wise man and many a talented eccentric has been numbered along with the inevitable bores and repeaters of platitudes. Russophobes have portrayed the Russian as a devil incarnate; Russophiles have idealised him; Russia-fanciers have patronised him as a 'holy fool' or saintly buffoon. Fortunately, though, there have been other, subtler observers who have discerned Russians as a manifestation far more complex.

Many foreign commentators have sought to analyse or explain Russian thought processes. Yet the enigma of the Russian mind seems to retain its secrets to this day. Still, four and a half centuries after Herberstein, the world's thirst for insights remains unslaked. Nor will the present study triumphantly unwrap some oracular riddle from its enveloping enigma and present it neatly solved in a brief, crisp, unambiguous formula. It is, however, hoped that readers may begin to find Russian behaviour, often so baffling to the outside observer, considerably less puzzling than it may previously have appeared.

To inquire into a people's mentality is to accept a challenge. Here is a collection of so many million human beings whose ways of thinking, past and present, must be ransacked for common denominators simultaneously typifying them while differentiating them from the rest of mankind, dead or alive. In an inquiry so broad, a knowledge of the country, a command of source materials, and a grasp of statistics, literature, history and thought are essential; but they are not enough. A study such as this must, in the last analysis, be a somewhat impressionistic personal statement. It must depend a great deal on 'hunches'—a consideration which imposes on the investigator the duty to cultivate modesty and caution, yet not to the extent of being deterred from stating the truth as he sees it.

While delving into the complexities of a single national psyche the investigator must also remember the wider picture. It has, accordingly, been helpful to forget from time to time that I happen to be an English student of Russia, and to think of the many studies, outside the Russian-English sphere, of one nationality contributed by the representative of another. They all tend to possess a particularly significant feature: the emphasis which the alien observer is apt to place on the uniquely paradoxical and self-contradictory nature of the national mentality under review. No one, perhaps, could be further removed from myself in background and outlook than a Spanish duke. And few peoples seem to resemble the Russians less than the Dutch. Yet here is the Spanish Duke de Baena's excellent study *The Dutch Puzzle* (1975) making the following points about a nation which has been the object of his profound scrutiny as ambassador to their country: 'Never in my long and adventurous life have I known a people so riddled with paradoxes as the Dutch.' The Dutch are, according to the Duke, 'passionately fond of freedom and equally servile to convention . . . tender and sentimental in [their] feelings, and also rude in [their] . . . manners; . . . both tolerant and fanatic . . . both grand and petty . . . excessively cautious and madly indiscreet . . . strongly materialistic and extremely religious, both sensuous and puritanical.'[1]

It chances, as will emerge from the material below, that every word in this summary of the Spaniard's assessment of the Dutch closely echoes my own assessment of the Russians. Can it then be human nature in general rather than Russian or Dutch, Spanish or English nature which is so riddled with incongruities? Can it, even, be human nature in general which the representative of Nationality

A tends, unconsciously, to have in mind when he thinks that he is focusing his gaze exclusively on Nationality B? This is a useful consideration to keep in mind. I have accordingly attempted, when examining Russia's many paradoxes, to consider whenever possible whether they may not be universally human rather than exclusively national. Still, one does acquire a certain patriotism by adoption about the object of one's most extensive observations. Though I can concede that the stolidity so misleadingly projected in Amsterdam or The Hague is a mirage, I still find it hard to believe in my heart that the Duke de Baena's Dutchmen can compete with my Russians in the generation of paradoxes.

Another difficulty presented by the investigation of a national mind is that which confronts an inquirer whose philosophical approach is as unfashionably individualist as mine happens to be: one whose natural instinct is never to find his own or anyone else's chief significance in his function as the representative of some class, income group, colour, race, creed or other category, including that of nationality. 'My attitude as a housewife, teenager, window-cleaner, ordinary this, average that . . .': such self-categorisation, frequently accompanied by the smirk of the inverted snob and encouraged nowadays by the pomposities of the media, seems to be increasing. This is regrettable, since to think of oneself as a status-geared unit typical of other, identical units, is to take a significant step towards adopting the mentality of a slave, cipher or automaton.

Fortunately contrary currents may also be observed, suggesting that typicality is not universally accepted as admirable. Such a disparaging streak may be traced in the language of insult. 'How typical of a man; how like a woman; I know your sort; I've met your kind before': the use of such formulas in an angry or disparaging sense is encouraging. It shows that ordinariness, averageness and typicality, though by no means necessarily disgraceful characteristics, need not always be automatically invoked as causes for complacency and self-congratulation. The existence of this disparaging attitude towards group allegiances suggests that there is no harm in having a collective phenomenon like the Russian mind examined from an avowedly non-collectivist viewpoint. There may, on the contrary, be considerable stimulus in surveying from such an angle a culture's characteristic structure of mental grooves,

(23)

verbal patterns, conventional responses—its thought formulas, its facial and other gesticulations, its unconscious taboos. These features owe part of their fascination to the potential danger which they represent; for what can pose a greater threat than the consolidated prejudices of 'ordinary people', especially if harnessed by political manipulators and officious do-gooders? Nor are such manifestations necessarily a less valuable or absorbing subject for study simply because they are less admirable and striking than are the achievements of remarkable individuals in overcoming their own national or other group limitations.

Great minds, whether they operate on Russian, American, British or any other soil, are surely far from 'thinking alike', as the proverb mistakenly claims. On the contrary, they are exceedingly prone to think unalike. It is, rather, minds of smaller calibre which incline to mimesis, conformism and taboo-acceptance. To study a nation's psychology is, therefore, in a sense to study its clichés, its conventions, its inhibitions—to wander along the beaten tracks of the foothills rather than to scale the heights. But the heights, too, are part of the landscape. It has not been found possible to calculate Russian intellectual common denominators without taking frequent sightings from the peaks and trig points represented by the country's many creative nonconformists—by such men as Pushkin, who ignored; Chekhov, who rejected; Dostoyevsky, who carried to extremes, and thereby transcended, the national norm. Nor will it be forgotten that an ability to rise superior to collective limitations is no monopoly of exceptionally gifted individuals. Many a more modestly endowed Russian has achieved such freedom of spirit, as any sensitive person who knows the country will confirm. Moreover, even the dullest conformists have an importance which one would be foolish to deny; they contribute to a society, for good or ill, that element of cohesiveness and stability without which there might not be any Russian or other collective mind to analyse. A community consisting solely of individualists is, happily, never likely to arise; but may heaven preserve mankind from a society which entirely lacks them.

There are those who believe the investigation of national characteristics to be mischievous and foredoomed, since it must inevitably become bogged down in vague generalisations which can neither be proved nor disproved, and which may turn out both misleading and offensive to the nation concerned. Much respecting this objection, I have tried to meet it in two ways. First, this study has been made as concrete and precise as possible, rather than abstract and portentous. Secondly, an attempt has been made to observe one simple rule of etiquette which should arguably be accepted as a cardinal element in civilised behaviour in any context: never to assume in advance that an unknown citizen of Russia or any other country will necessarily exhibit even a single characteristic, however minor, from among any amalgam which may be claimed as typical of the group as a whole.

To turn from the general to the particular difficulties of the subject is to be faced by the need to distinguish between the overlapping concepts of Russian and Soviet. The nationality which dominated the Tsardom of Muscovy, and later the huge, multinational Russian Empire, was transformed, in the years 1917–22, into the leading partner in the allegedly federal and to some extent notionally denationalised USSR. At the same time the Russian words for *Russia* and *Russian* were officially discouraged as smacking of the previous regime. That policy has long been abandoned, and national pride has been admitted, since the mid-1930s, as a legitimate and indeed obligatory element in the liturgy of institutionalised Soviet Russian self-praise. At the same time the official claim is also made that a new and superior psychological type—Soviet Man—has been evolved in the USSR. How much weight can be attached to this claim? To what extent is there a Soviet as opposed to a Russian mentality? These are some of the many problems on which glosses will be offered here. But a decision has been taken not to give undue prominence, in this survey of Russian attitudes throughout the ages, to the Soviet period. Postrevolutionary features will indeed be considered below in some detail. But they will not dominate a review which ranges through the centuries with a tendency to find the last six decades of the Empire (1855–1917) the richest source of inspiration.

Another difficulty is to decide precisely who the Russians are. In so far as they have a national territory it is now that of the Russian Soviet Federated Socialist Republic (RSFSR). This is the largest by far of the fifteen Union Republics into which the USSR is divided—so large, indeed, that it spans the entire six-thousand-mile stretch from Smolensk to Vladivostok. But many non-Russians inhabit this territory too, some of them in Autonomous Republics of their own. Russians also abound as sizeable minorities in the other fourteen Union Republics: the Ukraine, Belorussia, Moldavia, those of the Caucasus and Central Asia, and the formerly independent Baltic states. There are also Russian *émigrés*, millions of whom have enlivened the non-Russian scene in both hemispheres, and many of whom were originally refugees from the 1917 Bolshevik Revolution or the Second World War. Though they and their descendants have become increasingly assimilated in their countries of domicile, not a few still consider themselves Russian, and their mentality cannot be left out of account.

Such are some of the difficulties of defining the subject in the present century. To them must be added the complexities of the nation's evolution during an entire millennium. Should this investigation be taken back to AD 862—in which year, according to tradition, the Russian state was originally founded? How much attention is to be given to Kievan Russia: the first East Slav state, a loose confederation of competing principalities which was converted to Christianity in the late tenth century, and which flourished considerably before subsiding into insignificance and being finally destroyed by Tatar invaders in 1240? The subject is tempting, if only for some of the material in the early chronicles. There is the original invitation extended, according to legend, by the East Slav ancestors of the Russians to the Viking chieftains and raiders known as Varangians: 'Our land is large and there is no order in it —come and rule over us.' This probably apocryphal episode was to be invested by nineteenth-century Slavophile philosophers with symbolic significance based on the alleged voluntary as opposed to compulsory symbiosis of Russian rulers and Russian ruled throughout the ages.[2] Such speculations may safely be ignored, but there yet remains a kernel of symbolic truth in the story of the invitation extended to the Varangians. Russia indeed is large, far larger now than in Varangian times. Moreover, as will be noted, there has always been a tendency for lack of order to require correction by the imposition of excess of order, and often through the importation of non-Russian rulers, of whom—from the Varangians through the Mongol Khans and the German Catherine the Great to the Georgian Stalin—Russia's history has known not a few.

Despite such elements of continuity, there are reasons why Kievan Russia will not loom large in this investigation. Having a civilisation advanced by the standards of its own day and possessing intricate dynastic links with many another medieval kingdom, the Kievan state was less differentiated from contemporary Western European society than Russia has ever been since. Another consideration is that Kiev was not only the cultural, national and institutional ancestor of Russia herself, but also of two other important East Slav peoples: the Ukrainian and the Belorussian. Leaving the three nations to argue about which of them is the true heir of Kiev, the present investigation will concentrate on more recent times, only noting in passing that the strict differentiation of the three East Slav peoples is a twentieth-century phenomenon. Before 1917 the term *Russian* tended—decreasingly and despite growing nationalist objection—to cover all three, with 'Great Russian' as a semi-specialist term used, in contexts where it was necessary to distinguish what are now called 'Russians' from the Ukrainians (then officially called 'Little Russians') and the Belorussians.

The decline of Kiev in the twelfth and thirteenth centuries was accompanied by Russian colonisation of a forested mesopotamia to the north-east, in what is now central Russia. The earlier Finnic settlers were gradually ousted or assimilated as the small fortified settlement of Moscow, first mentioned in the Russian chronicles under the year 1147, gradually became a minor and then a major principality. Here, far more than in Kiev, one seems to recognise the cradle of the Great Russian people, whose physical features tend to include the high cheekbones and slanted eyes associated with the Finns—a characteristic not inherited by the Ukrainians and Belorussians. It also happens that the Great Russian people was, while yet in early process of formation, almost strangled at birth through the first and greatest of many major disasters. The invasion by Mongol-ruled Tatar cavalry hordes in and around the year 1240 devastated the country and subjected it to overlordship until roughly 1480, the year in which Muscovy is traditionally regarded as having ceased to pay tribute to the Tatars. To compute the effects of the Tatar Yoke on the Russian mentality, and with special reference to the key theme of Russian attitudes to authority, is another complex problem which must be faced later. For the moment it is important to note that the Russia with which this study is chiefly concerned is that which developed after the collapse of Tatar overlordship at the end of the fifteenth century: first as Muscovy; then, from 1721, as the Russian Empire; and later, from 1917, as the predominant Russian component of a new revolutionary state.

Though Muscovy threw off Tatar dependency in about 1480 and went on to the offensive in the following century, itself conquering many of the lands of its former masters, the peril had by no means been liquidated. Centuries of harassment by slave-trapping Tatar raiders and freebooters were to follow, an ordeal which only ended with the conquest of the Crimea under Catherine the Great in the late eighteenth century. The Tatars were, accordingly, the scourge of Russia from roughly 1240 to roughly 1783—more than half a millennium. The need to maintain a large standing army and a fortified line of outposts against Tatar marauders placed an excessive strain on Russia over many centuries, especially as the country was also exposed to other foreign enemies. Wars on and for her western frontiers, notably against the Poles and Swedes, were frequent from the sixteenth to the eighteenth century. More recently a series of major collisions of increasing severity—the Napoleonic invasion of 1812, the Great War of 1914–18, the Second World War—have helped to ensure for Russia an experience of mass suffering more extensive than any other large modern occidental or partly occidental state has experienced—so extensive as to create yet another barrier to the understanding of Russians by non-Russians. Russians make the most of this, seeking to enlist visitors' sympathy, not to mention negotiating and propaganda advantages, by retailing German atrocities committed between 1941 and 1945. No attempt will be made to minimise these, or the Russian losses in the First and Second World Wars; but it must also be pointed out that the ordeals imposed on Russia by foreign enemies have not fallen far short of those imposed on Russia by her own rulers; or, for that matter, on occupied foreign countries by Russian invaders. Of Russia's tyrants Joseph Stalin has been the most destructive, largely through casualties inflicted by concentration camp conditions, which led to many million fatalities. But Ivan the Terrible (ruled 1547–84) rivals Stalin in the percentage of the then much smaller Russian population which he liquidated. Ivan even

outdid the Georgian dictator in the element of apparent irrationality underlying the massacre of his subjects. Nor do these two
names exhaust the tally of Russia's despots, among whom Ivan the
Great in the late fifteenth and Peter the Great in the early eighteenth
century were outstandingly ruthless; but they appear to have concentrated more effectively on confining the slaughter of their subjects to contexts linked with the strengthening of state power.

Though Russia's sufferings owe so much to human agency,
whether foreign or native, they have also derived from environ-
mental factors. The excessively cold climate has captured the
world's imagination since travellers from Elizabethan England reported that a man's spittle was liable to hit the ground as a solid
gob of ice. In Russia the drunk and neglectful are likely to freeze
to death in the streets. But it is not so much the discomforts and
dangers of long, severe winters as the associated poor agricultural
conditions which have made the climate a source of special hardship. Since even the best agricultural land, the Black Earth belt of
central Russia, lies in an area of unfavourable precipitation, har-
vests have tended and still do tend to be sparse and unpredictable.
Terrible famines, in which the food-producing peasant has usually
been the worst sufferer, have punctuated the country's history.
Though the most recent occurred as long ago as 1932–3, agricultural conditions—additionally hampered by the notoriously
inefficient system of collective and state farming forcibly imposed
from 1929—have made it necessary for Russia to buy American
and Canadian wheat extensively in the 1970s. Furthermore, quite
apart from the hardship imposed by famine conditions, Russia's
inability to produce an adequate food surplus has all along hin-
dered the growth of her economy in general—notoriously primitive
until the late nineteenth century, even when compared with that of
some less advanced European states.

Territorial size has conditioned the Russian mentality for many
centuries. Consisting largely of a vast plain with no significant
natural barriers between its western frontiers and the far-distant
mountain ranges of central Siberia, the country has always lacked
defensible frontiers such as might have saved it from becoming
embroiled again and again in so many long, exhausting armed conflicts with its neighbours. Despite a network of navigable rivers, for
centuries the main arteries of communication, immense distances

have rendered travel and transport difficult, slow and hazardous: a further hindrance to the development of the economy and a handicap to effective administration. At the same time the availability of space in the south-east and east has contributed to a nomad psychology in the Russian peasant. Feeling less solidly grounded on his own plot of soil than the traditional peasant of other lands, he has stood poised to uproot himself and seek his fortune in what has been called Russia's Wild East. This had its own dangers and hazards, but was for several centuries relatively free from interference by the increasingly authoritarian central government. Hence the obsession with untrammelled spaciousness which has often been cited as a feature of the Russians. They are said to dislike rooms with low ceilings, and when visiting the city of Oxford they have expressed a preference for the wide-open reaches (small by their own standards) of Port Meadow over the willow-enclosed, claustrophobia-inducing banks of the River Cherwell. This same obsession with space once induced a Russian parish priest—one Father Vasily, a native of the central Russian plain—to complain during a visit to the spectacular Caucasus range that there was 'no scenery' in these parts; to those who found the statement difficult to understand he would explain that the mountains got in the way.[3]

Space and expansiveness provide a key to the Russian character, having played so great a part in the country's evolution. After shaking off Tatar dominion Russia has expanded, as the United States and Canada were later to expand, over an enormous integral territory rich in natural resources. Both territorially and in terms of population increase the expansion rate has been phenomenal over the centuries; the area of the country has swelled about fifty-fold, while the population—by conquest as well as by natural growth—has increased almost as much. As might be expected, the boost in territorial growth preceded the peak demographic explosion. In the century and a half between 1550 and 1700 Muscovy was *annually* adding to her territory an area equal to that of modern Holland.[4] Thereafter territorial expansion proceeded at a much slower rate, a mere fifty per cent having accrued since 1650, unless the 'satellite' states of Eastern Europe may be regarded as part of a greater Russian empire.

During the years of greatest territorial expansion demographic growth was comparatively modest: in the two centuries between

1550 and 1750 the population barely doubled, from roughly eight million to roughly seventeen million. But then it quadrupled in a century, to about 68 million in 1850; doubled again by 1900, to 126 million; and has now, in the 1970s, doubled yet again to over 250 million. The figures reflect expansion by self-colonisation within an integral sovereign territory which has been the largest in the world since 1650. They also help to show how a feeling of space and potential mobility—accompanied, since this is a land of extremes, by the contrary sensation of being hampered, constricted and confined—are so prominent in Russian psychology throughout the ages.

To feel freer, and yet somehow more cramped, than other peoples is one of those Russian characteristics, including not a few other polarised opposites, on which more must be said later in the argument. Fuller treatment will also be given at a later stage to further special features which are now briefly invoked in order to complete this short preliminary review of major factors hampering East–West understanding.

Not least among these factors is Russia's abiding consciousness, surprisingly little modified in recent years, of its backwardness when compared to the advanced nations of the West. Culturally, economically, industrially and above all administratively, owing to the two archaic institutions of serfdom (abolished 1861) and hereditary autocracy (abolished 1917), Russia long lagged behind. Hence the Russian love-hate hysteria about the West and other manifestations seeming to betray an inferiority complex, such as extreme national boastfulness combined with extreme self-deprecation.

Another feature differentiating Russia from the more advanced West is that of class structure and a slow rate of urbanisation. Throughout most of its history Russia has been a predominantly peasant society, so much so that despite intensive industrialisation over three-quarters of a century, the urban population did not begin to preponderate over the rural until about 1960. At the end of the nineteenth century, when Russia's industrial revolution was already well advanced, four-fifths of the population were still registered as peasants, while only thirteen per cent rated as town dwellers. In earlier times the proportion of town dwellers had been negligible: under 4·5 per cent in 1812. Towns were thus a rarity in imperial Russia, and large cities even more of a rarity. At the end of the nineteenth century, when London numbered about 6·5 million and New York about 3·5 million inhabitants, neither of Russia's two largest cities had gone far beyond the million mark.

These two metropolises, Moscow and Leningrad (formerly St Petersburg) occupy a special place in Russian attitudes. In 1897 each was more than twice as large as the nearest Russian rival, the Black Sea port of Odessa, and their character and history were in striking contrast. Moscow was the ancient capital of the Tsars of Muscovy, the stronghold of Russian nationalist feeling and of the Slavophile movement; whereas St Petersburg was the artificial creation of a single potent individual, Peter the Great, set up by a defiant act of will on a remote misty marsh in the north-western corner of his empire as a symbol of his determination to modernise and Europeanise his country. With the restoration of Moscow as the Soviet Russian capital in 1918, and the two renamings of St Petersburg (as Petrograd in 1914, as Leningrad in 1924) the former capital has fallen into second place, but without losing the intense local pride which presumably led Stalin to single out the city for discriminatory persecution outstanding even in an age of general severe oppression.

Another special feature is separate cultural and religious development. Unlike most of Europe, Russia never formed part of the Roman Empire and inherited neither Roman law nor Roman Christianity. Nor did Russia's adoption of Christianity in its Eastern, or Greek, form involve any consequential influence of classical Greek civilisation. Perhaps, as a recent Russian philosopher has splendidly suggested, it would indeed have been desirable for his country's leading minds to have been suckled on Aeschylus rather than on that (ultra-dreary) early Marxist thinker Karl Kautsky.[5] But it was not to be, since Greek civilisation, together with Roman, was to become the creative basis of the West's—not of the East's—cultural heritage, and to play its role in the Renaissance. For that development no parallel is to be found in the evolution of Muscovy, which was still struggling with the Tatar menace in the days of Michelangelo, da Vinci and Erasmus. Nor did Russia ever undergo any phase comparable to Europe's Reformation.

Above all, Russia's development has diverged from that of the West in the evolution of state authority. While authoritarian rule has however unevenly and sporadically, steadily declined in the

West over the centuries, a marked contrary trend is to be observed in Russia from the fifteenth century onwards—and that despite occasional phases, the early reign of Alexander II (from 1855) being the most striking, in which official regimentation was in retreat. The introduction of totalitarian rule under Lenin, and its consolidation under Stalin, did nothing to reverse the trend. Now, after so many years, the country still lacks any tradition of civil liberty, of rule by law binding on rulers as well as ruled. It has never possessed a politically influential upper, middle or any other class; never any powerful corporate body able to exert irresistible pressure on central authority. Thus Russia has presented its sons and daughters with features markedly different from those conditioning their Western brothers and sisters. This remains true however conscious one may be that 'the West' is far indeed from forming any integral entity, and that generalisations such as the above strictly speaking require a host of caveats and reservations which the reader has been spared.

THESIS OR ANTITHESIS?

Since the Russians have already been observed oscillating between the extremes of life-enhancement and life-denial, it will not be surprising if they also exhibit other opposed characteristics. Broad, yet narrow; reckless, yet cautious; tolerant, yet censorious; freedom-loving, yet slavish; independent, docile, tough, malleable, kind, cruel, loving, hating, energetic, lazy, naïve, cynical, polite, rude—they will be found veering in all these directions at some time or other; as what people will not? The Russian speciality is a tendency for a single individual or group to alternate between one extreme position and its opposite; or even, somehow, to occupy two or more mutually exclusive positions simultaneously.

A close examination of some of these pairs of polarised opposites may help to define the conditions in which one extreme rather than the other tends to become operative.

Are Russians energetic or lazy? Abundant evidence can be quoted to show them as both. Where one observer stresses their 'dynamic energy' and 'enthusiasm for work', another says that they cannot bear to exert themselves, and tend to 'be plagued by the curse of laziness'.[1] That 'Soviet Russians have . . . a far greater aversion than Americans to manual labour' is the opinion of an American specialist. A similar view was evidently held by that premier regimenter of Russians, Joseph Stalin; urging his subjects to cultivate 'a businesslike American attitude to work', he pointed out at the same time that mere Russian exuberance was not enough.[2]

That the Russian tends at any moment to be a prodigy of laziness or of energy—that he works, if at all, in spasms of momentary enthusiasm—is a common observation.[3] This pattern is often linked to the peasant psychology of a nation largely consisting until recent years of farm labourers accustomed to toil in a northern latitude where field work is concentrated within a short period, thus demanding greater efforts than milder climes impose. To his brief, violent spurt of annual labour the Russian peasant long ago gave the name *strada* (etymologically, 'suffering'). It is from the *strada*, according to the historian Klyuchevsky, that the people derives its talent for 'short, concentrated bursts of excessive exertion. Hence the routine of brisk, frenzied, effective toil followed by autumn's and winter's enforced idleness. No other nation in Europe can put forward such concentrated spasms of labour as the Russian. Nor, however, shall we find anywhere else in Europe such inexperience of steady, disciplined, evenly deployed work as in this same Russia.'[4]

So much for the national mentality as grounded in pre-revolutionary peasant tradition. But what of the peasant's master? He was easily visualised as a rural Oblomov. Sunk in torpor never relieved by spasms of application, he was apt to begin 'the labours of the day by resuming his seat at the open window and having his Turkish pipe filled and lighted by a boy whose special function is to keep his master's pipes in order'.[5] As for mental work, the Russian intellectual has been censured again and again for his inability to generate the kind of solid, unremitting application which forms the basis of a professional man's activities elsewhere; and for seeking to compensate for this lack of persistence by developing a superficial, frothy brilliance. 'For these people the enthusiasm of the moment is all that counts; they term it inspiration and nothing else matters to them . . . They call work pedantry.'[6]

The active-inactive polarisation has also communicated itself to

Russia's rulers, at least during the monarchic period, when individual autocrats tended to be active or passive—in either case to excess. The egregiously energetic sixteenth-century sovereign Ivan the Terrible was succeeded by that saintly and sluggish nonentity, his son Theodore I. With the Emperor Nicholas I, monster of despotic energy and scourge of early nineteenth-century revolutionaries, may be contrasted his namesake and great-grandson Nicholas II, that pious, unassertive but stubborn mediocrity butchered on Lenin's orders. As for the intervening eighteenth century, this polarising trend affected the Empresses too, 'among whom Catherine the Great was the outstanding trail-blazer, while Catherine I, Anne and . . . Elizabeth belonged rather to the quiescent order of rulers'.[7] Since many sovereigns were non-Russian or barely Russian by descent, here is confirmation of one thesis which seems to suggest itself: that it is not some pervasive gene, but the environment which provokes Russian-type reactions.

To the routine of rustic life as a factor illuminating Russian psychology may be appended, for the sake of the curious, an ingenious rider whereby behaviour patterns are attributed to a single detail in the life cycle of the muzhik ('peasant'). This is the swaddling of babies, a practice of the lower orders rather than the privileged classes, and one still widespread, though now said to be on the decline. Constricted and enshrouded during most of his day, when he can move only his eyes and must bottle up emotions of rage or joy, the mummified infant is periodically unwrapped for a delicious romp during which he can kick his legs about and relish a brief ecstasy or tantrum. Thus, according to the swaddling hypothesis, is the Russian programmed for life to oscillate between emotional extremes. The theory has been argued amusingly and with some scholarly reserve by the anthropologist Geoffrey Gorer; but he has not, unfortunately, proceeded to any systematic global diaperological survey which might conceivably have related the mentality of the Russians to that of other swaddled nations, while distinguishing it from that of the collective unswaddled. Nor has he demonstrated which categories of Russian babies have been swaddled, at what historical periods, and in what parts of the country. For these reasons his study may be accepted as a stimulating speculation which fails to prove its point.[8]

True or false, the swaddling theory emphasises that the drive to express emotions forcibly, while switching rapidly from one surge of feeling to its opposite, is a characteristic of the human infant in general, Russian or non-Russian, rather than of the human adult. Is the adult Russian, then, 'always a great, big grown-up child'?[9] He has been so described by the early twentieth-century British publicist and Russia-fancier Sir Bernard Pares; and one wonders in passing whether Pares's 'ordinary Russian' received a similar impression of his sometimes embarrassing observer. Still, though this witness may exaggerate, his thesis is widely accepted. 'It is in the expression of emotion that the childlike aspect of Russian adult behaviour becomes most apparent,' writes a more recent observer, Harvey Pitcher. 'Russian adults are at liberty to express their feelings in a way that we would find more appropriate and acceptable in the behaviour of a child.'[10] Here again one finds the quintessentially Russian qualities best expressed, as often, by that Russian of Russians, Dostoyevsky. Himself so addicted to strong sensations, at least until his middle forties, that he often seems to have preferred—as he most certainly courted—violent unhappiness to mild happiness, he created in his fiction a gallery of formidable, emotionally oscillating characters whose behaviour patterns, in adulthood, mirror those of children rather than of adults as commonly conceived outside Russia. 'What . . . is the emotional age of a typical character from Dostoyevsky? The parent of young children who is also a reader of his work might be inclined to put it at the two-year-old stage or even at that of the infant in arms.'[11] Such are the torrents of uninhibited emotion, such the love-hate oscillations to which the great novelist's brainchildren are prone. If, as seems possible, his appeal to readers derives partly from skill in causing them to relive the sensations of the cradle, thus performing on themselves a kind of psychoanalytical therapy, there may be a similar explanation for the fascination which the allegedly childlike adult Russians hold, even outside the pages of Russian novels, for the perhaps prematurely senile Western adult.

It is in the context of the capacity—whether or not inspired by intensive harvesting and swaddling routines—to concentrate enthusiasm and superhuman efforts on a limited, selected target, that one special Russian institution, here termed the prestige project, may be understood. Its pioneer was Peter the Great, and the most notable prestige project still remains St Petersburg, now

Leningrad. It was by an assertion of autocratic will that the Great Tsar caused this fine city to be erected from 1703 onwards, contrary to all logic and good sense, on an uninhabited swamp in a disputed corner of his realm. In this, the battle area of a war which he seemed to be losing, he drove to work tens of thousands of conscripted peasants, many of whom perished on the site. An act of grandiose folly? Or of prodigious statecraft? It is still possible to argue either case, and Russians themselves have done so endlessly.

Other prestige projects have included the purely frivolous. Such was the palace of ice erected at the behest of the Empress Anne on the River Neva during a bitter mid-eighteenth-century winter. With its columns of ice, its statues, its balconies, its ingenious lighting effects created by blazing oil, it was over a hundred yards long and contained among other absurdities a life-sized ice elephant mounted by an ice man in Persian dress. The whole folly was designed as the venue for a marriage which the Empress had decided to arrange, to while away the winter's tedium, between two court jesters: a hideous Kalmuck woman and a titled buffoon, one of the many Princes Golitsyn. Bride and groom were locked inside for the night, with sentries posted to prevent escape. 'It says much for their fortitude and ability to take a joke that both survived the nuptial slab.'[12]

Long after this grotesque hymeneal edifice had slumped into the thawing Neva, the same city witnessed another assertion of imperial will. In December 1837 the ornate Winter Palace, which had taken eight years to build from Rastrelli's plans in the previous century, was gutted by fire, whereupon the reigning monarch, Nicholas I, decreed that the structure should be restored in its original form within twelve months. Through haste and severe labour conditions the undertaking caused the high incidence of mortality traditional among workers engaged on a prestige project. But completed on time it was. 'So you see,' a contemporary French visitor was told, 'in your country people spend three years arguing about how to rebuild a village hall, while our Emperor restores the largest palace in the universe in a single year.'[13]

In the twentieth century similar boasts have been made about numerous exercises in ostentation, including some which possess more utility than the prestige project in its purest form—boasts made by Russians, but also by observers as dissimilar (albeit united by a love of sweeping false generalisations) as Bernard Shaw and Adolf Hitler. Stalin had 'solved' Russia's agricultural problem by collectivisation, Shaw incorrectly maintained, adding less misleadingly that the Soviet dictator had been 'founding new cities and colonies in two continents much faster than we can get a private bill through Parliament for a new tramline'. Hitler said that Stalin had constructed railways which were not even on German maps (some were not on Soviet soil either), and with more than Teutonic efficiency, completing these projects while mere Germans would still be arguing about the price of the tickets.[14]

Many of Stalin's prestige projects were architectural. Neglecting basic housing, he poured building resources into the 'wedding cake' monstrosities of his capital city: Moscow State University, the Ukraina Hotel, the Ministry of Foreign Affairs. But his main monument to constructional pretentiousness is Moscow's underground railway, the Metro: a symphony of veined marble, tinted granite, stained glass and glittering mosaics—part folly, part efficient public amenity. Nor did such mixed prestige projects end with Stalin, for they have included the post-Stalinist space programme, which combined technological research with status promotion, and was outstandingly successful until overtaken in both respects by American efforts. At the time, though, Russian achievements in space astonished the world, beginning with the launching of the first sputnik in October 1957 and continuing less than four years later with the first manned orbit of the earth.

Gifted in areas as varied as chess, rocketry and athletics, Russians are often successful when they turn their combined efforts to prestige projects, many of which are functionally effective as well as impressively decorated. One important secondary aim is to capture the imagination of foreign observers in the hope that some may be sufficiently dazzled to overlook the poor living conditions endured by the average citizen; for though the Russian is 'wonderfully sensitive to the seductive influence of grandiose projects', he is not unique in this respect.[15]

Spectacular as Russian prestige undertakings can be, and formidable as is the concentrated energy which they can focus, no one familiar with the country could miss the antithetical and no less characteristic qualities of vagueness, laziness, casualness, and unpunctuality. The usual complaint 'of people who have to work with them is that they are chronically unpunctual, wasteful, careless and so on'.[16] To these defects many Russians will own, sometimes making a virtue of them by contrast with the soulless efficiency of the German, and cheerfully attributing to themselves the quality of *bezalabershchina*, 'sloppiness', of which the prefix means 'lacking', while the root may derive from Latin *elaborare*. The word thus expresses an 'inability to work things through'. Hence Russian strictures on their habit of doing things 'any old way'; hence the insistence on the need 'to get rid of dreaminess and vague ideas . . . devoid of everything but the crackling and smoke of an over-heated imagination'. Referring to the 'utter slovenliness of everyone', the nineteenth-century memoirist and literary censor Alexander Nikitenko adds that 'all our enterprises begin with words and evaporate in words'.[17]

A similar point of view is attributed to Lenin as his thoughts are reconstructed by Alexander Solzhenitsyn. Why, the unhappy Bolshevik leader is made to ask himself, had he been doomed to originate in so uncouth a land? And why had fate hitched him to the 'ramshackle Russian rattletrap', when 'nothing in his character, his will, his inclinations made him kin to that slovenly, slapdash, eternally drunken country?' Lenin knew of nothing more revolting than 'back-slapping Russian hearties, tearful tavern penitents, self-styled geniuses bewailing their ruined lives'.[18]

These harsh judgements of an imaginary Lenin are echoed by the twentieth-century French ambassador to Russia, Maurice Paléologue, when he refers to the fluid, vague and inconsistent character of Russian schemes and notions. 'There is always a lack of co-ordination or continuity somewhere. The relationship between facts and ideas is hazy; calculations are merely approximate and perspectives blurred and uncertain . . . Russians see reality only through a mist of dreams, and never have precise notions of time or space!'[19]

That these remarks are not of universal application is illustrated by the success of so many prestige projects as invoked above: imperial as well as post-imperial and including the Trans-Siberian Railway begun in 1891, together with the hydro-electric stations and nuclear submarines of a later age. These are no ice palaces. Yet, despite so many impressive achievements, precision seems hard to attain, particularly where figures, and dates or other time contexts are involved. The disease has grown more acute since Stalin sought to correct it by issuing detailed economic statistics. Relating to such achievements as the over-fulfilment of work norms and the tonnage of pig-iron produced, they proved on examination to be incantational rather than informative, being virtually uninterpretable except by astrologers.

Wherever the concept of time arises in a Russian context, one seems to feel the presence of an occult force. For the fact that, in 1917, the 'February' Revolution took place in March, and the 'October' Revolution in November, a rational explanation may be found: the thirteen-day lag between the Julian calendar then used in Russia and the Gregorian calendar, used in Western Europe and adopted by Moscow in 1918. Still, the apparent date blur is typical, recalling the complications associated with the year 1700. At that time Russia, far from lagging thirteen days behind most of humanity, was 6,508 years ahead—until Peter the Great readjusted the date with typical decisiveness, happily ignoring contemporary predictions of the imminent end of the world.[20]

Of the many changes since Peter the Great none, perhaps, has been more striking than the inculcation of a sense of time, which the German Russia-watcher Klaus Mehnert believes to have been effected by the Bolsheviks. At the beginning of the twentieth century, according to him, young Russians were hardly aware of time; but they have since become thoroughly sensitised to the chronological dimension. 'For this the Bolshevik training has been less responsible than the facts of life in an industrialised society with its piece-rate wages.' Elsewhere Mehnert refers to the establishment of a feel for time as the field in which the Bolsheviks have attained their greatest success: he calls it a 'profound and apparently permanent transformation'. His opinion commands respect; yet, to the excessively time-geared Westerner, Russia still seems emancipated from the clock, resembling Spain rather than Germany, Britain or America in this respect. Here is one of the country's most attractive features—well evoked in symbolic form, so far as British parallels are concerned, by the observation that it is not the teapot, as in England, but the samovar which rules in Russia.[21]

Is the Russian kind or cruel? Both, naturally; and both, naturally, to excess. 'Of his [the Russian muzhik's] spontaneous kindness towards strangers there are innumerable testimonies,' according to the historian Richard Pipes. There was the peasant habit of bestowing gifts on exiles bound for Siberia, not out of sympathy for their cause or crime but because they were thought unfortunate. 'In the Second World War, Nazi soldiers who had come to conquer and kill met with similar acts of charity once they had been made prisoners.' Even when drunk, Russian peasants only became tender and maudlin instead of fighting and killing each other like drunken Frenchmen; such, at least, was the testimony of a nineteenth-century French nobleman generally considered hostile to the Russians.[22]

Contrary witness—that the Russians, as a people, are exceptionally cruel—is not lacking. In his essay 'On the Russian Peasantry' Gorky has characteristically overstated his case. Published in Berlin in 1922 in the wake of the Civil War, this pamphlet has been suppressed in its country of origin for obvious reasons. Gorky thinks that a 'special sense of cruelty, cold-blooded and seemingly devoted to probing human endurance of pain to the limit' is a quality as distinctive to the Russians as their much-advertised sense of humour is to the English. Drawing on the Civil War for atrocity stories, Gorky claims that Reds and Whites were equally cruel. 'After all, both are Russian . . . I ascribe the cruelties of the Revolution to the exceptional cruelty of the Russian people.'[23]

Here Gorky, carried away by natural revulsion, showed himself poorly attuned to the rhythms of history. That he does not exaggerate the horrors of the Civil War, the well documented record of that conflict confirms. But the unpalatable fact is that non-Russian wars have produced so many atrocities and horrors, both before and after Gorky's day. No one nation can claim any monopoly. One Western observer ascribes Russian cruelty to indifference and lack of imagination, not to the dedicated sadism which Gorky claimed to discern. 'It seems comprehensible that people who pay so little attention to their own physical sufferings should also ignore those of others . . . A good deal of behaviour which, if performed by occidentals, would be deliberate cruelty, should rather be described as indifference when performed by Russians.'[24]

To the Russian capacity for great kindness as well as great cruelty must be added a penchant for exhibiting both characteristics in turn. Such switches can often strike foreigners as dramatic or surprising, owing to the tendency to execute a sudden volte-face. The same point is expressed in different words by the anthropologist Margaret Mead when she writes of the Great Russians that 'in attitudes towards individuals an expectation that friends could behave like enemies was combined with an expectation that this behaviour could also be reversed'.[25] The tendency to oscillate between expressions of good will and hostility, which often alternate with bewildering rapidity, has helped to create that minor yet significant type, the malign buffoon or *faux bonhomme*. Of these Russian literature and life have each provided one outstanding representative in Dostoyevsky's Fyodor Pavlovich Karamazov (of *The Brothers Karamazov*) and in a recently deceased statesman, Nikita Sergeyevich Khrushchev.

Of Khrushchev in his role as a sinister clown it has been well said that Western journalists and politicians were far too ready to praise him as shrewd, jovial, human and candid—even as he was bloodily suppressing the Hungarian uprising of 1956; sabre-rattling during the Suez crisis; manufacturing crises in the Congo and Berlin; indulging in Russian nuclear roulette over Cuba.[26] One still remembers this genial, clubbable, sweating, folksy autocrat as he mocked foreign ambassadors at Moscow receptions; disrupted the United Nations by banging his shoe on the table; and, at home, hobnobbed with norm-exceeding pigmen, his face contorted in a rictus of simulated goodwill. Beloved of foreign journalists because his 'colourful' behaviour made such excellent copy, Nikita Sergeyevich was less popular at home, where his manners were considered compromisingly uncouth; and where his successor, the stolid Brezhnev, has proved in many ways more acceptable.

As for Fyodor Pavlovich Karamazov, that other malign buffoon or treacherous clown, one remembers him best for the scandal which he creates near the beginning of Dostoyevsky's novel, in the monastery where he has agreed to meet his estranged eldest son Dmitry with a view to reconciliation. After crossing himself before the icons with suspect zeal, Fyodor Pavlovich kneels—with a parade of fervour unnerving in the context—in front of the local holy man, Father Zosima, and asks, 'Master, what must I do to inherit eternal life?' Soon the clowning monster is parodying the biblical language in which the monks address each other, and eventually accuses them of hypocrisy and 'attempting to save their souls by living on cabbage'. Then he tells an anecdote, unseemly in these pious surroundings, about a man who was murdered in a brothel and nailed in a box while prostitutes sang comic songs—all this as a prelude to threatening his son Dmitry with a duel instead of extending his fatherly forgiveness, the ostensible purpose of their meeting.[27]

That Russians have the capacity for friendliness and hostility, and both in extreme degree, does not distinguish them from non-Russians so much as the apparent ease with which they can make the transition from one condition to the other. For such 'breadth' of behaviour, alike unusually oscillatory and unusually intense, they are inclined to claim credit with foreigners whenever conversation turns to the problem of comparative national psychology. 'It was an article of faith for the intelligentsia (not entirely unfounded in fact), that the Russian people were endowed with a "broad nature", expansive and generous, a nature which it was impossible to restrict within the narrow confines of legalistic formulae.'[28]

The same generosity of soul was lavishly bestowed by Dostoyevsky on the above-mentioned Dmitry Fyodorovich Karamazov, whose broad Russian nature is emphasised throughout the novel. This 'breadth' includes the elements of recklessness, exuberance, panache, verve, commitment and enthusiasm, as covered by the commonly invoked term *razmakh*, which embraces all the above qualities. From displaying *razmakh*—or 'letting himself go'—the more hidebound foreigner is temperamentally disqualified; or so the Russian will often 'tactfully' imply. Nor, if the same miserable manikin of a foreigner should ever be persuaded to embark on a drinking bout, is he likely to do so with sufficient *élan* to qualify the operation as a sample of *razgul*: a full-blooded orgy *à la russe*. Nor yet will the foreigner be credited with the capacity to appreciate another of these *raz*-prefixed words: *razdolye*, that sense of spaciousness which the Russian feels to be beyond the ken of the inhibited alien. From the special function of the *raz* prefix, suggesting vigorous expansion in all directions, the Russian mentality might be characterised as centrifugal and extrovert by comparison with that of the inward-turned, self-restricting, strait-jacketed, centripetal non-Russian.

Russian generosity of spirit extends, naturally enough, into the financial sphere. The Russian is liable to lend or give away his last rouble, and to borrow someone else's—both with equal unconcern.

(43)

To this must be added a sense of property so alien to the non-Russian mentality that the language does not possess a proper verb for 'to lend' or 'to borrow'; the translation into Russian of such a phrase as Shakespeare's 'neither a borrower nor a lender be' therefore presents linguistic problems. 'A Russian student does not expect to *ask* if he can borrow something—he just takes it. He will go into a friend's room and immediately start rummaging for the cigarettes, whether the other student is there or not.'[29] As for saving money, the notion is incompatible with the Russian's ideal conception of himself, being more suitable to the calculating, despised yet admired German.

In this connection I recall a discussion in which I took part when visiting the country on a journalistic assignment, briefed to discover how the 'ordinary' Russian lives. Striking up a conversation with a well-dressed youngish man in a restaurant, and learning that he was an engineer, I profited by the convention whereby such inquiries are rarely resented in Russia to discover how many roubles a month he earned; and then asked whether he was in the habit of saving. The question aroused mild resentment. Did I take him for a German or an Englishman? The suggestion was insulting. A little later, though, relations having been re-established in accordance with the conventions of volte-face, I asked how much my new friend had paid for the well-cut suit which he was wearing. He named a sum roughly equal to his monthly salary.

'But how could you afford it, Vyacheslav Mikhaylovich?'

'Saved up, of course.'

At this point interrogator and informant remembered the latter's recent denial that a true Russian could demean himself by *saving*, and the conversation dissolved in laughter, having reached one of those cruces where the English, Russian and perhaps other senses of humour coincide. This trivial episode illustrates a tendency of the Russian which must be further examined below: to keep two separate mental account books, the one for ideal, the other for actual transactions.

Apt to see and project his personality in terms of an ideal image, the Russian will emphasise among the traits which he attributes to himself a reckless, devil-may-care attitude. Hence the rejection of saving money as a characteristic unworthy of a full-blooded man. Hence too a style of hospitality which, though it may be kindly intended, is apt to become burdensome; and of which one cannot positively assert that it is in every case inspired by unalloyed benevolence.

In the nineteenth century 'the hospitality of the great Russian houses could probably not be duplicated anywhere else in Europe'; Russian grandees kept open house and consumed more champagne each year than was produced in all the vineyards of France.[30] This was much appreciated by the numerous jesters, buffoons, parasites and hangers-on who attached themselves to these same great houses. But what of guests less willing? Many are the tales of bored country squires who would waylay passing strangers and force food and drink on them, having first immobilised them by removing, for example, a wheel from their tarantass. One such incident, attributed to the year 1871, involved an unwilling guest being kidnapped, incarcerated and plied with food and drink for forty-eight hours by a man whom he had never seen before. In the end the conscripted guest escaped by bribing the servants of his tyrannical—but by now no doubt incapacitated—host. Another sceptical view of Russian hospitality is that of Custine, who reckoned it an excuse for spying on the suspect foreigner. 'They refuse you nothing, but they accompany you everywhere. Politeness is here a surveillance technique.'[31]

That the use of hospitality as a weapon has not died out, many a recent visitor to the country can testify. Genuine kindness may remain the dominant impression, but it is difficult to forget other occasions when 'delegations' to the USSR have been plied with food and drink by all means short of intravenous injection. These operations tend to become competitions in national prestige whereby 'the honest, hearty, all-embracing Russian stomach' is, so to speak, held out for comparison against its 'squeamish and etiolated' non-Russian counterpart.[32] Can it be that to cause a guest to vomit, or to suffer distressing after-effects, qualifies a Russian host for bonus points on some award scheme? There are those among them who seem to confuse hospitality with hospitalisation. To such over-zealous dispensers of good cheer nothing short of their guests' collective expiry through surfeit of alcohol, caviare and sucking pig could, it seems, be accepted as an adequate response. Here, not for the first time, excess of zeal must be recorded as a feature of Russian *mœurs*.

While thus competing with foreigners in a duel by food and drink, the Russian male often seems from his general posture to be confusing ingestive with sexual athleticism. Is the operation sometimes inspired by that classic symptom of insecurity, the need to mount a public demonstration of superior virility? To reflect on this aspect of East–West conviviality is to be reminded of a notable libel impartially directed against the Persian Orient and the Greek Occident in 425 BC through the dialogue of Aristophanes' *Acharnians*.

> ENVOY: Only the greatest gluttons and boozers are proper men, according to the barbarians.
> DIKAIOPOLIS: Now, with us Athenians it's always the buggers and the fornicators.[33]

While admitting excess of Eastern hospitality to be more exceptional than Western sexual misdemeanours, one may yet sympathise with the German woman whose husband has written that 'When we were among Russians she always felt rather ill at ease, because they seemed to expect her to demonstrate openly and enthusiastically the same good fellowship that came naturally to them. If she sat somewhat bewildered and unintentionally stiff in her chair, someone was liable to rush up and ask, "Why don't you like us?"'[34]

Russian recklessness and addiction to extreme sensations find expression in what some have regarded as the nation's chief hobby: the consumption of alcohol. Though hard liquor also plays a prominent part in the routines of many non-Russians dwelling in comparable northern latitudes with their long, harsh winters which must somehow be endured, there does seem to be a special relationship between Russians and alcohol—and that from earliest times. In the tenth century Grand Prince Vladimir of Kiev is said to have rejected Islam as the infant nation's religion on the ground that his fellow countrymen enjoyed drinking and 'couldn't do without it'. Yet it was not until the sixteenth century that Russians learned the craft of distilling spirits—from the Tatars, perhaps the most significant legacy of so many years of Russo-Tatar symbiosis. That the nation as a whole at once took to imbibing with characteristic *razmakh* has been the impression of many a foreign traveller from the early sixteenth century onwards.

'Drinke is their whole desire, the pot is all their pride,
The sobrest head doeth once a day stand needfull of a guide.'

Such is the verdict of the versifying diplomatic secretary George
Turbervile on his visit of 1568. Another English envoy, Giles
Fletcher, who visited the country a few years later, has described a
typical Russian meal as one at which all concerned drink themselves speechless; it was usual for them to get drunk on every day
of the week. The seventeenth-century German scholar and traveller
Olearius calls Russians the tipsiest people in the world, describing
drunkenness as a universal vice to which clergy and laity, men and
women, all ages and stations, were equally prone; they commonly
dropped dead in public from overindulgence.[35]

Early developed, too, were those technical devices, some still
operative, whereby the hospitable Russian ensures that his foreign
guest shall drink himself into insensibility. Herberstein records the
custom whereby each banqueter must invert his goblet over his
head after a toast has been drunk, as proof that every drop has been
drained. But this faint-hearted envoy would contrive to escape. 'I
had no alternative but to assume the appearance of being drunk,
or to say that I was too sleepy to drink any more.'[36] It was to
thwart such evasions that Peter the Great, two centuries later,
introduced his special drinking horn, now exposed to view in the
Moscow Kremlin's Armoury. This vessel was so devised that it
could not be placed on the table without falling over, a safeguard
against any dereliction of duty by the insatiable Tsar-Emperor's
conscripted guests. I once interpreted a long explanation of this dia-
bolical contrivance into English while suffering (the word is not
used lightly) from a hangover induced by the kind of trick which
the vessel so depressingly called to mind: a quintessentially Russian situation.

For centuries what is in effect an official campaign to promote
drunkenness has coincided with an official campaign to eliminate
drunkenness: yet another example of the principle of polarised
opposites. For instance, a ban on the private retailing of vodka and
beer (ineffectual, like most Russian bans) was declared by Tsar
Alexis and the Patriarch of Moscow in 1644;[37] similarly, the sale of
spirits, as prejudicial to martial effectiveness, was prohibited on the
outbreak of war in 1914. In modern times, as the most superficial

reader of the press must be aware, official campaigns against drunkenness succeed each other with monotonous inevitability. On the evils of the 'green snake' (alcohol) the newspapers publish moral tales, often describing the ingenuity with which addicts frustrate attempts to restrict their supply. Some high-minded doctors have even refused treatment to people injured on the roads, on the grounds that their breath smelled of alcohol: an offence so grave, one infers, as to suspend the operation of the Hippocratic Oath.[38]

No statistics are available on the present-day Russian consumption of alcohol, but this may be less impressive than a reading of the press would suggest. In the late nineteenth century, when statistics were available, *per capita* consumption was low compared with that of France, Britain, Germany and Denmark.[39] The point was, and perhaps still is, not so much that the Russian regularly consumes more alcohol than anyone else, as that he tends to proceed, as in other walks of life, in a series of spasms or peristaltic jerks. When he does become drunk he likes to do so wholeheartedly, and he particularly likes—as will be further noted below—to be seen to be drunk. But he may plunge into his intervening bouts of abstinence with equal zeal.

To these attitudes towards drunkenness must be added the high regard, respect, tenderness and even affection with which the average sober Russian seems to regard any intoxicated person. One might suppose that to achieve a condition of alcoholic befuddlement was a feat meritorious, arduous and attainable only after years of apprenticeship. In minor criminal cases, such as assault and 'hooliganism', drunkenness may—though not during one of the successive anti-drunkenness campaigns—be pleaded in mitigation, rather than being considered an aggravation.

A tolerance of alcoholism may perhaps be invoked as a further example of the Russian breadth of mind, especially as the addiction is sometimes implied by Russians to constitute evidence of possessing such virtues as charity, generosity and compassion. This view is linked with another tendency: to depersonalise such concepts as crime and sin, while claiming that a specific criminal or sinner should not be regarded too harshly on the grounds that 'we' are all guilty in some manner deeply felt yet rarely specified. Hence a nineteenth-century Scotsman's comment: 'One constantly meets in Russian society persons who are known to have been guilty of flagrant dishonesty, and we find that men who are themselves honourable enough associate with them on friendly terms.'[40]

Allied with breadth of character and generosity is the acceptance and understanding of others which Russians claim for themselves. In his novel *A Hero of Our Time* Lermontov writes that he 'could not help being struck by the Russian's ability to adjust to the customs of the peoples among whom he happens to live. Whether this quality of mind is deplorable or praiseworthy I don't know; but it does show the Russian's extraordinary adaptability, and a lucid common sense which forgives evil when he sees that it can neither be dispensed with nor eliminated.'[41]

Dostoyevsky makes the same point more forcefully when he claims the Russian as endowed with a unique ability to 'get inside the skin' of foreigners. Whereas, for example, Shakespeare's numerous Italians are all Englishmen in disguise, Pushkin's *Stone Guest*, set in Spain, might be mistaken for the work of a Spaniard were it not for Pushkin's signature. So Dostoyevsky claims; but advances no evidence. He ascribes this adaptability to that special 'universality' and 'omnihumanity' which, he maintains, distinguishes the Russian from the non-Russian.[42] Though this is surely the merest mumbo-jumbo, the Russians may yet be credited, in their foreign contacts, with a degree of flexibility perhaps generated by centuries of experience in managing a multi-national empire. That other peoples may practise different religions, have different complexions and facial appearance, talk a different language—these discoveries surprise, dismay and shock them less than peoples more insular in outlook. Their tolerance has also been traditionally extended to the religious sphere. Early nineteenth-century English Quakers who, when visiting Russia, refused to remove their hats in the presence of the Tsar and even of holy icons, were not ridiculed for these outrages, but treated with great respect; perhaps they were mistaken for the foreign equivalent of that traditional native phenomenon, the *yurodivy*, or 'holy fool'? As was noted by one early nineteenth-century observer, J. G. Kohl, Russian priests were then 'distinguished for their tolerance in religious matters'.[43] In modern times high officials—Party members committed to militant atheism as part of their political philosophy—may speak with affection and respect of the Christian faith practised by their grandmothers.

That the people is comparatively free from malice and vengeful-
ness in relations with its enemies seems confirmed when one contrasts the vindictiveness of a Stalin (no Russian, but a Georgian
reared on the traditions of the blood feud) with the cruelties of
ethnically Russian rulers—far less directed to revenge on individuals against whom a grudge has been harboured over the decades.
Even Ivan the Terrible, who contravened this generalisation, may
have been acting out paranoiac fantasies rather than working off old
scores à la Stalin, when he engineered the painful death of so large
a section of his population. Lack of grudge-bearing, as imputed to
the Russians, receives confirmation from witnesses whose record
exempts them from the charge of Russia-fancying. Speaking of an
'inability to bear malice', Pitcher adds that 'Russians have long
memories of the last war, which is not surprising when one remembers the depth of their suffering, but it is an abstract kind of hatred
seldom extended to flesh and blood Germans.' To this the impas-
sive, by no means vengeful, reaction of the Russian public to a
parade of 55,000 German prisoners through Moscow (in the summer of 1944) bears witness. Mackenzie Wallace, perhaps the most
judicious nineteenth-century foreign observer of Russians, admits
that they can be violent when their patriotic feelings are aroused;
but he also claims that they are, 'individually and as a nation
singularly free from rancour and the spirit of revenge'.[44]
Are the admittedly broad, generous, reckless Russians liable to
lurch into equally extreme narrowness, meanness and calculation?
Naturally this element can be traced too, and it seems particularly
evident where government and administration are concerned,
whether one thinks of the cold and often sadistic practices of a
Nicholas I or Stalin (neither being Russian by descent); or of the
caution and calculation imposed on many of their subjects by the
hosts of bureaucrats who have made the pre-revolutionary term for
official—*chinovnik*—a synonym for petty, officious interference.
The work of Michael Saltykov, Russia's most renowned nineteenth-
century satirist, abounds in such figures, immediately recognised
as lifelike by his many readers. There must evidently be something
small and niggling as well as something broad and impulsive about
the Russian soul if such characters as Plyushkin and Korobochka
(in Gogol's *Dead Souls*) could so readily be accepted as typical. The
same may be said of Chekhov's hidebound schoolmaster Belikov

(the tyrant of a provincial town in the story *A Hard Case*) and of his Sergeant Prishibeyev, from the story of the same name, a prototype of the future concentration camp guard. That these figures also, alas, exemplify a common human type is another consideration which may be worth adding. One thinks, too, of those thin-lipped, self-righteous Soviet matrons who are so often found issuing orders and interfering, Belikov-like and Prishibeyev-like, in the affairs of others. But though such narrowness of spirit as one detects in Russians is not confined to the political sphere, where it looms particularly large, the dominant impression remains that typical Russians err, if at all, rather from excess of generosity or pseudo-generosity than from pettiness of spirit.

II
Communication
Systems

SIGNALLING DEVICES

The working of a mind, whether individual or collective, can only be studied in terms of the signals—words, grunts, gesticulations and so on—which it transmits, and it is therefore necessary to consider the techniques whereby Russians communicate with each other. Do they put out different signals to foreigners? Are there areas in which they communicate with particular freedom? And others in which their lips are sealed? To what distortions, deliberate or otherwise, and in what contexts, are these messages liable?

Personal names are usually the first feature to attract the foreign reader of Russian novels as peculiarly Russian. That every Russian possesses three basic names soon becomes apparent. There is the first name, which it becomes increasingly anachronistic to call 'Christian'; then the patronymic, consisting of the father's first name with an attached suffix (usually *-ovich/-evich* for men, *-ovna/-evna* for women); and finally the surname. Hence such triple combinations as 'Dmitry Pavlovich Karamazov', 'Anna Arkadyevna Karenin', or—by no means unknown—'Ivan Ivanovich Ivanov'. But who are all these Mitenkas, Annushkas, and Vanyas, who are also frequently encountered? Any reader with a talent for elementary code-breaking soon catches on, learning to equate a 'Sasha' with an 'Alexander' or 'Alexandra', and even a 'Dunechka' with an 'Avdotya'; and deducing correctly that these are affectionate ways of referring to someone who may elsewhere figure as an 'Alexander Pavlovich' or an 'Avdotya Romanovna'. The difficulty is not to understand the system, but to retain in one's head the identity of characters of whom there seem to be far more than necessary, and to distinguish in each case the numerous and various names under which they are known.

Of the admissible combinations, that consisting of first name and patronymic is perhaps the most significant. To address someone in this way, for example as 'Ivan Ivanovich', is to achieve an inter-mediate point of cordiality between, on the one hand, the familiar 'Ivan' with its still more familiar derivatives 'Vanya', 'Vanichka', and so on; and, on the other hand, the relatively curt or formal 'Ivanov', 'Comrade Ivanov' and the like.

Much of the interest of Russian name usage lies in such atmo-spheric nuance, but no less in the sheer frequency and persistence with which—even when no third party is present and there can be no question of mistaken identity—two Russians will incessantly address each other as 'Nikolay Gavrilovich', 'Marfa Timofeyevna', 'Antosha', or 'Lizochka', almost as if these were radio call-signs. It is as though each speaker had contracted to confirm the fact of the other's existence in return for a similar courtesy. This habit of repeating an interlocutor's name in dialogue is often considered characteristic American usage: not least in conversation between comparative strangers, who are apt to address each other repeatedly as 'Mr Smith', 'Dr Jones', 'Tom', 'Dick' or 'Mary' in contexts where neither speaker seems in danger of forgetting his identity. In England this custom has tended to be confined to salesmen and others with a professional interest in communication. Such matey-ness is possibly less welcome the more densely populated a country is, belonging properly to the lands of prairie, steppe and other wide open spaces.

Russians and Americans are akin in this usage, then, but the Russian variation places more strain on the memory. To observe decent etiquette with even the most casual Russian acquaintance two names must be retained as well as the surname, since to call a Timofey Matveyevich 'Matvey Timofeyevich' is a grave solecism. It is not enough to know that the same man is surnamed 'Kuzne-tsov' or 'Sidorov'; whereas a Smith, a Jones, a Robinson might work in an English-speaking office all his life without any of his colleagues learning what his father's first name is. But, though Russian usage places a strain on anyone with an extensive acquain-tance, the national mind is conditioned to such special efforts from birth; and necessarily so, since it may be inacceptable for a Russian to write to another Russian unless he knows his addressee's name and patronymic. He may therefore need to send another letter first, to a common acquaintance with a known name and patronymic, in order to obtain the necessary particulars.

That mnemonic feats are expected from readers of Russian novels is notorious. Reviewing Solzhenitsyn's *August 1914* a few years ago, I wrote that I was 'saddened to find myself yet again expected to remember some Zhenya who resurfaces on page 551 after nothing has been heard of her for five hundred pages—expected, moreover, to distinguish her from some equally unremarkable and long-neglected Ksenya.'[1]

Denseness of allusion can be as grave an obstacle as sparseness. In the first thirty-three pages of his novel *Dr Zhivago*, Pasternak introduces no less than thirty-three differently named characters. Nor is perversity over names confined to such technically limited practitioners of the art of prose fiction as these. It is also cultivated by more impressive craftsmen. The first ten lines of Chekhov's story *The Russian Master* name three horses (Count Nulin, Giant and Mayka); an elderly man, old Shelestov; his daughter Masha. Of her we further learn, not only that she was known under the pet names Manya and Manyusya, but also that, when a circus had been in town, she had enjoyed it so much that her family had nicknamed her 'Marie Godefroi' after a celebrated equestrienne of the era. By the twelfth line of the story the reader is already judged fit to meet other characters: Masha's sister Varya, a 'Nikitin', various officers. Nor is this an isolated aberration. Another of Chekhov's finest stories, *A Hard Case*, introduces within a comparably short space a village, Mironositskoye; a village elder, Prokofy; and two hunters: 'Ivan Ivanovich, a veterinary surgeon, and Burkin, a grammar-school teacher'. And was it really necessary for the vet to have 'a rather odd and quite unsuitable surname: Chimsha-Gimalaysky'? At this point the non-Russian reader or critic might dismiss the passage as incompetently written, were he not usually so bemused by the Russian atmosphere as to suspend judgement on the grounds that the sequence must possess incantational or occult significance. But to the Russian, schooled as he is in proper names and their variations, it is all straightforward and acceptable.

Another refinement in the use of names, the atmospheric variations obtainable by change of suffix, is illustrated by Yekaterina (Catherine) Maslov, heroine of Tolstoy's novel *Resurrection*. We learn that the child Yekaterina's domestic status had been ambiguous, neither that of a maid nor that of a daughter; 'so they called her by the half-way name of Katyusha: not Katka or Katenka'.[2]

That Katka is coarser and Katenka more genteel than the intermediate Katyusha, Tolstoy can assume as evident to his Russian
reader. Then again, there is the folksy practice of referring to
someone of mature years or senior status by the (when possible)
abbreviated patronymic alone: for example, as 'Ivanych'. This
implies a peculiarly Russian combination of respect and familiarity,
resembling English use of 'the Gaffer', 'the Boss', 'the Old Boy',
or even 'His Nibs'. Lenin is accordingly referred to in certain contexts (for example, if reported conferring with dear old peasant
women) as 'Ilyich', a locution which carries a strong emotional
charge of respectful affection, whether genuine or simulated for
propaganda purposes. In the case of the grim Stalin, by contrast,
no such cosy, folksy atmosphere could be generated even for propaganda purposes, since his oppressions were even more extensive
and spread over a far longer period than Lenin's. In other words,
no dear old crone is likely to have addressed that feared tyrant with
the semi-playful 'Vissarionych'. Stalin, indeed, even disliked being
called by the relatively neutral 'Joseph Vissarionovich', preferring
the distant 'Comrade Stalin'. As for top men of intermediate status
in propaganda-registered popular affection, Khrushchev figured
most naturally as 'Nikita Sergeyevich', not as the cosy 'Sergeich'.
Brezhnev is a 'Leonid Ilyich'; and for reasons of copyright, as it
were, could not conceivably be referred to by the patronymic
Ilyich alone, since that would be to claim for him parity of status
with the sanctified Lenin.

Children may address adult strangers as *dyadya*, 'uncle', corresponding in context with English 'mister', and as *tyotya*, 'aunt', or,
with the addition of the wheedling suffix *-enka*, as *tyotenka* and
dyadenka. Adults may accost coevals as their little brothers, tending to reserve the no less affectionate 'little mother', 'little father'
for those senior in age. For a man to call his wife *mamasha*,
'mother', as Dymov does in Chekhov's *Butterfly*, is paralleled in
English regional usage. But in Russian a man can call another man
by another variant of the word for mother, *matushka*; for that
matter, he may well call him his 'little pigeon' (*golubchik ty moy*)
without this being interpreted as a form of 'camp' or homosexual
endearment.

The prime function of such locutions is defined by Madame
Jarintzov. Listing certain affectionate and other variants of the

first name Dmitry as 'Mityusha', 'Mityushka', 'Mitik', 'Mitenka', 'Mityunchik' and 'Mityunya', she points out that 'You only have to select this or that ending . . . and your feelings, your attitude at the given moment towards the addressed person is sun-clear!'[3] Here is a significant point: elusive Russians may be in some ways, but in the field of emotional response they are correspondingly anxious to make their feelings, or what they wish to be thought their feelings, abundantly manifest. That a non-Russian might positively prefer, in casual contact with strangers, to keep his emotional responses to himself, to have them fog-blurred rather than sun-clear, they may not understand—for which reason they may feel ill at ease among the restraints of a non-Russian milieu. 'On coming to live here [in England], we [Russians] sometimes feel quite awkward in being spoken to as if we were nonentities, without any names or personalities . . . With us . . . something or other is always there, besprinkling the speech, so that you feel sure that it is you whom the speaker keeps in his mind and not the general public.'[4]

So much for personal names. But what of the stranger whose name is unknown? 'Hey, girl' (*devushka*) or 'Hey, spinster' (*devitsa*) may be used to hail females, while the unknown male is liable to be accosted—especially if he wears sandals or a beard, or is in breach of some other taboo—either as *molodoy chelovek*, 'young fellow', or as *starik*, 'old man'. But why are younger men commonly addressed as *starik*, whereas many a *molodoy chelovek* might easily be, from his appearance, at least an octogenarian? I do not know. Nor, in general, can I explain this insistence on repeating names and labels. Is it a need for repeated assurance that they are heeded and appreciated? Or do they crave something more basic: confirmation that they exist in the fullest ontological sense and possess a discernible identity? Whatever the urge underlying the practice, it seems to minister to some drive from which representatives of many other nationalities are relatively immune.

The desire to repeat proper names may be further stimulated by a craving for stability and the special need for mnemonic aid created by a marked lack of continuity in the designations of persons and places. Was there ever a nation so addicted to changing labels, often suddenly, often for reasons of policy or decorum? That a town called Black Muck (Chornaya Gryaz) should have been renamed as the more ennobling Empressville (Tsaritsyno) is understandable, and might have happened anywhere. Less easily paralleled is the evolution of a similarly named city, Tsaritsyn, which first became Stalingrad for a political reason (Stalinisation) before relapsing, again for a political reason (de-Stalinisation), into the neutral and safer Volgograd, (Volga-town), which it remains at the time of going to press. Similarly, the ancient city of Perm became Molotov in 1940 before reverting to Perm in 1957 with the disgrace of the honorand, Vyacheslav Mikhaylovich Molotov. That he was born a Skryabin and that Stalin, who inspired the now-suspended town names Stalino, Staliniri, Stalinogorsk and many another such as well as Stalingrad, was born a Dzhugashvili: such details further emphasise the mobility of Russian names, both native and colonial.

Then again, the same bridge may be Holy Trinity Bridge, Equality Bridge, and Kirov Bridge in bewilderingly rapid succession.[5] What more natural in a city which has itself progressed from St Petersburg to Petrograd before being named Leningrad—and that after Vladimir Ilyich Ulyanov. As this reminds one, Lenin and other Russian revolutionaries almost all adopted aliases in the pre-1917 period—partly for security, partly as a matter of style. Lenin, Gorky, Trotsky for the original Ulyanov, Peshkov, Bronstein—these are only a few among legion. This practice of name variation makes the reading of a map, gazetteer or telephone directory—assuming such an object to be obtainable—a more difficult operation than it is in countries where the labels are more stable.

To turn from the use of proper names to the use of language in general is to find a similar emphasis on emotional nuances. Like ordinary first names, ordinary nouns tend to possess diminutive and other similar forms, exploiting a wide range of suffixes to express variations of mood: for example, not only *domik*, 'a dear little house', but also *domishche*, 'a bloody great house'. The term *diminutive* is misleading if taken to refer solely to size; rather does its use reflect the speaker's mood. To call someone a *durak*, 'fool', is offensive; but to call him a *durachok*, 'a bit of an ass', can be affectionate. In many cases diminutives are 'really meant to imply smallness', admits the pioneer English grammarian of Russian, Nevill Forbes; but he adds that they are often used 'merely as a means of expressing affection, politeness or good humour, and as such they are difficult, if not impossible, to translate into English'.

Forbes also points out that when a train conductor asks to see your *biletiki*, 'little tickets', this does not imply that the tickets are small, merely that he would not refuse a drink.[6]

As for the ever-sensitive topic of liquor, and also food, the appropriate diminutive is practically compulsory unless the speaker wishes to emphasise that he is out of humour. *Kak nash-chot vodochki?* ('How about a spot of vodka?') The diminutive *vodochka*, rather than the balder *vodka*, is the natural form for a convivial Russian to use. And he will similarly refer to another drink as *chayok* rather than *chay*. *Chayku by mne*, 'I'd like a spot of tea [a "cuppa"].' Similarly, a relaxed Russian will demonstrate the national attitude to time by saying that he will be ready *chasika cherez dva*, 'in a couple of hourlets'.

Emotional flexibility is enhanced by the existence of two forms for 'you' when reference is to only one person. *Ty*, 'thou', is used when addressing intimates, small children, animals, lunatics, drunks and God; *vy*, 'you', is the more formal mode of address, which foreigners are recommended to employ unless they are sure of their ground. One British grammarian of Russian misrepresents usage when he invokes the use of *ty* in converse with servants, peasants and other inferiors as a 'grave social error' in present-day Russia.[7] It is in fact normal in that highly stratified society for an official to address, say, his chauffeur as *ty*, while requiring the respectful *vy* in return. He will happily do so in the presence of foreigners, showing that in this context the preservation of hierarchic differences takes precedence over the contrary urge: to treat, or to pretend to wish to treat, all men as equals. In this matter Russian usage differs from that of French and some of the many other languages which also preserve the distinction between an intimate and a polite form of the second person singular; here of course English, with its single undifferentiated 'you', is the exception among the world's leading tongues, and it is Russian which follows the norm.

Another, more specialised, feature of the language has fascinated non-Russian dabblers in the arcana of linguistics: the so-called aspects, imperfective and perfective, of the verb. For this English and the other major Western languages furnish no close parallel, in that the typical Russian verb has two distinct sets of forms—the aspects, perfective and imperfective—where other tongues tend to have only one. The perfective aspect lays emphasis on the result of an action, the element of achievement; whereas to use the imperfective is to stress the process of the action together with its accompanying emotional resonance. The perfective describes what was done, the imperfective how it felt—which obviously makes the imperfective the more 'Russian' of the two. The point has been made by an English student of the subject and authority on ancient Greek religion, Jane Harrison. In a pamphlet published in 1915, *Russia and the Russian Verb*, she claims that the aspects furnish 'one clue to the reading of the Russian soul'. It is the imperfectiveness, she says, which readers seek and find in the Russian novel, especially in Dostoyevsky, because the imperfective is the aspect of emotion and sympathy. Pointing out that the Russian verb is relatively weak in its tense structure, she relates this deficiency to Russian vagueness about time, whereas 'the Latin languages love order and are precise as to time'.[8] She also disparages a group of people whom she terms 'we': representatives, it seems, of Western, non-Russian civilisation in general. 'We draw sharp lines, we circumscribe, we leave no open field for imagination and sympathy, and here we may well learn from the Russian.' She further adds: 'I want to use these aspects, I long to be able to, I need them, they feed me spiritually.' Here is a case of the transfer of *umileniye*, 'gush', across national barriers, and it may seem heartless or soulless to point out that the statistically scrutinised Russian employs the perfective more commonly than the imperfective: out of every hundred verbs 53·1 per cent of those used in conversation and 57·5 per cent of those used in non-conversation have been recorded as perfective.[9]

A contemporary reviewer of Miss Harrison's work congratulated her on the rich experience awaiting her 'when she arrives at the stage of attempting the translation of a really skilled artificer in imperfective aspects, such as Chekhov'.[10] Though she never seems to have embarked on such self-indulgence, I have myself translated a million-odd words of Chekhov; but without, it now occurs for the first time, consciously considering the problem of aspect. On reflection I feel that Chekhov, like many other Russian authors, makes skilled use of the past tense of the imperfective aspect to describe actions which are conceived as typical or repetitive without the author necessarily committing himself on whether they even took place or not. It is consistent with Miss Harrison's findings to link this usage with that habitual vagueness and imprecision which, in certain contexts, seems typical of the Russian and which can be so stimulating or infuriating. The imperfective can also be regarded as the aspect of the ruled and of the more inactive rulers. That 'most gentle' seventeenth-century Tsar Alexis Mikhaylovich may well have mooned through his reign in an imperfective state of mind. But a Peter the Great and a Stalin were more inclined to employ the perfective, with its emphasis on results. To these social engineers the aspect of emotion, of savouring the process rather than of achieving the goal, was of no interest.

Not that these two rulers left the niceties of Russian usage unaffected. Peter the Great temporarily reduced the language to a 'hideous jargon',[11] through the importation of imperfectly digested Polish, Dutch, English and other loan-words and calques. Stalin, who spoke Russian with a strong Georgian accent all his life, yet developed his own brand of Russian linguistic chauvinism. In his article 'On Marxism and Linguistics' he describes Russian as a victorious language which has always absorbed other tongues, and which is therefore destined to influence the world language of the remote Communist future.[12] Meanwhile this linguistic imperialist was ordering the arrest of anyone ever known to have expressed interest in another candidate world language, Esperanto, though himself once an unsuccessful student of that synthetic tongue.

Since this brief survey of one language, Russian, is written in another, English, it is worth considering claims about the comparative merits of these two major tongues. To Madame Jarintzov Russian is much to be preferred. 'The luxuries of speech which we possess and you don't are so numerous that they overwhelmed me.' That there are many words in English for which Russian has no equivalent she admits, but finds it instructive to consider what these words are. Russian has no word for 'kick', for instance. Nor can something be described as 'shocking' except by use of the obviously borrowed verb *shokirovat*—and this, clearly, because the urbane and supremely tolerant Russian is not subject to the inhibited timidity and shockability of the typical Anglo-Saxon. Still less does the Russian—emancipated, devil-may-care, un-bourgeois, with soul unbuttoned—have a word for 'respectability'. ('We don't need this characteristic, somehow!') To fill the gap another ludi-

(60)

crous borrowing, *respektabelnost*, must be made to serve. Nor, she further points out, does Russian possess native words for 'job', 'business' or 'weekend'.[13]

Fascinating as Madame Jarintzov's arguments are, not least for the grotesque English in which she claims that English is an inferior language, a more authoritative view is that of the *émigré* Russian writer Vladimir Nabokov, who employed both tongues with panache in his novels and other works. Many of his writings are especially instructive through having appeared in both languages in the author's own version. A comparison of parallel English and Russian passages in Nabokov is a rewarding process for the light which it sheds, not only on the author's psychology, but also on the languages, native Russian and adoptive English, which he uses. It may be significant that, after writing his best-selling novel *Lolita* in English, the language in which it was first published, he later rendered it into Russian while expressly confessing, in a postscript, that he considered the English version the better. The exercise of back-translation had convinced him that Russian was a green and immature tongue, whereas English resembled a succulent plum, ripe or over-ripe with the wisdom of the ages. He defined the main advantage of English, over Russian, as its ability to flick at meanings in contexts where the Russian must be painfully explicit.[14] Perhaps. But long experience of the opposite process, that of teaching advanced Russian prose composition, suggests that a richly allusive and intonationally subtle English author—an Anthony Powell, an Evelyn Waugh, a Norman Douglas—can, by dint of hard work and sympathy, eventually be rendered into suitably responsive Russian. As between the opposing views of the two Russians, Jarintzov and Nabokov, I therefore find it hard to adjudicate, and would be more inclined to declare a dead heat.

DISPLAY POSTURES

Does the Russian reveal, as a communicator, the tendency to oscillate between extremes noted above? So it appears from the evidence of many witnesses who portray him in one of two opposed guises: either as a truthful, open, sincere, frank, extrovert, delightfully natural human being; or as an obsessively secretive, devious,

cynical, mendacious creature whose every word must be scrutinised in case it may not even mean the opposite of its purport.
Never, according to one section of the evidence, was there anyone
more delightfully self-revealing and open to inspection. 'It is the
best part of a Russian,' writes a Russian of a former generation,
'that you always know where you are when you have to deal with
him.' 'Russians behave,' writes an Englishman of a later generation,
'so much more openly and naturally than we do.' A second English
witness testifies to the 'natural frankness in the Russian's approach
to his fellow beings', while a third speaks of honesty as a quality
for which the Russians are unmatched by any other nation. A
young American woman loves the Russians' 'incredible lack of
artifice'; a German of more mature years speaks of their 'uninhibited naturalness and candour'.[1]

Contrasting such testimony with the enigmatic qualities which
others (including Winston Churchill) have attributed to the Russian, a hypothesis suggests itself. Can it be that the Russian's
secretiveness is confined to the mundane world of fact, which he
finds boring and fundamentally unreal; whereas, where emotion—
the true stuff of life—is concerned, he delights in communicating
his reactions? Should a foreigner stop him in Moscow's Gorky
Street and ask the way to Red Square, he might (according to an
extrapolation of this hypothesis) refuse to disclose the information
as belonging to the world of fact and therefore lacking significance.
Yet he might immediately explain that the inquirer resembled his
deceased father, son, brother, aunt or mother-in-law whom he
loved or hated under circumstances which he will readily detail.
Such a theory would explain the psychological impasse which often
exists between a Russian and a Western citizen, since the latter
tends to be more at home exchanging information than emotional
responses, at least with comparative strangers. It is not, according
to this theory, that the Russian is more or less communicative than
the non-Russian; but that the areas within which these qualities
are displayed tend to be mutually exclusive.

This hypothesis would also help to explain the frequent claims
made by and on behalf of Russians that they are peculiarly spontaneous, 'warm', natural, sincere. On first meeting someone, 'we
frequently burst out with something . . . omitting even the word
of greeting', writes a Russian, also claiming credit for an unusual

capacity to become intimate with strangers. 'How often we make thorough acquaintance in the course of the first conversation with a stranger who appeals to us, telling and asking each other with equal straightforwardness dozens of things of a personal nature.' The Russian 'allows himself to be openly angry when he feels angry, just as he allows his heart to go out to people when they do appeal to him. We are not capable of concealing fermentation, whether with wrath or exaltation.' Not that Russians wear their hearts on their sleeves; it is just that 'some power, without asking our permission, has concealed little X-ray cameras against our hearts'.[2]

Nowhere is the emphasis on emotion more characteristically displayed than in the genre of the memoir and autobiography, to which Russians have made many outstanding contributions, as well as some on a mediocre level. In such works one may read that 'father positively exuded secretions of sincerity' (*ot ottsa tak i iskhodili flyuidy serdechnosti*). There is often an insistence on the vitality, dynamism and verve of the main characters, and of the world in general: a hearty, all-jolly-Russians-together atmosphere which seems to generate an effect contrary to that apparently intended. 'Life at Skuchishchevo was always a-bubble' (*tak i kipela*); Uncle Gleb 'literally sprayed everyone (*bukvalno opryskival vsekh*) with merry witticisms and lighthearted puns'; Cousin Boris 'simply spluttered with *joie-de-vivre*' (*ot nego tak i pryskalo zhizneradostnostyu*). Such is the common coin of Russian memoirists—that is, if one is unkind enough to pick out some of the more undignified effusions and translate them literally. And what a mood of impending doom or inspissated lugubriousness such heartiness can create in the reader.

These examples have been deliberately chosen as grotesque, and one can go too far in reacting against such exuberance. Nor need too much be made of the references to the soul with which Russian speech abounds. A Russian will address his friend or spouse as 'my soul' (*dusha moya*); or refer to a particularly close friend as *zadushevny*, 'a behind-the-soul one'. One is struck, too, by the concrete images in which the Russian soul can figure. A comic writer can express anguish, whimsically, by saying that 'Cats scratched my soul.' And the Russian frequently refers to himself as wearing his soul, as one may a shirt, 'unbuttoned' (*naraspashku*).

(63)

The Russian soul is no longer the target for indiscriminate admiration which it once was. Nor is the decline surprising: hard statistics show the use of *dusha* to have declined by about fifty per cent since 1918. But the concept was much in vogue in the West during the First World War—the years when an epidemic of cultural Russomania swept the world. During this period an illustrated miscellany of articles, *The Soul of Russia*, was published as a book in London in aid of Russian refugees, and the notion fascinated English critics and writers of the period. While Jane Harrison, as quoted above, was seeking the soul in the aspects of the verb, Virginia Woolf was identifying it as the chief character of Russian fiction: 'this perplexed liquid, this cloudy, yeasty, precious stuff, the soul'. She also says that 'in reading Tchekov we find ourselves repeating the word "soul" again and again. It sprinkles his pages.' Not surprisingly if, as one Russian has it, there is 'a passionate love for the soul of Nature which radiates human warmth and sympathy winding its way through the whole of Russian literature'.[3]

As the last quotation reminds us, the Russian is rarely inhibited by fear that the word *love* may become debased by over-use. 'Russians love to love . . . What a power of loving there is granted to the Slav.'[4] To such claims can be added those of a non-Russian witness: 'Chekhov loved people. He crammed his life with them . . . Wherever he went he knew everybody, talked to everybody, listened to everybody, liked everybody.'[5] Thus reads the introduction to a translation of Chekhov's selected stories into English —a statement which reference to almost any page of the author's correspondence refutes. Chekhov was no misanthrope, lacking any generalised attitude to humanity; but he had a genius for scathing comment on the many individuals who irritated him.

It is well to bear such possibilities in mind since one might otherwise judge the Russians to be all dedicated to the cult of *umileniye*. For this common but notoriously untranslatable word, the dictionaries have 'tenderness', but one is tempted to call it 'gush', 'emotional self-indulgence'. I have also heard it rendered 'the self-congratulatory jactitation of simulated emotion'. That *umileniye*, however defined, indeed is a common feature in their projection of feeling, cannot be denied. But it is not universal. Nothing could be more misleading than to regard all Russians as the emotionally incontinent beings of popular misconception.

They can be as reserved as the most tight-lipped of proverbial Anglo-Saxons, for there is as much scope for variety in Russian as in any other national psychology.

According to Custine, an 'absence of soul' betrays itself in all Russian contexts.[6] It might be hard to substantiate that claim, but one may at least defuse the sentimentality fathered on Chekhov. For instance, the frequent occurrence of the word 'soul' (in the versions of his works presumably read by Virginia Woolf) was due to coarse translation: where Russian *dusha*, conventionally rendered 'soul', is used, some other rendering such as 'heart' is often nearer to English usage. Thus, *ot vsey dushi* usually translates better as 'with all my heart' than as 'from the bottom of my soul'. When I was first translating Chekhov I pointed out that it was 'not necessary to bring in the soul wherever the Russian has *dusha*, since the English use of "soul" is now almost confined to theological contexts.'[7]

So far was Chekhov from wallowing in soulfulness that he rejected such sentimentality even when its source was the person with whom he was most intimate. His wife, the actress Olga Knipper—herself of German parentage, incidentally, but Russian by upbringing—once wrote to him that 'My soul aches when I remember the quiet anguish which seems so deeply seated in *your* soul.' The husband's reply was brief. 'What nonsense, darling.'[8] Turning from domestic to literary emotions, one again finds Chekhov displaying his usual austerity when he considers the sentimental heroines of Turgenev's fiction. Those pure, idealistic young women were 'intolerably affected and bogus', he once said.[9] He even wrote a literary parody on the situation so often provoked in Turgenev when such a young girl suddenly 'drops everything' to follow her—usually highly unsuitable—lover to the ends of the earth. As such a young woman Chekhov's heroine Zinaida, in his *Anonymous Story*, is revealed when she dutifully leaves her husband and joins her lover. But that cynical, ironical and urbane character, one Gregory Orlov, is no Turgenev hero, and he spoils the pattern by treating his mistress's unheralded arrival in his home as a major disaster, not as the prelude to a New Life. Far from conveying the intruding Zinaida to the uttermost ends of the earth, he is chiefly concerned to disembarrass himself of an encumbrance. 'Yes, old boy,' he tells a friend, 'the prescription is

Turgenev's, but it's me who has to take the bloody medicine.'
'I am not a Turgenev hero,' he later complains, adding that 'Should
I ever require to liberate Bulgaria I could dispense with any
female escort.' Here is a dig at Turgenev's *On the Eve*, which
describes the Bulgarian freedom-fighter Insarov as being followed
part of the way to the 'ends of the earth' by his devoted Helen.[10]

In the context of Turgenev's novels it is instructive to find an
Englishman, not a Russian, displaying emotional incontinence.
'This pure girl, with passionate courageous soul,' oozed Edward
Garnett, writing of *Virgin Soil*'s heroine Marianna, 'is in fact the
Liberty of Russia . . . In her figure is personified the power of the
Russian youth.'[11] 'What nonsense, Garnett,' Chekhov might have
replied, had this exercise in *umileniye* been brought to his notice.

As Chekhov's comments on Turgenev remind us, it is nearly
always a Russian who proves the most effective corrector of the
typical Russian faults—that is, if one is justified in assigning over-
emotionalism to the category of defect. But Chekhov's corrections
went largely unheeded. Nor could he protect himself against the
false reverence and automatic piety which leading writers often
attract, not only in Russia. Here again it is another Russian writer
—Chekhov's friend, the even more caustic, the even less sentimental Ivan Bunin—who rescues good taste. Criticising commentators for over-emphasising Chekhov's tenderness, sadness and
warmth, Bunin remarked that he could just imagine what Chekhov's feelings 'would have been if he had read about the tenderness. As for the warmth and the sadness, they would have disgusted
him even more.'[12]

From Bunin on Chekhov, and bringing this review of unsentimental Russians into modern times while advancing ever further
from *umileniye*, one may turn to the novelist Vladimir Nabokov on
Bunin. In his autobiography, *Speak Memory*, Nabokov describes
how the elderly Bunin, flushed with the recent award of a Nobel
Prize, invited him, the then-youthful Nabokov, out to a meal at a
time when both authors were living in Parisian emigration. In
issuing the invitation Bunin had been unaware that this young
man, whom he rashly sought to patronise, had a morbid dislike of
restaurants and cafés; besides which, 'heart-to-heart talks, confessions in the Dostoyevskian manner are . . . not in my [Nabokov's]
line'. Nabokov describes Bunin as a spry old gentleman 'puzzled by

my irresponsiveness to the hazel grouse of which I had enough in my childhood and exasperated by my refusal to discuss eschatological matters.'[13] Such is the English version. In the earlier, Russian, rendering of his autobiography, Nabokov had put the last phrase differently—Bunin is 'irritated by my refusal to unbutton my soul'. In both versions of the episode Nabokov firmly rejects *umileniye*.

If, then, Russians have sometimes been prone to overdose themselves with emotional self-indulgence, let them also have the credit for having evolved their own antidote. Nor are the Chekhovs, the Bunins and the Nabokovs as rare as Russia-fanciers often pretend. One such unsentimental figure is Alexander Nikitenko. Such a witness, simply because he can also be so caustic about his fellow countrymen on occasion, commands respect when he makes statements that sound unconvincing when made by a Pares or a Jarintzov. Nikitenko claims that 'In our hearts and emotions we Russians are more richly endowed than all other European peoples ... What an amazing people the Russians are. They are almost impossible to live with. Yet you feel drawn to them by something so kind, intelligent and enchanting that no German, Frenchman, *or even Englishman*, can compare with them.'[14] Disarmed by the anglophile phrase here italicised, I should have liked to leave Nikitenko with the last word on the Russian tradition of communicating emotion. However, it is also necessary to cover certain serious reservations to which Russian emotionalism and its prophets can give rise. It has, or can have, disturbing qualities not yet discussed. Though sufficiently exceptional not to invalidate Nikitenko's favourable verdict, these are yet obtrusive enough—and above all, sufficiently neglected by other commentators—to demand their place in the reckoning.

How different from Nikitenko's witness is the common insinuation that emotion, as expressed by a Russian, is automatically stronger and more laudable than that to which the non-Russian can aspire. For example, Madame Jarintzov writes of a poor Russian peasant woman during the First World War 'with large tears standing in her eyes as she hands a pot of milk to the wounded on a passing train, calls them *rodnyye* [darlings] under her breath, for each of them is as much *rodnoy* to her heart as the one boy who is fighting somewhere far, far away.'[15] There seems to be a strong suggestion in the context that no 'simple' woman of any other nationality could be moved by compassion for her wounded menfolk, or that, if she were, the feeling must somehow rate as immeasurably inferior to that of the, by definition, super-sincere Russian.

The Russian, this same informant elsewhere stresses, loves passionately: other people, snow, frost, natural scenery, lying on the grass. No doubt. But the main urge behind the purveying of these data seems a wish to deride the miserable, repressed Englishman, here portrayed as glumly taking part in organised games and solemnly plodding about in his woollen underwear while the Russian is lavishing love in all directions. If Madame Jarintzov's Englishmen use the word *love* at all it is to speak of a lovely dinner or a lovely piece of bacon.[16] Here is a shrewd dig at a traditional feature of English behaviour, and it would be humourlessly unconvincing to pretend that the charge was unfounded. What one must reject is, rather, the assumption that Russian exuberance and self-revelation are always preferable. Though I find Madame Jarintzov's long-buried denunciations of the British or English amusing, I am unwilling even at this distance in time to capitulate abjectly in the Russia-fancying manner.

Here is a characteristic sample of Russian self-praise designed, it seems, to convince the bemused alien that it is somehow 'charming', a key word in the context; he is to be indoctrinated with the patter and sent forth repeating it as his independent judgement. Thus may the uninstructed non-Russian be found bewailing his own inferiority, his incapacity to feel true emotion by comparison with the vivid, colourful, uninhibited, outgoing, extrovert Slav. And how rarely such Russia-fanciers confine their self-abasement to the first person singular. Influenced, again, by Russians, they tend to speak as representatives of a group which certainly never elected them its spokesmen, causing their confessions of emotional atrophy to embrace not only their own persons, but 'the West', 'the British', 'Americans' or some never-defined community called 'we'. A recent English witness praises the absence, in Russia, of what he has been taught to call *hypocrisie anglaise*. Virginia Woolf goes further. Speaking of the Russian writer's simplicity and absence of effort, she contrasts the stilted and self-conscious Anglo-Saxon. '*We* become awkward and self-conscious; denying our own qualities, *we* write with an affectation of goodness and sincerity which is nauseating in the extreme.'[17]

Another such propaganda casualty has described the tragic première of Chekhov's *Cherry Orchard* in Moscow on 27 January 1904, when the dying, jubilee-detesting author was cajoled into attending a celebration enacted on stage in honour of the twenty-fifth anniversary of his literary début. Of that moving—but to Chekhov acutely painful—experience, the following comment is made. '*It is difficult for anyone except a Russian to appreciate* the warm personal feeling with which he was greeted that night.'[18] But is it really so difficult for a moderately sensitive person, however ethnically preconditioned, to make this empathetic leap? Have the Russians indeed cornered the higher sensibilities, as is here implied? The author of the above lines was, alas, myself in youth. When, therefore, in the present study, I chide Russia-fanciers and propaganda casualties for mindlessly repeating the patter, I am also criticising myself—or at least myself of the year 1950.

Quick to volunteer information on aspects of their lives which others would regard as private, Russians also demand similar information in the opposite direction. Hence the impression of inquisitiveness which they can make on those schooled in other conventions. One early nineteenth-century foreign observer found such intrusions offensive: Dr Robert Lyall, who spent several years in Russia after 1812 and who married a Russian woman. 'With as much ease as they say, "How do you do?" [they] . . . ask the most impertinent questions, with respect to your connections and family, your property and revenues, and your secret affairs and private opinions. An evasive answer only prompts their curiosity.'[19] This trait has not disappeared over the centuries, as foreign visitors to the Soviet Union can testify. *Zachem, pochemu, otchevo, dlya chego, chego, na koy chort*: the language seems to possess, and to need, an infinite number of words for 'why'. Why, why, why? Why do you not grow a beard, why do you not shave off your beard? Why do you never say what you mean? Why did you learn Russian, why do you not learn Russian? Why don't you like me? Why do you like me? Do you love your wife, hate your children? What are your impressions of Soviet Man? Such questions can irritate a sensitive ear—particularly since, as Dr Lyall also noticed, a polite evasion will not usually be accepted. As for inter-Russian communication on home soil, native inquisitiveness has been further encouraged by official insistence, in the totalitarian period, that everyone must directly concern himself with such matters as his neighbour's efficiency at his work, together with his attitudes to topics as varied as art, literature and his father-in-law. Thus is the Russians' innate 'inquisitiveness of big children',[20] as Pares defined it, further reinforced as part of the officially inculcated Soviet ethos.

To concede that Russians are prone to utter emotionally charged statements in the presence of strangers—this is not necessarily to accept certain corollaries commonly assumed to follow. Among them is the imputation that the expression and the feeling of strong emotion are closely correlated, whereas the opposite can sometimes be the case. The second assumption is that to express strong emotion is meritorious in itself, placing the emotion-displayer on a pedestal of moral superiority without regard to context and good taste. Thirdly, there is the common assumption that 'sincerity' can be measured, in a Russian or anyone else, by persons who present no credentials of competence in performing so complex an act of divination; and who never seem to recognise that the accurate assessment of an individual's—still more a nation's—collective sincerity would (even assuming it to be possible) be an operation of the utmost delicacy. A Bernard Pares, a Virginia Woolf, may lecture the world on Russian 'genuineness', 'naturalness', and 'simplicity'. But how did they acquire such confidence as arbiters of these qualities? Does the 'sincere' man splutter, does he work his facial muscles, his intonational pitch, his gesticulations in some 'genuine' way which can at once be recognised—if only by some other, equally sincere, genuine individual? Such judgements would be more convincing if some of those who make them presented evidence, as Nikitenko and Bunin do in their writings as a whole, that they possess the precious gifts of sensitivity and good taste.

To deny that the over-projection of emotion *à la russe* is necessarily more laudable than its under-projection *à l'anglaise*—this is not to assert the opposite. Believing neither that all Russians over-project, nor that all non-Russians under-project, I would not pose as an arbiter in the comparative evaluation of these practices. I would suggest, though, that if a person of whatever nationality prefers not to express his feelings in public, no conclusions whatever may legitimately be drawn by strangers as to the strength or quality of those feelings; nor are they the rightful concern of anyone but the individual concerned and those with whom he chooses to be intimate. Conversely, if someone chooses to express his feelings more openly, he is entitled to do so. But let neither type seek to claim credit points for exercising its own option. Over-projectors or under-projectors—what does it matter? Stimulating and boring, kind and callous, sensitive and crude individuals may be found in both categories; and these qualities should count more than reserve or effusiveness. As for their proportionate distribution between persons of restrained and exhibitionist habit, one suspects it to be on a roughly equivalent basis.

The point is not that restraint is always good and lack of restraint always bad; merely that the reverse assumption, common in the present context, is unjustified.

To features in the communication of emotion already discussed must be added a passion for self-dramatisation. Histrionically gifted, Russians tend to be alert to audience reaction. Where 'Western civilisation has bred in us an aversion to being conspicuous in public, a horror of being involved in "scenes", such reluctance is not . . . found among Russians.' Making this point, Mehnert contrasts the readiness of a typical woman shoplifter in Germany to 'go quietly' when apprehended, and to attract as little attention as possible, with some Russian woman whom he once chanced to see arrested in Moscow for illegal street trading. She 'screamed like one possessed and fought tooth and nail until the police finally threw her bodily into an open truck'.[21] Such too was the robust attitude to public disgrace displayed by 'Grandma' in Chekhov's *Peasants*. Far from hiding her head in shame when her treasured samovar was carried off by the village elder in lieu of tax arrears, she rushed after him shrieking in a sobbing chant, and beating her breast like a heroine from Greek tragedy. 'Good Christians and believers in God! Neighbours, they have ill-treated me! Kind friends, they have oppressed me! Oh, oh! dear people, take my part.'[22]

Self-dramatisation often seems present when Russians undertake, as they often do, the consumption of food and drink on a scale beyond their means. A lower-paid worker will go to a restaurant at the weekend and order black caviare with his vodka—not, according to Harvey Pitcher, because he can afford it, or even because he likes caviare, but *'to show that* he is as capable of doing this as the next man, and as an example of the broad, expansive nature on which Russians have always prided themselves'.[23] It is not enough for him to indulge in such recklessness privily: he must be manifestly seen to do so, whether he happens to be Pitcher's worker or one of Dostoyevsky's fellow-convicts from the prison at Omsk a hundred years earlier. As described in his *Memoirs from the House of the Dead*, they were often able to smuggle liquor into jail, and then to indulge in solitary drinking bouts—but solitary only in the sense that the drinker would keep all the precious fluid to himself. Audience reaction was of the essence on these occasions, when the celebrant 'would get as drunk as an owl and make a point of staggering and blundering round the prison, trying *to show everyone* that he was drunk, that he was "on the binge"—and thereby to earn general respect'.[24]

Dostoyevsky has also noticed the Russian tendency to 'fall in love with the injuries done and insults offered to them' (*polyubit svoyu obidu*), and to make self-pity a basis for theatrical behaviour. His tempestuous heroine Nastasya Filippovna, once seduced in youth by a middle-aged roué, proceeds (in *The Idiot*) to build her entire life-style around the dubious thesis that she is a 'fallen woman'. On a more trivial level such histrionic self-pity *à la* Dostoyevsky can come into play when some well-meaning foreign visitor chances to offer a tip to a self-respecting citizen of the modern age. This can be a delicate manœuvre in a society where tipping, on the one hand officially abolished as inconsistent with the dignity of Soviet Man, is on the other hand a widespread practice. An Intourist official once told me how an American visitor had insulted him in this way, proffering a one-rouble gratuity in return for some service. However tactless this *faux pas* may have been, the injured party seemed to protest, and to enjoy protesting, too much. He seemed, like Nastasya Filippovna before him, to propose building his future emotional life around this petty incident. Yet the entire protest was obviously, *au fond*, a joke, game or charade to him—as will become clearer below, where the neglected phenomenon of the Russian leg-pull is to be scrutinised.

Such a contretemps can erupt on a grander scale, as witness a similar incident in 1959, when Richard Nixon visited the Soviet

Union as Vice-President of the United States. Believed, probably through some misunderstanding, to have offered a tip or bribe to a humble meat-weigher, one Smakhtin, encountered during a good-will tour to 'meet the people', Mr Nixon alerted the media and plunged the country into Dostoyevskian self-pity. Meat-weigher Smakhtin, having thus had greatness thrust upon him, appeared on Moscow radio to bewail the insult offered to an 'ordinary Russian working man', and sent a letter to *Pravda* describing how he had proudly thrust aside the wallet of the trans-atlantic gentleman.[25] This episode, which shows self-dramatisation harnessed by the department of agitation and propaganda, was allowed to smoulder on for an unconscionable time. Soon after-wards, on a still higher level, Nikita Khrushchev was directing similar tantrums at President Eisenhower at the summit confer-ence held in Paris in the wake of the U-2 spy-plane scandal—a connoisseur's specimen of the hammed-up disproportionate reaction.

Politics everywhere tend to involve play-acting and buffoonery such as has not been confined, in Russia, to the totalitarian period. The Emperor Nicholas I could never forget for a second who he was. 'He postures incessantly, with the result that he is never natural even when he is sincere.' A similar claim has been made for that emperor's, and his successors', bitterest foes: Russia's pio-neer revolutionaries. 'All you want is to play a part and posture to the mob for the sake of applause'—thus Nikitenko apostrophises the followers of his *bête noire*, the radical publicist Herzen. And again, 'These ultra-progressives . . . want to posture on the stage, they want to play at making history.' But Nikitenko does not go so far as another authority, who has dismissed the whole of Russian civilisation as pure play-acting. 'They are much less interested in being civilised than in making us believe them so.'[26]

This histrionic tendency helps to explain the national love of *skandaly*, 'scenes'. 'A Russian takes incredible delight in every kind of scandalous public upheaval,' wrote Dostoyevsky when intro-ducing what must be the greatest *skandal* sequence in literature: the scene (in *Devils*) where a gang of malicious, semi-politically motivated hooligans or nihilists wreck an already preposterous public literary conference, thereby triggering the moral dis-integration of the unnamed provincial town which is the scene of the action. Wherever the outward decorum of everyday life shows signs of breaking down, the average Russian still seems inclined to foster such disruptive tendencies—no matter how trivial their origin, such as an argument about the quality of a single potato offered for sale in a collective farm market. Everyone in hearing joins in, accusations and counter-accusations fly about until sooner or later authority steps in, if only in the person of a humble militia-man, and decorum is restored—until the next *skandal* rears its always-enticing head. The whole of Russian history can be plausibly related to the rhythm of the *skandal* and subsequent tamping-down operation or counter-*skandal*. *Zamyat*, 'to hush up', is a verb which frequently occurs in this context.

Small wonder that the rulers of a nation so histrionically inclined should have resorted to theatrical devices when seeking to bolster their authority. The most spectacular example was the trilogy of Stalinist show trials of 1936–8. The available surviving senior colleagues of Lenin were paraded in court, where they vied with each other in confessing to espionage, economic sabotage, assassination plots and other forms of terrorism—virtually all fiction, and all part of an elaborate script taught to them at the behest of the producer-in-chief, Stalin, by various forms of persuasion, including appeals to Party discipline, threats to relatives and torture.

Similarly, on a humbler level, use is still made in factories, universities and other institutions, of 'boards of shame' on which delinquent individuals are pilloried for failing to have their hair cut, cheating in examinations, seducing girls, neglecting to follow prescribed safety regulations—and of course for drunkenness. There are also show trials of a kind, still: the semi-public self-criticism sessions or kangaroo courts at which an erring individual may be called to order by his self-righteous workmates. One may read in the press many a cautionary tale, such as that of a worker in a match factory detected listening to foreign broadcasts. Hailed before his mates, he was bullied until he broke down, confessed his sins, bowed to his fellow workers and thanked them for standing bail for his future conduct and thus showing their trust in him.[27] Such episodes are obviously rigged from start to finish by local Party officials, activists and busybodies, but even so they could probably not take place at all but for the general love of self-projection, particularly where highly dramatised repentance and contrition is involved. In this way the aggressively secular state has harnessed traditional religious reactions, a topic which must be considered in a later chapter.

The same histrionic urge perhaps explains the people's fondness for political demonstrations—no matter that, under totalitarian conditions, they are often organised by and for the authorities; less commonly against them, as in other societies. 'Set a collection of Russians down in a street, tell them to start walking in the same direction, and in no time they will all be singing together and smiling.' The fiction that such officially rigged demonstrations are spontaneous can the more easily be sustained since it involves injecting the element of leg-pull, always an acceptable spicing, into a situation already theatrical. Such are the occasional spontaneous (that is, officially rigged) demonstrations staged by 'ordinary workers impelled by elemental righteous indignation' (that is, those detailed by officials to take part) against foreign embassies in Moscow in order to point up some international squabble. One such performance was mounted outside the British Embassy in 1956 at the time of the Suez crisis, when a well-regimented shouting 'mob' flourished placards ('Dirty Hands off Egypt') on the perimeter. But the obliging fur-capped major-general of police who was in charge was able to inform an inquiring Embassy official of the exact hour at which the spontaneous explosion of the people's wrath was scheduled to end.[28]

An example of similar 'spontaneity' on an individual level is found in Pitcher's analysis of 'Kolya', an enthusiastic young Party member with whom, as a visiting student, he shared a room in Leningrad. Considering it his duty to project *bodrost* (a buoyant, optimistic approach to life), Kolya would switch on his ideal personality when required. 'Whenever a stranger came into the room —whether a Russian or a Westerner—Kolya's "liveliness index" would immediately shoot up several points.' He would become instantly livelier, more talkative and cheery. ' "You'll be able to go back to England and tell them how jolly Soviet students are," he would comment after this sort of performance.'[29]

Such posturing is a significant national characteristic. 'Just you watch me being spontaneous' is the formula which most effectively covers it. But there is, of course, something highly paradoxical about the kind of 'spontaneous', sincere, natural and so on behaviour

(75)

which is not merely ostentatiously labelled as such by those
who stage it, but can also be announced in advance—and even
timed to end at a predetermined moment. This becomes still more
ludicrous when accompanied by 'tactful' allusions to the alleged
lack of spontaneity of the American, German et cetera, person who
has been chosen as audience or target for the exhibition. The same
point is made in a less irreverent and more Russia-fancying way
by another observer. 'The Russian . . . displays that naturalness
which has so often enchanted foreigners.'[30] *Displays!* Precisely.

Yet the Russian manages to 'display' all this naturalness without
really possessing a word for 'spontaneous' or 'spontaneity', for he
has had recourse to borrowing the forms *spontanny* and *spontannost*
—than which, etymologically, nothing could be less Slav. Why
does the language lack the terms? Two mutually exclusive explana-
tions suggest themselves. Either the Russian is so spontaneous and
natural that the very concept can be taken for granted and needs
no words to express it. Alternatively, the very possibility of any
human reaction not being dictated by deep-laid guile is so totally
excluded as to exempt the language from filling what, in any other
tongue, might be found a serious lacuna.

In any case Russians are obviously not the only people given to
the sin or feat of self-projection. Nor can all Russians be accused
of constantly seeing themselves on stage with the spotlight playing
on them. Chekhov, for example, least of all men sought to cultivate
an 'image', as he showed when someone accused him of betraying,
in his story *The Party*, a fear of being considered a liberal. 'I think
that I can be accused of gluttony, drunkenness, frivolity, frigidity,
or of any crime in the calendar rather than of wishing to seem or of
wishing not to seem something.'[31]

Though Russians can appear comic when enacting the carefully
prescribed and pre-scripted motions of self-criticism in kangaroo
courts and the like, it should not be forgotten that they also have,
as a nation, a remarkable record for detecting and analysing their
own shortcomings in a more dignified yet hard-hitting style free from
paranoia and ostentatious self-disparagement. Even Custine, one of
their severest critics, admitted this when he wrote, 'Fundamentally
they judge their country more harshly than I.'[32] So indeed
they do. One thinks of the pictures of provincial life conveyed
in Gogol's *Dead Souls* and *Inspector General*; of Chaadayev's

denunciation of Russia's past, present and future in his *First Philosophical Letter*; of Saltykov's picture of Russian officialdom; of the criticism of the Russian intelligentsia in the symposium *Landmarks* of 1909; of Gorky's above-quoted diatribe against the Russian peasantry. One also thinks of the satire of the 1920s: of Zamyatin, of Ilf and Petrov, and of many another. As these instances show, the Russians may be accused of many crimes, not excluding that of bombastic self-glorification. But one cannot accuse them, as a nation, of ignoring their own defects—which, as so much else, they seem to exaggerate with their usual exuberance and *razmakh*.

CAMOUFLAGE DRILL

Few analyses of the Russian psyche even mention one key concept: *vranyo*, the national brand of leg-pulling, ribbing or blarney. It is defined by one dictionary as 'lies, fibbing, nonsense, rot', and by another as 'idle talk, twaddle'.

Vranyo is the more innocent of two distinct terms denoting the dissemination of untruths, its more serious equivalent being *lozh*. To impute *vranyo* involves little more than the affectionate charge of possessing a lively imagination: *vryote*, 'You're having me on.' But to accuse someone of *lozh* is harsh: *lzhosh*, 'You bloody liar!' The roots of both words are rich in derivatives such as *zaviratsya*: crudely translated, 'to prevaricate oneself into a condition of trance'. Indeed, Russian may possess almost as large a vocabulary for terminological inexactitude as Arabic has for different kinds of camel.

The distinction between these two brands of prevarication is drawn in a notable essay, 'Pan-Russian Vranyo', by the pre-revolutionary short-story writer and dramatist Leonid Andreyev. He claims—unfairly perhaps—that Russians have no talent for *lozh*, and he calls this more serious brand of misrepresentation 'an art, difficult and demanding intelligence, talent, character, stamina'. A good *lozh*-type liar is Shakespeare's Iago—whose skill is beyond any Russian's, says Andreyev. 'Yes,' he continues, 'the Russian is incapable of telling downright lies [*lozh*]; but he seems equally incapable of telling the truth. The intermediate phenomenon, for which he feels the utmost love and tenderness, resembles neither truth nor *lozh*. It is *vranyo*. Like our native aspen, it pops up uninvited everywhere, choking other varieties; like the aspen, it is no use for firewood or carpentry; and, again like the aspen, it is sometimes beautiful.' As an example Andreyev quotes someone who, after conversing normally for a while, suddenly announces that his aunt has died—and this though 'far from being deceased . . . she is about to turn up in half an hour, as everyone knows. He has no way of benefiting from his aunt's supposed death, and why he uttered the *vranyo* is a mystery.'[1] To this may be added Potugin's story (in Turgenev's *Smoke*) of the sportsman who, while beating an unfamiliar countryside for game, was directed by a helpful rustic to a near-by marsh offering a profusion of wild fowl helpfully waiting to be shot. The huntsman trudged on, only to discover, alas, that both marsh and birds were mirages.[2]

Such is *vranyo* at its simplest, in which form it has outlived the nineteenth century. I was once present when a USSR-domiciled Russian visitor to England spoke to a British host about a Russian *émigré* known to both of them. According to the visitor, one of the *émigré*'s sons had recently returned to Moscow after a stay in Paris; had published a book of which the exact title was given; had changed his name; had undergone various other adventures. The host listened with a straight face, thus preserving the conventions, though he was a close friend of the family concerned and knew that every word was untrue. Did the narrator realise that he had been identified as purveying *vranyo*? Yes and no. That, as will be seen below, is the point.

Here, then, is the kind of fantasy in which Andreyev claims a Russian monopoly. As his country's true representative he singles out Khlestakov, that ingenious hero of Gogol's *Inspector General* whose skill lies in juggling with fantastic improvisations, and who, according to Andreyev, constitutes something uniquely Russian, 'like a samovar'.[3]

On so Russian a phenomenon as *vranyo* the arch-patriot Dostoyevsky has inevitably made the most memorable contributions. He has spouted it himself, not least in his famous 'Pushkin Speech' of 1880. He has analysed its theory, especially in the article 'A Word or Two about Vranyo', published in his *Diary of a Writer* for 1873. And he has created many a notable *vranyo*-monger in his fiction.

Among these General Ivolgin of *The Idiot* holds pride of place. Most readers remember Ivolgin for his account of an alleged experience in a railway compartment which he had once purportedly shared with a woman and her lapdog. Objecting to his smoking, she had (according to Ivolgin) snatched his cigar and thrown it out of the window, whereupon Ivolgin had avenged himself by tossing her lapdog after it. Unfortunately a member of his audience, unsympathetic to *vranyo*, then broke the conventions by remarking that the incident had recently been reported in a Belgian newspaper, from which the inference followed that the General had not been concerned in it at all.

As the episode confirms, *vranyo* at its best represents an art form, not a means of gaining personal advantage. Its function is to provide light amid the encircling gloom. This point is also made in Andreyev's essay, where he has one of his *vranyo*-purveyors say that he does not mind being caught out. 'It's only right that truth should triumph—I value truth and respect it. But before you're found out *you do seem to come to life for a moment*.'[4] Indeed, *vranyo*'s continuing late twentieth-century vogue may well derive from its function of enlivening the drabness of modernity, since the official doctrine that totalitarian Russian life is somehow more exhilarating than life elsewhere is itself so extreme an example of creative fantasy.

To invoke totalitarian fantasy-mongering is to be reminded that the subject has so far been considered only in a relatively private or intimate context, as it develops in *tête-à-tête* dialogue or small social gatherings. But what of public *vranyo*, as developed by Russia's rulers, statesmen and official spokesmen, not merely since 1917, but throughout the ages? Here the Russian claim to a monopoly is less firmly founded, since public *vranyo* tends to become fused with and indistinguishable from public political bombast in general—for instance, with that found incised on the obelisks of the Pharaohs; with the grandiloquent addresses directed by such un-Russian figures as the poets Virgil and Horace to the Emperor Augustus. But how prosaic those stolid Romans were by comparison with the public *vranyo*-purveyors of a later, larger, more ebullient empire.

Among pioneers of Russia-based *vranyo* was the Empress Catherine the Great, who, as has been said, 'erected self-advertisement into a system of government'.[5] One example was the elaborate

Instruction framed by her in 1765–7 for the guidance of a specially summoned Legislative Commission charged with drawing up a new legal code. But there was, it seems, no prospect of any practical outcome to the harangues on the desirability of equality, justice and other abstract nouns with which the Empress, versed in Montesquieu's *L'Esprit des lois* and other foreign sources, had adorned her *Instruction*. The operation was an exercise in official *vranyo*. That this kind of operation, already detected in ancient Egypt and ancient Rome as well as Russia, has been prevalent in most countries and ages, need hardly be argued. It was the nineteenth-century Church of England, not Catherine's Russia, which Samuel Butler most directly satirised with the 'musical banks' where all respectable citizens of his imagined state Erewhon kept accounts in a notional or ideal currency of purely decorative and symbolical significance—currency parallel to and entirely separated from the real coin of the realm, with which alone it was possible to make purchases. Long before *Erewhon* this principle had been translated into visual terms by Catherine's most celebrated favourite, Potemkin, creator of those renowned 'villages' which remain to this day the prime emblem of Russian *pokazukha* ('bull') and *ochkovtiratelstvo* ('eyewash'). They were mere two-dimensional stage props erected in sight of the River Dnieper, being designed to impress upon the touring sovereign, as she glided downstream with a flotilla of notables, the comforting illusion that the wilderness around her was a prosperous, densely populated province of her realm. Well might Michael Speransky, the statesman who served the Empress's grandsons Alexander I and Nicholas I, complain in another context that 'in no other State do political words stand in such contrast to reality as in Russia'.[6]

Though *pokazukha* on the scale of a Potemkin and a Catherine had receded in Speransky's day, the nineteenth century by no means renounced her legacy. One observer lamented that 'Any traveller who let himself be indoctrinated by the locals could traverse the length and breadth of the Empire and return home having done nothing but tour a sequence of façades.'[7] Another hundred years later many façades had been hauled down, but far more new ones had been put up in their place. Yet only since Stalin's death has *vranyo* emerged as a key element in totalitarian public posture. One might over-simplify and call the age of Lenin the age of truth, since it was also an age of faith. When official spokesmen then promised the people that they faced a glorious future, that they would overtake America, and that revolution was shortly about to erupt in Germany, they were speaking the truth in the sense that on the whole they believed these promises to be well founded. Then came the age of Stalin, that era of *lozh* militant, when a sincere belief in anything—especially in Stalin himself— could become a passport to disgrace and arrest. When Stalinist spokesmen referred to millions of peasants voluntarily joining the collective farms, this was no *vranyo*, but just a deliberate *lozh*-type lie. Not until the era of Khrushchev did *vranyo* come into its own as a factor influencing public behaviour, partly through the personal example of the new leader, whose statements on cultivating maize, catching up America and the like often carried so strong a whiff of fantasy, and were obviously made partly for fun. But the spread of *vranyo* then derived less from Khrushchev's own shining example than from the relaxations over which he presided by enabling more communication to take place—both internally, between citizens; and externally, between natives and foreigners. This relaxation of controls released a torrent which had been dammed for decades, and which has since been canalised and exploited under the leadership of Brezhnev—himself, by contrast with his predecessor and to humanity's loss, no great *vranyo*-monger.

Vranyo has changed since Catherine's and Dostoyevsky's days, having become more of a ritual. Its subject matter now runs in prescribed grooves. Whereas the traditional purveyor of *vranyo* could improvise as he wished, and enjoyed amateur status, one now finds officially licensed greeters or contact men—Intourist guides, members of delegations and so on—who bear the signs of having been drilled in the technique of manipulating foreigners at some highly secret central school of *vranyo*. Approved topics include the frequent denial that begging, tipping and prostitution exist within the Kremlin's sway. But these are only fields for negative *vranyo*, an unimportant by-product of the genre, since it is hard for even the most experienced practitioner to embellish the *absence* of something with the vital element of elaborate embroidery —especially when that something does not happen to be absent at all.

For embroidery purposes a positive topic is needed. One example is the fiction, widely propagated of late, that tens of millions of 'workers' may be observed every summer as they drive their families along the main roads of the country towards the Black Sea resorts 'in their own cars'. When once listening to such a recital I must have committed 'facecrime'—conveyed disbelief by my facial expression—because the speaker, a woman, quickly remarked that there were 'some workers who don't yet have cars of their own'. This comment brings out a modern refinement beyond the ken of Dostoyevsky's contemporaries, that of oblique *vranyo*: the various 'defects' or disadvantages of the country are 'frankly' admitted, an admission designed to underline, by implication, the reliability of the performance as a whole. The above episode also illustrates another difference between present-day and nineteenth-century *vranyo*. With double chauvinism Dostoyevsky claimed the practice as unique to the Russian male. This is no longer true, for here as elsewhere the equality of the sexes has been very properly asserted.

The changes since Dostoyevsky's day have not been all gain, for it is now common practice to dilute *vranyo* with injections of truth. One finds this in the endless 'building stories', one of the staples of modern *vranyo* which few foreign visitors to Moscow escape. The presentation is unrolled with traditional ceremony, with accounts about how there was 'nothing here, nothing' except swamp and shacks a few months ago, whereas there is now some vast suburb containing so many million square metres of living space. Such achievements are explained with certain accompaniments not yet mentioned: expansive gestures, a piercing glance, a swelling neck, an empurpled face, and that curious constricted voice which suggests that the speaker is on the point of choking. But something is wrong; for the apartment blocks—even if not built as quickly as indicated—are visibly present. Thus a fine old tradition has been adulterated and diluted in the modern age, though of course *vranyo*'s loss has been the Muscovite's gain. One should not, however, underestimate the fantasy element in traditional construction stories. Precisely the same stories, told with precisely the same physical symptoms on the part of the narrators, had been put out by precisely the same spokesmen in earlier years when (they now 'frankly' admit) the building programme had been grossly inadequate. It could of course be argued that this has involved no adulteration, but an even greater sophistication: in earlier times *vranyo* had to be untrue, but nowadays its connection with truth has become so obscure that it no longer matters.

To what extent does the *vranyo* artist believe his own fantasies? He obviously differs from the *lozh*-purveyor, who well knows that he is lying. But still less does he believe himself to be telling the truth, occupying rather an intermediate position. Can it be that he simultaneously believes and does not believe the creative fictions which he disseminates? No. More probably, he does not believe them as he begins his harangue; but then suddenly becomes convinced by his eloquence in mid-career—a phenomenon which may be termed the take-off. Such at least is Dostoyevsky's view. In his essay on *vranyo* he addresses a typical adept as follows: 'You have told such fantastic stories . . . that, though you have started to believe in yourself half-way through your story (for one always does begin to believe in oneself half-way through a story), nevertheless when you go to bed at night and have enjoyable memories about the pleasant impression made on your listener, you suddenly pause and remark involuntarily, "Heavens, what rubbish I talked." '[8]

It seems likely, therefore, that the typical *vranyo* dispenser at any given moment either believes or does not believe whole-heartedly in what he is saying, and that he oscillates between these two conditions. Since the more distressing physical symptoms—mentioned above as including the strained voice, bulging eyes and purple face—are associated with the period of take-off, during which he comes to believe himself, it seems possible that the recurrent gusts of clear-headedness are nature's way of providing relief.

To consider this is to touch on an elusive problem, the nature of belief. It is a puzzle intractable anywhere, but doubly so in a totalitarian context, since too little is known about the effect on the brain of being compelled year in and year out to repeat statements known or suspected to be untrue. The evidence of refugees from totalitarian countries shows that many persons of high intelligence have emerged from decades of conditioning surprisingly unscathed. Some had adapted to their environment by developing controlled schizophrenia, whereby private thoughts and compulsory official mendacity were, so to speak, confined in separate compartments of the brain.

In some cases, though—as observation of 'capitalist' politicians also confirms—the repeated acting of a false part may wear a groove in the actor's brain until he comes to believe propositions which he originally knew to be absurd. That this may prove dangerous is suggested, again by Leonid Andreyev, in his story *Thought*. It describes a man who has decided to murder his wife, and who, wishing to evade criminal proceedings, prepares his defence in advance by faking insanity. He indulges, that is, in a series of carefully planned eccentricities—none serious enough to cause him to be confined in a mental home, but all sufficiently suggestive of an unbalanced mind as to make it appear obvious, after the murder, that he had been mad all along. So convincingly, however, does he act his part as a madman that, in the end, he genuinely loses, or appears to lose, his sanity, an important point of the story being the impossibility of assessing his, or perhaps anyone's, true mental state. Now, a lifelong addiction to *vranyo* may produce some similar dislocation in the brain, a possibility which discourages any temptation to regard the modern Russian adept as a comic character. He might instead be a *pagliaccio* or tragic clown, increasingly ill at ease each time he dons the motley. General Ivolgin, that grand master of *vranyo*, is in many ways such a tragic figure; but even Ivolgin was not compelled to indulge in *vranyo* by forces outside himself.

How much more painful, then, must be the predicament of an internally protesting Soviet *vranyo*-monger who is humiliated by the obligation to produce officially sponsored fantasies. Perhaps he wishes to protest and dissociate himself from the performance, yet he is not prepared to face the penalties for failing to produce *vranyo* at all—or, still worse, for substituting the truth in its place. There is, however, one kind of protest which he can make with relative safety. By subtly overdoing his performance, he can deride the whole process, separate himself mentally from his humiliating position, and thus preserve a measure of self-respect. He is safe in doing so, for who can be certain that the exaggeration is deliberate? Moreover, though interfering 'activists' can easily embarrass someone who shows insufficient zeal, they are less favourably placed when confronted by one who shows an approved brand of zeal, however synthetic, in excess. In attempting to harass him, they might easily find themselves in trouble.

Recent literature provides many examples of such counterfeit displays of excessive zeal by way of protest, perhaps none more striking than that at the deathbed of Professor Skutarevsky's son in Leonid Leonov's novel *Skutarevsky* (1932). The son, implicated in counter-revolutionary activity, has attempted to commit suicide by shooting himself in the stomach. As he lies in hospital, dying and unable to speak, his father directs at him an interminable enthusiastic political harangue. Leonov cannot have been serious in writing this and other similar passages in his works; rather was he mocking indoctrinational literature. This was daring, since many of his presumably satirical sallies were published under Stalin; but it was safe, for what censor would dare suggest that they were written with tongue in cheek? Such protesting mimicry may play a greater part in inspiring modern *vranyo* than one might imagine. It also calls to mind a traditional practice of pre-1917 Russian revolutionaries which will be further discussed below: that of supporting and attempting to intensify reactionary governmental policies with the aim of discrediting the government through its own increasingly absurd measures, and thus rendering its violent overthrow more likely. Given the Russian's acute sensitivity to audience reactions, as noted in the previous section, one is not surprised to find *vranyo* incorporating this element. It requires not only its purveyor or donor, but also its recipient or recipients. *Vranyo* differs in this important respect from *lozh*, which can operate through radio broadcasts and diplomatic notes no less than in the *tête-à-tête*, whereas the true *vranyo* artist can only give his best in the presence of a partner or straight-feed man—the role in which the now-forgotten Marshal Bulganin once served the ebullient Khrushchev. The fact that *vranyo* is a two-way process is stressed again and again in the literature of the subject; and, as the following key quotation from Dostoyevsky's above-mentioned essay shows, facial expression has an important part to play. 'Have you never told an anecdote, an alleged personal experience, to someone who originally told that very same story to you about himself? Have you really forgotten how, half way through the story you suddenly remembered this fact . . . also confirmed by *the suffering glance of the listener, fixed firmly upon you, for in such cases people somehow do stare into each other's eyes with tenfold intensity?*'[9]

As this passage illustrates, the relations between purveyor and recipient are of the essence. Perhaps the greatest passage of *vranyo* in fiction is the scene in *The Idiot* where General Ivolgin tells Prince Myshkin a tall story about his supposed childhood experiences during the Napoleonic invasion of 1812. Ivolgin claims that Napoleon appointed him his page during the occupation of Moscow, and the zenith of the *vranyo* is attained when Napoleon is described as ordering the French retreat on the infant Ivolgin's advice to 'Buzz off home, General.' Throughout this preposterous account Ivolgin studies Myshkin's expression. 'He squinted mistrustfully at the Prince, saying, "You are smiling, Prince, you are looking at my face," ' and so on. After Ivolgin had left, the recipient 'had a premonition that he [Ivolgin] belonged to that category of liars who, although they lie to the point of sensual self-indulgence and even to a condition of trance, nevertheless suspect that they are not and cannot be believed.' Myshkin had heard Ivolgin's absurdities out with a straight face, hoping to minister to the General's self-respect; but he had failed, for he received a note from Ivolgin that same evening breaking off all relations.

Prince Myshkin's experience is a warning to all visitors to Russia. When confronted with *vranyo* they should assume a serious, respectful expression, thus avoiding 'facecrime'. Surely that is not too much to ask. Many a *vranyo*-monger is a decent enough man, after all; and if it is his official duty to bemuse foreigners with misleading signals, that is no reason for humiliating him by showing obvious signs of disbelief; still less by trying to catch him out. It may be irritating to be told, as has often happened to foreign students in Russia, that all readers in Moscow's Lenin Library can easily obtain access to any book they want, including the works of Trotsky, Zinovyev, Bukharin, and—for such attempts have been made—myself. But this, again, is no reason for imitating those visitors who have been known to make the offending *vrun* show them all the various catalogues in order to expose the story as an invention. Some things do not need disproving. Moreover, those who seek to demonstrate the falsehood of a given piece of *vranyo* may unwittingly offend some harmless fantasist by implying that it was a piece of *lozh* all along.

Given the vogue of creative fancy-mongering, it is no surprise that visitors from Russia often imagine themselves exposed to Western *vranyo* when they are not. I have noticed this when conducting Russian visitors around Oxford colleges. One has only to make an innocent remark of indisputable veracity, such as, 'Here is a typical undergraduate's room,' to see a change come over the visitor's face as he composes it in an attitude of respectful serious-ness—which may not, however, conceal his disbelief. *The vranyo has begun*, he has concluded; and, as one man of the world talking to another, he proposes to receive it with due solemnity. His own turn will come later, after all. There has to be give and take in these matters; for, as Dostoyevsky enunciated nearly a century ago, 'A delicate reciprocity of *vranyo* is almost the first condition of Rus-sian society, of all Russian meetings, parties, clubs, learned societies and the like.'[10]

While the *vranyo* artist does not expect to be disproved or un-masked, and is entitled to this courtesy, a key question remains: does he expect to be believed? Not at all. There could be no greater error than to conclude that these creative effusions are meant to be taken seriously. They are intended to be accepted with a serious and respectful countenance, but that is a different matter. By believing, literally, a piece of *vranyo*—a reaction surprisingly com-mon among more gullible Western visitors to Russia—the recipi-ent gravely insults his host's inventive powers, implying in effect that they have not been called into play. There is no satisfaction in dispensing *vranyo* to an innocent who happily accepts it at its face value. Consequently official *vranyo* purveyors often prefer, when dealing with Western visitors, a tactful sceptic to a duped fellow traveller. In Russia the latter can easily seem more sinister than he is; for there must be something wrong, it is felt, with someone who swallows official handouts while under no compulsion to do so.

Even in the totalitarian period some Russians have not hesitated to satirise aspects of official *vranyo*; for, despite all official controls, one may still find traces of that healthy early tradition whereby it is Russians themselves who most expertly mock the incongruities and pretences of their society. Such protests are usually on a muted level, being linked to minor targets and restricted by the conven-tions of officially licensed 'self-criticism'. However, in phases of political relaxation there have been occasions when the basis of society has been called in question with a verve reminiscent of such as Radishchev, Chaadayev, Gogol and Saltykov, those scourges of the pre-revolutionary musical-bank network. Such an exceptional work was Alexander Yashin's story of 1956, *Levers*. Here members of a collective farm's Party organisation are found discussing the miserable condition of their fief: the widespread poverty, the shortage of livestock, the squalor, the mess, the meaninglessness of official catch-phrases. But then they suddenly pull themselves up, reverting with the ease born of long practice from real speech to the musical currency of official *vranyo*, and begin intoning those same meaningless catchwords which, in the previous phase, they had ridiculed.[11]

Yashin's story illustrates the two-compartment mentality which the Russian official has cultivated since long before the revolutions. It also illustrates my own long-standing contention that there are two distinct Russian languages: the low-style or demotic tongue, based ultimately on peasant usage, in which ordinary events such as the loss of a collar-stud or the price of a bottle of vodka may be discussed; and the priestly or hieratic argot, deriving partly from Church Slavonic, in which such matters as the notional fulfilment of notional norms, the 'achievements' of 'workers' and other liturgical or 'musical' material is traditionally couched.

DECEPTION TACTICS

Now that the practice of *vranyo* has been reviewed, the more serious kind of distortion must be considered: *lozh*, 'lies'.

To claim that all men are liars is to exaggerate; but it is not straining credulity to suggest that some Russians, like some Frenchmen, Englishmen or Greeks, do occasionally lapse into terminological inexactitude in a grosser form than *vranyo*. How far can one determine whether this is so? Do Russians exhibit any specific national characteristic when indulging, if they do, in the common human practice of affirming what one knows not to be and of denying what one knows to be?

That all Russians were liars was a common impression of the earliest Western travellers to the country. The sixteenth-century British trader Antony Jenkinson referred to them as 'great talkers and liars, flatterers and dissemblers'.[1] His successor, the ambassador Giles Fletcher, made the same point. 'From the great to the small (except some few that will scarcely be found) the Russ neither believeth anything that another man speaketh, nor speaketh anything himself worthy to be believed.' Fletcher also contrasts the double-dealing Russians with their scrupulously honest Tatar subjects, repelled by Christianity because of the duplicity of the Orthodox.[2] An extreme statement or libel on these lines is that of a sixteenth-century Lithuanian traveller. Describing the sale of captured Russians, which regularly took place at Crimean Tatar slave auctions, he asserted that the auctioneer always tried to pass off his stock as Polish rather than Russian, 'for the Muscovite race, being crafty and deceitful, does not bring a good price'. The seventeenth-century traveller Olearius describes the Russians as cunning and unscrupulous in dealing with each other, and as even less sincere when dealing with foreigners; incapable of friendship, they simulate good will only in order to exploit another's benevolence for their own purposes. Two centuries later Dostoyevsky too came near to saying that all Russians are liars. 'Among our Russian intellectual classes the very existence of a non-liar is an impossibility, the reason being that in Russia even honest men can lie.' He then continues, qualifying this harsh judgement, 'I am convinced that in other nations, for the great majority, it is only scoundrels who lie; they lie for practical advantage: that is, with directly criminal aims.' Though this passage comes from Dostoyevsky's essay on *vranyo*, mentioned above, it is the *lozh* root which he employs here.[3]

The Russia-baiter Custine voices similar sentiments; he speaks of members of all classes conspiring with miraculous accord to bring about the triumph of duplicity. 'They have a dexterity in lying, an aptitude for the bogus so effective that it affronts my integrity.' Custine elsewhere denounced Russian mendacity as less than dexterous; he felt insulted, he said, by the low level of the deceits practised on him, considering them 'infantile ruses'. The same point is also made by Mackenzie Wallace. 'When we [foreign visitors] happen to detect positive dishonesty, it seems to us especially heinous, because the trickery employed is more primitive and awkward than that to which we are accustomed.' One sympathises with the Russians: dismissed as liars—and incompetent liars at that—not merely by the hostile witness Custine, but also by one of their most objective nineteenth-century observers. The same point is put in a different way by a twentieth-century Russia-watcher, Sally Belfrage, who, after noting Russians' 'incredible lack of artifice' goes on to correct herself with 'or at least hopeless inability to put artifice over'.[4]

Miss Belfrage's perceptive comment conveniently straddles the contrary witness of those quoted immediately above who emphasise the supreme mendacity of the Russians, and of those whose witness was invoked on an earlier page as stressing their supreme honesty. Claims were there cited to the effect that one always knows where one is when dealing with a Russian, that Russians exhibit a degree of honesty unparalleled among other nations, and so on.[5] One might also have added, had it not seemed premature before the phenomenon of *vranyo* had been explained, the frequently voiced obsession with *pravda* ('truth', 'justice'), on 'seeking' which Russians, whether peasants or intellectuals, have constantly affirmed themselves to be engaged, though just what they understand by this quest is hard to say. Yet to a Russian, according to Gorer, the gradual discovery and application of the Truth (*pravda*) is the most significant activity of mankind. 'In the Russian conception of the universe, their concept of Truth holds an extremely important place.'[6] The concept is all the more vital to the Russian owing to his tendency, reinforced by exposure to a dogmatic ideology, to assume that, in any given situation, however complex, there can be only one Truth.

Bearing in mind such testimony, one may consider what defence can be made against those many native and foreign witnesses who have found it practically inconceivable that a Russian should open his mouth except to tell a lie. At least it is only in earlier centuries that witnesses to Russian mendacity seem so outspoken and unanimous, which suggests that standards of truthfulness have improved over the ages. One must adjust one's aim very slightly, though, owing to the appearance in modern times of the Russia-fancier— the witness who, whenever he makes what might sound a disparaging remark on the country or people, is subject to an automatic urge to correct the balance, and display his own objectivity by some form of words designed to soften the impact of adverse criticism. From this kind of flaccid, mechanical fair-mindedness such robust witnesses as a Jenkinson, a Fletcher, an Olearius, a Custine, a Dostoyevsky, a Mackenzie Wallace and a Chekhov were immune, living as they did in those happy eras when no one felt impelled to cultivate an 'image' of this kind.

In what other ways can one modify the absurd yet so frequently advanced imputation that all Russians lie all the time? Certainly the incidence of mendacity can be shown to vary according to who is talking to whom, when, about what topic and—perhaps most important of all—in what mood. Owing to the usual emphasis on emotion and relative unconcern with fact, it is in the former area that one is more likely to encounter the kind of trenchant honesty which has impressed so many witnesses in the Russia-favouring camp.

In the nineteenth century mendacity tended, according to some, to be more widely cultivated among the privileged than among the unprivileged section of society. Though Nikitenko calls the muzhik 'almost a perfect savage' in his diary, adding that he is also a drunkard and a thief, he goes on to say that he is 'incomparably superior to the so-called educated and intellectual. The muzhik is sincere. He does not try to seem what he is not . . . But the educated Russian is bogus through and through.'[7] A contemporary, the influential political *émigré* Alexander Herzen, claims that all familiar with the Russian peasantry, as he himself was only in limited degree, would agree that peasants rarely deceive each other; that they have almost unlimited trust in each other 'without need for formal contracts and written conditions'.[8] Of peasant relations with the authorities Herzen gives a different picture, describing the traditional subterfuges employed by the muzhik in his undeclared war against landowners and officials. So do others who treat the theme, not excluding Soviet-published authors. Sholokhov's collectivised rustics, in his novel *Virgin Soil Upturned*, tend to share the nineteenth-century muzhik's attitude towards authority, defined by Mackenzie Wallace as follows: 'Russian peasants, when dealing with the authorities, consider the most patent and barefaced falsehoods as a fair means of self-defence.' It was only when the muzhik came into contact with the authorities that he functioned as an expert fabricator of falsehoods. 'In this there is nothing that need surprise us. For ages the peasantry were exposed to the arbitrary power and ruthless exactions of those who were placed over them; and as the law gave them no means of legally protecting themselves, their only means of self-defence lay in cunning and deceit.'[9]

If ordinary Russians have for centuries lied to their authorities, those authorities have been in no position to complain, owing to

the institutionalised mendacity which they themselves have practised and which has not been calculated to set a good example to
the lower orders.

The regime of Nicholas I has been described as cynical and
seemingly based on the cultivation of a series of massive fictions:
there were 'two images of Russian reality—the country as it actually was and as the authorities wished it to appear'.[10] If 1839
should be compared with 1939 this impression would be enhanced
by the political fictions and myths in which Stalin's subjects were
not necessarily expected to believe, but of which they were required to affirm their acceptance as a form of ritual obeisance.
These included the claim that Bolshevik theory is scientifically
based; that socialism had been achieved by the late 1930s; that the
Soviet people was politically and morally united; that power was in
the hands of the workers. 'By restricting the public utterances of
. . . citizens almost solely to reciting parts of the theory and glorify-
ing its creator, Stalin demonstrated the extent to which they were
in his power.'[11]

Authority has always tended to provoke passive resistance. But
so too have foreigners—no doubt because, during so many years of
Russian history, the foreigner has often represented or been equated with authority. From the Mongol Khans through the Tatar
Tsar Boris Godunov, the German Empress Catherine the Great
and the nineteenth-century Tsar-Emperors—increasingly and in
the end overwhelmingly German by blood—to the part-German,
part-Kalmuck Lenin and the Georgian Stalin, the country has
often been ruled at the summit by non-Russians endowed with
absolute power. They have included some of the bloodiest of the
country's many tyrants. Meanwhile the local boss, from general
and high official down to bailiff and factory manager, has often
been some alien, or someone whom the muzhik considered a foreigner even if he was not. For these reasons foreigners have
traditionally activated the self-protective evasive tactics of Russia's
lower orders as much as any home-grown authority. This point
must be borne in mind when one tries to assess the many alien
witnesses who have for centuries furnished a high proportion of the
source materials on the history of a people which long ago learned
the unwisdom of volunteering evidence on matters of public
interest; or, indeed, on anything at all.

That a foreigner who harps on Russian truthfulness and sincerity has often been fed such sentiments for mechanical repetition as 'patter'—this has already been noted. No less suspect, it must now be added, is the witness of those foreigners who stress the nation's inevitable unreliability, duplicity and general untruthfulness.

SEALED LIPS

Ways in which the Russian exposes himself, either excessively or misleadingly, have been scrutinised, and the time has come to examine those areas in which he assumes the opposite guise of compulsive under-communicator.

Ever since Muscovy first became accessible to the intruding foreigner, there has been a tendency for information about the country to be kept a closely guarded secret, access to which must be denied to foreigners and citizens alike. Little did Ambassador Herberstein suspect this when he arrived in Moscow in April 1516, and embarked on seeking and imparting information. He offered, for example, to elucidate certain maps which he had brought with him; but which, as it turned out, aroused the gravest suspicions in his hosts. The result of this imprudence was that observers were quartered in his residence, and that he was permitted to receive visitors only under the eyes of these official scrutineers.[1] Far harsher was the treatment suffered by the learned foreign monk Maxim the Greek. Reaching Muscovy in 1518, only two years after Herberstein's first visit, to conduct a revision of liturgical texts at the invitation of Grand Prince Basil III, he was never permitted to return to his native land despite attempts, spread over several decades, to secure the sixteenth-century equivalent of an exit visa. He died in a monastery near Moscow in 1556, after the reason for his detention had been made explicit in terms reflecting a dominant streak in his hosts' mentality. 'We are in fear: thou, a man of learning, comest to us and hast seen here of our best and worst, and when thou goest hence *thou wilt tell of everything*.'[2]

Secretiveness has persisted through the centuries, ebbing or flowing according to the degree of relaxation obtaining at a given period. It was still in evidence when the Scottish scholar William Richardson, a visitor to St Petersburg in the 1760s, lamented that he could obtain no information from the newspapers: 'Half of Russia may be destroyed and the other half know nothing about the matter.' Similarly, Madame de Staël complained, when in Russia as a refugee from Napoleon in 1812, that she could discover nothing about the course of the Russo-French War.[3] And yet, little as foreigners may have been permitted to learn about the country, they have often enjoyed more privileged access to information than is conceded to nationals: 'No native could have been given the chance of visiting the prisons, hospitals, transport columns and barges that George Kennan was given, nor of holding conversations with political prisoners, even with police and governors.'[4] The reference is to the American journalist George Kennan, who toured Siberia's penal establishments in the 1880s, and whose description of them in his *Siberia and the Exile System* is an important historical source. The comment remains valid, even though it seems slightly misleading when one remembers the facilities afforded to that native student of Russian penology, Anton Chekhov, when he visited the convict settlement on the Island of Sakhalin shortly afterwards. As this reminds one, the latter decades of the Empire, including even the notoriously reactionary reign of Alexander III, were not one of those periods when the flow of information was most rigorously restricted.

The restriction of information has also involved trivial and individual issues. For example, no accident or suicide statistics were published in early nineteenth-century Russia. It was then possible for several hundred—or could it be thousand?—persons to perish in small boats in a single storm in the Gulf of Finland without the matter being mentioned in the newspapers of near-by St Petersburg, and without the gaiety of court celebrations being affected. No one could be induced to talk of it at all.[5] Similarly, in the totalitarian period, such disasters as aeroplane crashes in which no foreigner is involved, and which can therefore more easily be hushed up; the Tashkent earthquake of 1966; a forest fire in the Vladimir area, followed by a local potato famine in 1972—all have been ignored by the media, and have only come to notice long after the event.[6] During Hitler's mass onslaught on the USSR on 22 June 1941, 'While German planes and tanks were screaming into action in the forenoon . . . Radio Moscow blandly ignored these irrelevancies for several hours—continuing to broadcast a routine programme on physical training and cataloguing the "achievements" of Soviet workers in normal peacetime style."[7]

For obvious reasons the pretence that Hitler's invasion was not occurring could not, in June 1941, long be sustained. But many another momentous event of the past has been consigned to compulsory oblivion. After Ivan the Terrible's murderous enforcement agency, the *oprichnina*, had been wound up in 1572, the very mention of that defunct body was forbidden on pain of death. Similarly, the assassination of the Emperor Paul, in 1801, was still officially a non-event forty years later; no reference to it might be made in public, and passers-by would avert their eyes as they hurried past the scene of the murder: the Mikhaylovsky Palace in St Petersburg.[8] Another notable non-event was the Decembrist Rising which followed the death of Alexander I in 1825; all mention of it was forbidden throughout the thirty-year reign of the new monarch, Nicholas I, the executed and imprisoned rebels being relegated to the category of unpersons. Similarly, to take an eloquent example from the many suppressions of more recent years, it was possible for Stalin to deport an entire small nation of 200,000 persons (the Meskhetians) without this ever being officially admitted—indeed, without even the bare fact becoming known to the world at large for more than twenty years.[9] As for unpersons from Trotsky downwards, recent history is littered with them. Trotsky himself, though second only to Lenin as the initiator of the October Revolution of 1917, is regularly denied an entry in Soviet encyclopedias published since his disgrace, though the abstract noun *Trotskyism* rates a heading.

A monument to such liquidated or demoted phantoms could once, and for all I know still may, be observed in the colossal mosaics embellishing the roof of the Komsomol Square Station of the Moscow Metro. One of these panoramas depicted a notable scene of 1945, the surrender of captured German banners with their swastika emblems before a line of political dignitaries headed by Stalin. But of nine Politburo members portrayed, only three were still recognisable when I last visited the shrine in 1960. Six had suffered the whitewashing of their facial features, of which only the ghostly outline remained. There one could behold the spectral images of Beria, Molotov, Kaganovich and others who had incurred disgrace since Stalin's death—as indeed had Stalin

(95)

himself in part, but without ever achieving unperson status. How durable an institution unpersonship is one may be reminded by the nineteenth-century comment, that 'in Russia, on the day that a minister falls from favour, his friends become deaf and blind. No one dares to remember that he is living, nor even to believe that he ever lived. A man is as it were buried the moment he appears to be disgraced.'[10]

Comparable elusiveness is found in the area of historical record. In the first place, 'Most of the fundamental laws affecting Russia's system of government and the status of its citizens were never at all promulgated in any formal way.' These have included such basic institutions as the attachment of peasants to the soil and of urban inhabitants to the cities (serfdom), which had existed for more than two centuries before the emancipation act of 1861; the associated authority of landlords over peasants; the introduction (as well as the liquidation) of Ivan the Terrible's *oprichnina*; the system of automatic promotion by seniority within the civil service; the foundation of the first centralised political police organ, the Pre-obrazhensky Prikaz, under Peter the Great.[11] Secondly, one may contrast with these institutions—existing *de facto* but apparently not *de jure*—later, no less elusive institutions which have existed *de jure* but not *de facto*. The most prominent has been the Stalin Constitution of 1937, whereby the population was guaranteed widespread civil rights which, far from being assertable in practice, were contravened through mass arrest, torture and widespread relegation to concentration camps without due process of law. Bukharin, the main framer of this document, was himself framed and judicially murdered by show trial when the ink was barely dry on his signature to the draft constitution.

In a context so fluid and confusing it is no surprise to find that suspicion has been cast on so many historical and literary documents. The greatest monument of Russian medieval literature, *The Lay of Igor's Raid*, commemorates a minor skirmish of the year 1185 in language admittedly memorable, but of what date? Is this oft-acclaimed work of genius a near-contemporary poem, and in an idiom of which no other specimen happens to survive, as patriotic Russian scholarship maintains? Or is the *Lay*, as some have maintained, an eighteenth-century forgery based on a fifteenth-century document, the *Zadonshchina*? Or was the

Zadonshchina cribbed from the *Lay*? This is no place to offer solutions to a problem which has perplexed specialists for well over a century. Whatever the truth may be, the fact is that the document's authenticity is rejected by a number of reputable scholars. Its first publishers pointed with unconscious irony to the 'Ossianic Spirit' of the work, not realising that the semi-mythical Gaelic bard Ossian was hardly even an unperson—a reminder that such episodes are no Russian monopoly.

Another historical document to fall under suspicion is the purportedly sixteenth-century correspondence between Ivan the Terrible and a renegade nobleman, Prince Andrew Kurbsky. Long accepted as one of the most valuable medieval Russian sources, extensively quarried for the light which it seems to shed on a vital epoch in Russian history and on a maniac ruler of fascinating psychological make-up, it is now claimed by Edward L. Keenan to be a concoction of the following century. His conclusions, though strenuously contested, have placed the Ivan-Kurbsky correspondence under suspicion which later researches may—but, given the elusiveness of matters Russian, very likely will not—decisively confirm or refute. Whatever the outcome of the debate, the fact remains that 'In the sixteenth and seventeenth centuries, forgery was used with the definite aim of improving a pedigree, giving an improved title to land ownership, and in political controversy.'[12]

Confusingly authenticated too is a key document of the present century, the famous 'secret speech' delivered by Nikita Khrushchev to a closed session of the Supreme Soviet of the USSR on 25 February 1956. It first became available in an English translation issued, without attribution of source, by the American State Department in the same year. Though official USSR sources have neither confirmed nor rejected the authenticity of this pronouncement—the most important in the complex history of de-Stalinisation—Western scholars have displayed more collective assurance of its authenticity than *The Lay of Igor's Raid*, and even the Ivan-Kurbsky correspondence, now enjoy. Still, authentic though the 'secret speech' surely is, its status as a historical document remains elusive in view of the failure of the authorities in the country of origin either to confirm or to disavow so widely disseminated a statement by their leading politician of the time. Khrushchev's name was to figure again when, in 1971, the first, huge, instalment of his alleged 'memoirs' was launched by an American publisher without proper explanation of their provenance. Could these seemingly senile babblings, consistent in tone with what is known of their alleged author's character, indeed be his *ipsissima verba*? It was hard to decide. However, after the publication (in 1974) of a further massive instalment, at least one scholar has proclaimed the authenticity of the two-tier effusion as 'established beyond reasonable doubt'. He also adds that its 'value as a historical source remain[s] disappointing'.[13] The reason is, of course, that the Khrushchev material is too saturated with *vranyo* to be taken as evidence of much beyond its originator's psychological condition.

To all this may be added another notable twentieth-century document. The best-known novel of the Soviet period, Michael Sholokhov's *Quiet Don*, has been proclaimed in part a plagiaristic work filched from the writings of an obscure Cossack memoirist of the Civil War. Whether the accusation may stand or not again remains obscure; one of its leading sponsors is another prominent writer of the Soviet period, Alexander Solzhenitsyn, whose opinions command respect.

It is as if *Beowulf*, Magna Carta, the Gettysburg Address and President Eisenhower's memoirs should suddenly dissolve and enter a limbo in which their authenticity could no longer be established—nor yet impugned—while large parts of Hemingway's *For Whom the Bell Tolls* were suddenly revealed as possibly, but also very possibly not, lifted from the writings of an obscure war correspondent whose papers (if they ever existed) disappeared during the siege of Madrid. So much for certain literary and historical records. What of non-records? The papers of Michael Speransky, perhaps the most gifted statesman and administrator of Russia's imperial period, who died in 1839, waited until the year 1961 to be published—an astonishing tribute to the security-mindedness of Tsarist and post-Tsarist Russia alike. It is also a reminder that Speransky himself had become, in 1812, the victim of one of those sudden, volte-face disgraces which have characterised both major Russian regimes: he left the Emperor Alexander I after a friendly chat, only to be arrested and transported to Siberia while the monarch's affable words were still ringing in his ears.[14] True, Speransky was reinstated under Nicholas I, but there is something curiously enduring about Russian political disgrace, even when it has been nominally rescinded. Moreover, this gap of 122 years, not to mention three revolutions, between the man's death and the publication of his papers, prompts one to wonder how many other key documents may be mouldering unread in the archives—documents touching perhaps on such episodes as the death of the uncooperative Tsarevich Alexis in 1718, knouted or not knouted out of this life on the orders of his father Peter the Great.

To speak of secrecy is to be reminded of censorship, that archetypally Russian institution with a history too complex to permit more than a few fleeting observations on its general character. In Nicholas I's reign Alexander Nikitenko, himself a censor, reckoned that the number of officials engaged in censoring books exceeded the number of books published in a year.[15] But these were easy times for the censored compared with a century later. A former Soviet editor now domiciled in the West, Leonid Vladimirov, has reckoned the total of censorship officials in recent times at seventy thousand. He also speaks of a three-hundred-page index of banned subjects, colloquially known as the Talmud, with the aid of which the broadcast and printed word is kept free of reference, not only to such natural disasters as the above-mentioned Tashkent earthquake, but also to food shortages, price increases, the names of KGB operatives other than the head of that institution, the earnings of Party and government officials, and also—not surprisingly—the very institution of censorship itself.[16]

Nor is such secrecy confined to domestic affairs. For example, the American Watergate scandal of 1973–4 was long concealed by the Russian media. Yet, in reflecting discredit on the United States, the traditional major target for hostile propaganda, the affair might have seemed to cry out for exposure. Two considerations were probably operating here. As a sponsor of that modern form of appeasement misnamed *détente*, President Nixon enjoyed a measure of Kremlinite approval. His reputation must therefore be bolstered as long as possible. Secondly, if a figure as august as an American President could fall into disrepute, might not the sacred concept of authority in general—domestic as well as foreign— become devalued?

Foreigners have occasionally been enlisted in Soviet censorship or cover-up operations. As a subscriber to the Great Soviet Encyclopedia in the early 1950s, I recall being issued with a special page, largely devoted to supplementary material with which the entry 'Beria' in Volume Five (1949) was to be replaced. The point was that Beria, still honoured in 1949, had since suffered execution and the imposition of unperson status, a grave embarrassment to librarians and archivists. Subscribers were accordingly instructed to cut the page containing the entry Beria 'with scissors or a razor blade, while preserving the margin near the binding'. To fill the generous space formerly allotted to the then in-person Beria, a diarist, Friedrich Berkholz, was rescued from perhaps unmerited oblivion, together with several pictures of dead whales and walruses as snapped in the no less alphabetically convenient Bering Sea. Here is the kind of topic with which the satirist Saltykov had been filling his writings nearly a century earlier. There is, too, more than a whiff of Gogol about the affair.[17]

Sounding such information—highly restricted at source, now filtered out, now suddenly withdrawn or disavowed—foreign Kremlin-watchers have learnt to gauge the undertows of Soviet politics through analysis of such seeming trivialities as *Pravda*'s typographical house rules. Was Nikita Khrushchev properly described as a first secretary, a First secretary or a First Secretary of the Communist Party of the Soviet Union?[18] His influence fluctuated as the honorific capitals came and went; and the tracking of such signals is even more vital to native officials (whose careers and livelihood can depend on them) than to foreign commentators.

It is in this context of official secretiveness that Russian imaginative literature has acquired its special status as a source of insights, not otherwise obtainable, into Russian life. The point has been made many times: for instance, in an English review, dated 14 September 1878, of Turgenev's novel *Virgin Soil*. Commenting on the difficulty of obtaining information on Russia's internal condition, the reviewer, Richard Littledale, wrote that 'It is only books like the present that enable outsiders to guess at it with any approach to correctness.'[19] The same point has been made for a later era by the economist Alec Nove. Noting the difficulty of obtaining information on agriculture in the Soviet period, he adds that 'The best material about the village appears in the literary monthlies.'[20] And so one is often compelled to treat imaginative writing as a historical source because other evidence is unsatisfactory. Once again, though, Russia is not unique, for reference to the eminent Egyptologist Sir Alan Gardiner suggests a close parallel several thousand years ago in the land of the Pharaohs. 'If we ask where our best historical material is to be found our answer may seem to be almost a contradiction in terms; it is to be found in Egyptian fiction, where the authors were able to depict existing conditions and to vent their feelings with a freedom impossible when the predominant intention was that of boasting.'[21]

It is such considerations which have led to Russian history being described as part of the 'crown domain', and as 'a state secret, one closely but by no means efficiently guarded'.[22]

III
Group
Consciousness

TOGETHERNESS

After reviewing Russians as communicators the argument now
focuses on their collective responses to aspects of the world outside
and inside their own country. These will include the wider affiliations of religion, political party, nationality and class, and also the
intimate world of domestic, family and sexual relations. First, however, the Russian's general characteristics as a social being must be
considered. Is he, as often claimed, the most gregarious of humans,
is he endowed with a special gift for communication with his fellows? Or is he the opposite: a creature unusually ill-adapted for
co-operation?

To find competent observers, Russian and foreign, making extreme claims on both sides is to be expected. 'The communal spirit
is the basis, the foundation of all Russian history, past, present and
future. The seed and the root of everything that appears on the
surface lies buried in its fertile depths': thus the leading Slavophile Yury Samarin, in 1847.[1] A century later Klaus Mehnert
points out the special pleasure which the average Russian derives
from the company of his fellows, even without the help of alcohol,
and links this sociability with the pre-revolutionary village commune, the *mir*, as also with the proliferation of various 'collectives'
under communism.[2] Russians are described as thinking themselves
members of one vast family. They 'do not seem to feel that enforced close company is [a] ... threat to individual identity ...
the lack of physical elbow-room does not mean a lack of elbow-
room for the spirit.' When a factory inspector visited a Russian
sugar factory in 1903 he found the workers living in dormitories,
and insisted that partitions should be put up so that each individual
could enjoy some privacy in a small cubicle. But this was not what
they wanted. 'Are we cattle that we should be thus cooped in
stalls?'[3]

A love of togetherness can be traced in many aspects of Russian life, nowhere more than in the previously invoked *mir* or village commune. The institution consisted of an assemblage of heads of village households, meeting in an informal spirit and usually in the open air; and legally required from 1861 onwards to take certain decisions regarding military recruitment, taxation and public order. Informal though the atmosphere generally was, the *mir*'s discussions invariably ended, owing to some special ingredient in the Russian genius, in unanimous resolutions. 'Peasants do not understand decisions by majority vote.' All members of the *mir* were required to engage on a united search for a true and just solution to their problems, and anyone unable to accept the consensus could only leave his village and cut himself off from it. Similarly, in more modern times, a member of the Komsomol remarks: 'I say "my generation" all the time and not "I" because we never thought of ourselves individually, but always as a whole group.'4 The compulsory unanimity of the *mir*'s decisions has been transferred to the totalitarian electoral system, but with the slight relaxation that a majority of, say, 99·23 per cent is considered acceptable instead of the hundred per cent conformity which national tradition would demand.

In more violent contexts too the Russians have been credited with a tendency to react collectively. Gorky goes out of his way to identify the exceptional cruelty, in his view, of the Russian muzhik as a communal sport; he speaks of the peasantry enjoying the infliction of torture on a collective basis. Even in his atrocities, according to this witness, the Russian cleaves to his traditional togetherness.5

By many analysts the spirit of secular collectivism has been linked with the special communal spirit known as *sobornost*, 'community-mindedness', often claimed as unique to the Russian Orthodox Church. One modern Russia-watcher speaks of the spirit of Orthodox Christianity combining with that of the *mir* to create in Russians a conviction that, in the common sharing of an experience—divine in Church worship, man-made in Communist achievement—'they preserve a truer humanity than a Westerner can partake of in his over-cultivation of the individual.'6 Here once again is a modern, foreign authority echoing Slavophile doctrine of the nineteenth century. In this view the whole of Western culture has been corrupted by excessive rationalism deriving from the influence of classical Greece and Rome, while the Russian Orthodox Church owes its superiority to collective wisdom transcending that of any individual, however wise.

Religious togetherness received eloquent expression in Dostoyevsky's polemical writings. An extreme traditionalist both in religion and politics, and prone to unite these two elements in his many impassioned harangues, he spoke of the 'spiritual indivisibility of the millions of our people, and their closest communion with the Monarch'.[7] During the Stalin period and thereafter such spiritual indivisibility has been expressed or simulated, not only by the officially rigged near-unanimous elections to which reference was made above, but also in pre-scripted political meetings or pageants at which the dragooned congregation is periodically induced to rise to its collective feet uttering tumultuous applause. When a twelve-sided gramophone recording of one of Stalin's speeches was issued, the whole of the last side was assigned to the clapping and cheering which concluded the performance. A similar manifestation is reported in Solzhenitsyn's *Gulag Archipelago*, where a regional Party conference applauds a motion of loyalty to Stalin over a period of five minutes. They seem doomed to continue for ever, since no one dares incur the charge of disloyalty by being seen to desist first. In the end the director of a paper factory takes the initiative and sits down firmly, whereupon total silence follows. But he is arrested that same night.[8]

Such collective responses are strikingly 'Russian', and one could continue quoting them. But that would be to conceal another, less obtrusive feature: anti-collectivism. One modern observer bases his analysis not so much on the people's unique togetherness as on the tension between their strong centripetal urges and other—less obtruded but no less significant—centrifugal drives: 'the painful conflict between collectivism and self-assertion that the dualistic response to life was expressly designed to avoid'.[9] Looking back into history, this observer finds an even balance between the collective pull of the Church, which urged the peasants to sink their differences in common submission to God, and the individual pull of peasant behaviour.

To accept Russian claims to be animated by a uniquely corporate spirit might naturally be to expect that this spirit would be expressed in some equally outstanding capacity for corporate action. In fact the opposite seems to be the case. It is, for example, the relatively individualist British who sink their differences and combine to create that triumph of modern civilisation, an orderly queue. To see the doors of a Moscow underground train stormed with much self-defeating shoving and fighting is to marvel at the Russian's capacity for collective counter-functional behaviour. It is also to wonder at the good humour commonly preserved on these occasions, when no one seems to take offence at the buffeting—perhaps because, as one witness puts it, they feel it to be the crowd which pushes rather than the individuals of which the crowd is composed.[10] Nor are these conflicts confined to the hectic metropolis. Comparable hazards are involved in catching a bus in Vladimir or Smolensk.

All Russian enterprises, great and small, tend to fall foul of this inability to co-operate. 'When three or four of us Russians gather together to promote some idea or common cause you may absolutely depend on it that we'll quarrel, play each other scurvy tricks and split up by day two or three.' Making this point, Nikitenko adds that 'Our only salvation lies in the intervention of authority.'[11] In other words, though Russians may *feel* themselves at one with each other to an extent unusual among peoples, they yet seem exceptionally ill adapted for effective corporate *action* unless they can, in effect, sense the likelihood of punitive sanctions in the background.

Many prestige projects, as discussed above—a St Petersburg, a White Sea Canal, a Moscow Metro—were the work of conscripted or convict labour. One may therefore understand how, since so many collective achievements have been effected under compulsion, it is possible for a well-informed observer to deny that the country possesses any corporate spirit.[12] Its corporate institutions, too, have tended to prove impotent except as channels for imposing control from above. Of the pre-revolutionary social estates—gentry, clergy, artisans, peasants—only the clergy possessed a national organisation, and that was headed by a lay government appointee: the Procurator of the Holy Synod, in effect a Minister for Religion. And though the totalitarian period has seen the establishment of numerous nominally autonomous collective associations, the taking of corporate initiative seems virtually ruled out by the technique of intermeshing them with Party and security bodies briefed from on high. An authority on the Soviet professional classes is not exaggerating when he claims that 'Professional associations in the narrow sense of the term . . . are relatively unimportant in the Soviet Union.'[13] Many professions lack any national corporate association: lawyers, doctors, engineers, for example. One of the most active and politically important, the Soviet Writers' Union, is largely a docile instrument of the state. Yet it can acquire significance on the not infrequent occasions when minor rifts are reported as occurring inside it: a sign, usually, of the temporary relaxation of official controls.

Togetherness thus turns out no less elusive than other aspects of the Russian mind. Tempted though one may be to make much of the ability to dispense with privacy (a privilege which a Western citizen may regard as almost as important as the air he breathes), and encouraging though it may be to build inferences on the lack of any word for 'privacy' in their language, the fact yet remains that Russians do prize this amenity—and more, not less, than does many a philosopher of the subject. One may praise the Russians' ability to huddle together happily in communal flats and communal kitchens, and no doubt they do make the most of these inconveniences. But there can be no doubt that most of them vastly prefer, constantly seek, and sometimes achieve a place of their own. To find foreign Russia-fanciers rhapsodising from a safe distance over the communal cooking stove as an embodiment of the principles of *sobornost* and the village commune—this must be exasperating to such few Russians as are not mercifully unaware of these well-meaning patrons. The average Russian does not put up with queueing for use of the gas ring out of a yearning for spiritual oneness with humanity. He does so because he has no choice. He tends, moreover, to develop special skills in cultivating seclusion, living as he does in an ambience where everyone is officially encouraged to assume that his neighbour's business is his own. A private Russian may be comparatively rare; but he tends to be a very private person indeed.

As for the apparent conflict between the corporate spirit and corporate ineffectiveness, except under compulsion by all-powerful authority—at least the seeming contradiction helps to explain a difference of opinion over the interpretation of Chekhov's controversial drama. I have always been impressed, along with many others, by the primacy of 'failure to communicate' as a Chekhovian theme. One may instance, for example, the refusal of his *Cherry Orchard*'s feckless owners to take notice, or even to listen, when the self-made man Lopakhin explains that their ancestral home will be auctioned around their heads unless they immediately adopt certain measures. Here is a failure to communicate as complete as can be conceived—but only on the mundane level of information, common sense and practical affairs. For Lopakhin and his feckless friends are as closely attuned as possible on an emotional level, as any sensitive production of the play must show. Communication is nil, but sympathy total, since Chekhov creates between his characters an 'interplay of emotion' or electrical field which transcends their many disagreements on practicalities.[14]

SUPRANATIONALIST

No account of Russian collective responses can be complete unless it takes in the nation's relations to two supranational organisations, both of which make sweeping or absolute claims in the sphere of ideology, and neither of which possesses a unified global organisation. These are the Christian Church and the world Communist movement. Each has played, each still is playing, a key role in the development of the Russian mentality.

Brief reference has already been made to the special place of Russia's religious evolution in the history of Europe.

At the end of the tenth century the Russians began to adopt the Eastern form of Christianity, and thus joined a loose international religious community which became formally separated from the Western Church in 1054. It lacked any single centre comparable to Rome, consisting of a group of autocephalous churches, of which the Russian Orthodox communion, based on Moscow, became the most influential and extensive with the fall of Constantinople to the Turks in 1453. Under the already disappearing Tatar Yoke, the Russian Church had enjoyed a marked degree of tolerance, including freedom from taxation, and had contributed much to the salvaging or creation of national unity and consciousness under alien oppression.

After the assertion of national independence the Church became an enthusiastic ally of Moscow's Grand Princes, soon entitled Tsars with full ecclesiastical blessing and encouragement. The Church promoted national self-admiration by sponsoring a campaign claiming Moscow as the Third Rome, but no effective attempt was—or, probably, could have been—made to assert ecclesiastical independence of a secular power itself not answerable to any extra-territorial clerical authority. So it continued throughout the ages. In the sixteenth century Ivan the Terrible had a Metropolitan of Moscow and two Archbishops of Novgorod murdered. In 1589, during the next reign, the Regent Boris Godunov sought the Church's favour by securing the promotion of the sitting Metropolitan of Moscow to the highest Eastern ecclesiastical rank, hitherto held only outside Russia: that of Patriarch. Seven years later the Patriarch Job persuaded the feignedly reluctant Regent to assume the rank of Tsar. But the Patriarchate was to last little over a century. Peter the Great allowed it to lapse in 1700 (it was to be revived in subservient form in the totalitarian period), replacing it by a corporate body, the Holy Synod. Thus casually, not even by a stroke of a pen, could a domineering sovereign overthrow the Church's constitution. Even a weak emperor, Peter the Great's grandson Peter III, contrived the feat of sequestrating the Church's land during his six-month reign (1761–2)—again without evoking significant ecclesiastical protests.

The only notable believers' mutiny arose from concern with the minutiae of ritual and liturgy, matters always prominent in the preoccupations of the Orthodox. It was the state-supported decision of an unusually forceful seventeenth-century Patriarch, Nikon, to impose versions of the Russian liturgical texts as revised by comparison with the Greek originals, which sparked off a revolt among those whose devotion to the letter of scriptural law was so profound that they were prepared, nay eager, to sacrifice their lives in the interests of certain disputed—and false!—textual readings. Just what the mass suicides of some twenty thousand of these persecuted Old Believers, often by burning themselves in their own churches, teaches about the Russian character is difficult to specify; but a passionate dislike of the intrusion of rationality into the domain spiritual is surely a significant factor.

Despite their earlier habit of self-immolation, Russia's Old

Believers have flourished and proliferated in their various forms, and are by no means extinguished to this day. But the body from which they split off, the Russian Orthodox Church, was little more than a department of state during the Empire's last two centuries. It was centrally administered from St Petersburg by a layman, the Procurator of the Holy Synod. Its priests maintained an attitude so lacking in independence that they often seemed like another—befrocked, rather than uniformed—variety of *chinovnik* or official. Many sank to denouncing the political misdemeanours of their flocks to the authorities. Nor, as has already been indicated, did the typical Russian village cleric inspire his parishioners with the respect which a German pastor or English rector could command. Notoriously fond of their vodka, priests were not only the butts of the equally tipsy squirearchy, but were also mocked by the not-always-sober peasantry, being traduced in dozens of homely and traditional proverbs, and tending to be valued solely for the ritual functions which they alone could perform: especially conducting services and administering the sacraments of baptism, marriage and burial.

To argue from the dependence of the Russian Church on the state, or from the lowly status of the village priest, that the Russians set little store by their religion would be misleading. At the lowest level the muzhik found his dull, hard, featureless everyday life vastly enriched by the candles, the icons, the iconostases, the antique liturgy, the vestments, the onion domes, the music of his church services—all features which might have been expressly designed to provide psychological relief from the drabness of his environment. Religion was thus, to the average pre-revolutionary villager, an element without which life was barely thinkable. It was also indissolubly fused with the idea of Russianness. A peasant would ask a stranger if he was Orthodox, meaning 'Are you a Russian?' As has often been remarked, there is symbolic significance in the fact that the word for 'peasant' and the word for 'Christian' are etymologically identical (*krestyanin, khristiyanin*).

Thus was the pre-revolutionary peasant's life seemingly governed at every turn, if only in externals, by his church. He dutifully abstained from various forms of food and drink on every Wednesday and Friday, also keeping Lent and the many other extended and taxing fasts of the Orthodox calendar. He celebrated Christmas,

and above all Easter, in a manner so memorable that many an unbeliever could take an enthusiastic part in such ecclesiastical
ceremonies; they might mean nothing to him in a religious sense,
yet remained a familiar and beloved feature of his annual routine.

That the externals of Russian religion held great significance,
and for the uneducated Russian in particular, is common ground.
Where observers differ is on the degree of true spirituality underlying the many religious practices of the people. One school of
thought, which included the nineteenth-century Slavophiles and
has since influenced the accounts of foreign Russia-fanciers, makes
extravagant claims. Dostoyevsky, whose assertions were perhaps
the most extravagant of all, believed in a phenomenon termed the
Russian Christ, about whom he provided no precise information
beyond asserting his measureless superiority over any non-
Russian Christ. A special Russian mission to pronounce a mysterious so-called New Word supposedly destined to bring about a
spiritual regeneration of humanity at large—that too was a prominent feature of Dostoyevsky's teaching; and the (never spoken)
New Word was apt to be linked with that other no less baffling
national activity, the so-called Quest for Truth. Nor, seemingly,
has humanity heard the last of such claims. For instance, the
dissident author Valery Tarsis, who left the Soviet Union in 1966,
has since incorporated dithyrambs to the suffering Russian soul in
his book *Russia and the Russians*. Discounting Communist assertions to the contrary, he claims that his fellow-countrymen are still
uniquely religious, even if they are themselves no longer aware of
the intense devotion to the Orthodox Church which pulsates inside
them. In the end, he grotesquely prophesies, their collective farms
will be transformed into monasteries for the masses.[1]

That the average present-day Russian is more truly religious
than the average non-Russian, is a thesis difficult to sustain. But
what of his past? Has he ever, at any time, been the uniquely
spiritual creature of Dostoyevsky's and Tarsis's harangues? Or was
religion to him more a matter of superstition, mumbo-jumbo and
magical incantation? These are issues so imponderable that one
again marvels at the confidence with which so many observers have
pronounced on them. Moreover, those who contradict the thesis
ascribing a special degree of spirituality to the Russians are at least
as strident in their assertions as are their opponents. It was on this

point that the radical literary critic Belinsky took issue with the fiction-writing religious fanatic Gogol, addressing to him in 1847 a famous open letter—one of the most remarkable of Russia's nineteenth-century cultural documents. Gogol's thesis that the Russians are the most religious people in the world was a downright lie, according to Belinsky. The Russians were, on the contrary, by nature a profoundly atheistic people. They still retained much superstition, but not a trace of true religious faith. As for Russia's priests, their distinguishing marks were their fat bellies, their barbarous ignorance and their total indifference to matters of faith.[2]

A similar argument was put forward nearly a century later by Gorky, who at least offered evidence of a sort—a rarity indeed among pronouncements on Russian religion. According to him, the Revolution convincingly laid bare the absence of any deep religious faith in the Russian village. The point was not that the peasant permitted theatres and clubs to be set up in his village church, which he did, but that he did not even protest against the desecration of such revered shrines as the Kiev-Pechersky Monastery and that of the Trinity and St Sergius. These former objects of reverence seemed to have lost their magic overnight. But when it came to the stocks of grain which so many peasants were secretly hoarding, and which were badly needed to feed starving Moscow and St Petersburg, the same villagers had been prepared to do what they would never do for their saints, relics and shrines: go out gun in hand and beat off assailants and requisitioners.[3]

Religious life has changed almost more than any other aspect of existence since the revolutions. Militantly atheist in its philosophy and militant in exacting affirmations of faith in the new secular creed from most of those who wish to make a career within the new structure, the new state has persecuted religion on a persistent but fluctuating basis over a period of six decades. These efforts have, despite Tarsis's claim to the contrary, reinforced a decline in religion which (since it is general in the modern world) would surely have taken place in Russia without the benefit of governmental persecution. Even at its worst, however—even with the closing of churches, the execution or incarceration of priests and believers, the infiltration of the priesthood with pseudo-priests, and the recruitment of priests as police agents—the government has stopped well short of the systematic massacre of the devout. While successfully subverting or terrorising the lukewarm into apostatising, these efforts have only reinforced the faith of the faithful—whose numbers, though probably dwindling and in any case incomputable, still remain substantial. In the dissident movement of the 1970s Russian Christians occupy a prominent place. They still have their martyrs. And church-going, though practised most sedulously by grandmothers and their infant charges, is by no means confined to such. Among the congregations of the Orthodox, as also of the Baptists—a particularly flourishing denomination which seems to attract a higher proportion of the young and able-bodied—even an unbeliever may sense, or feel that he senses, a vibrant religious fervour such as he may never have observed before. In such a context it is easy to understand how the mid-nineteenth-century Canon H. P. Liddon could assert, after a visit to Russia in 1867, that 'The sense of God's presence—of the supernatural—seems to me to penetrate Russian life more completely than that of any of the Western nations.'[4] If that could be so even when the Church was protected by the state, how much the more so is it now when the faithful have, as it were, nothing but their faith to support them.

How far can the officially imposed Marxist-Leninist creed be accurately described as a new, secular religion which has supplanted the old? One can have an amusing game playing with a set of paradoxical comparisons. Like some canting priest, Stalin intoned over the newly dead Lenin's body, in 1924, a repetitive litany couched in the Old Church Slavonic which the speaker had learned as a highly unsatisfactory pupil of the Tiflis Orthodox Seminary. He then had the remains embalmed and placed on show in Moscow's Red Square for the benefit of pilgrims. Himself mummified and exhibited beside Lenin from 1953, he was—in accordance with the rhythm of the *skandal*—semi-disgraced, demummified and interred in comparative obscurity eight years later. Meanwhile the practice of carrying Lenin's and other leaders' huge portraits in procession—like *khorugvi* (church banners)—has persisted. One may even read placards asserting the actual and coming reincarnation of Russian Communism's premier messiah: LENIN LIVED, LIVES AND SHALL LIVE. Icons or graven images of the various leaders are prominently displayed in offices and public places. Like the now persecuted Orthodox Church, the new dispensation claims to be 'the executor of a species of [Marxist] scriptural revelation'. It has evolved its own devils, martyrs and angels, 'surrounding itself with a largely similar iconography, even down to the mummification of saints, and distinguished from its predecessor primarily by its concentration on the material aspects of existence here below, by its attempt to remove from the next world to this both the promise of heaven and the reality of hell.'[5]

From the Orthodox Church the Communist Party differs by exacting from its members repeated and positive affirmations of faith in the Marxist-Leninist creed, as also in the various successive and overlapping campaigns, political and economic, which are constantly and stridently promoted. It is also an elitist minority organisation which subjects the applications of would-be members to the strictest examination and to probationary scrutiny. How far this is from the purely nominal allegiance required of the Orthodox Christian! Of nineteenth-century Russian Christianity it has been said that 'So long as a member refrains from openly attacking the Church and from passing over to another confession, he may entirely neglect all religious ordinances and publicly profess scientific theories logically inconsistent with any kind of religious belief, without the slightest danger of incurring ecclesiastical censure.'[6] But now, after the dethronement of religion, the new dispensation extends no comparable degree of tolerance in the opposite direction.

Despite the obligation to offer repeated affirmations of faith in the Marxist-Leninist creed and its varying ramifications, one rarely seems to detect, on personal contact with the new faithful, the presence of any profound underlying conviction. Such affirmations are among the formal, routine requirements of a man's career: to be soberly discharged without revealing the inner cynicism which one sometimes seems to sense behind them. But this is, after all, only to be expected from a political creed which has received established status, and to a far greater extent than most established religions. For more obvious signs of Communist political fervour one has to seek among the sometimes persecuted minorities in non-Communist countries, just as one appears to detect the truest religious zeal among the persecuted faithful in the Communist world.

Concern with ultimate profundities, religious or political, has not prevented the Russian from taking a lively interest in mundane affairs, not least those of other countries and peoples, and it is his attitudes as a citizen of the world that must now be considered.

Remembering the care which Russian governments have taken throughout the ages to guard their frontiers, and to segregate their citizens from contact with the polluting alien, one is amazed at the degree to which the country's evolution has nevertheless been intertwined with that of the non-Russian world. It was largely as a by-product of the trading activities of other peoples, Viking and Greek, that the Kievan state first came into being; and Kiev's international relations—dynastic, diplomatic, commercial—remained extensive. In the next major phase of Russian history, that of the Tatar Yoke, a severe quarantine was imposed on foreign contacts, except of course that the Tatar was himself a foreign contact, however unwelcome; and remained one, either as a peaceable subject of the fast-expanding Russian Empire and USSR to the present day, or as an external foe until the end of the eighteenth century. Meanwhile another ancient Russian centre, Novgorod—tributary to the Tatars, but never conquered by them—had kept up lively trade with Western Europe as a member of the Hanseatic League. When Novgorod's independence was eventually extinguished in the late fifteenth century the agent was not Tatary but Moscow, herself newly Tatar-free.

In the middle of the following century Richard Chancellor's adventurous expedition from London to Moscow, via the North Cape and the Northern Dvina, was welcomed by Ivan the Terrible. The London-based Muscovy Company was founded in consequence, after which relations between Russia and Western Europe, albeit closely monitored and sporadically hampered by Muscovite authority, were to grow ever closer in succeeding years. Many of these contacts came through wars with Western states— Sweden, Poland, Livonia—which were Muscovy's superior in technology: wars from which Muscovy eventually benefited through being forced to adopt or improve on the methods of its adversaries. Long before Peter the Great embarked on the europeanisation of Russia's upper class, his predecessors had been welcoming to their service English, Scots, French, German and other Western or Central European soldiers, traders, craftsmen and professional men. Many chose to resist assimilation, retaining their national identity, customs and religion; others were transformed in a generation or two, through conversion to Orthodoxy and learning to speak the language, into Russians indistinguishable from other Russians, except perhaps by an outlandish surname. The registers of the Russian nobility and gentry came to include such representatives of Western civilisation as Polish noblemen and titled Germans from the Baltic lands along with Caucasian and Tatar princes. More than two-thirds of the late seventeenth-century gentry were of foreign extraction:[1] an astounding figure, eloquent on the interpenetration of Russian and non-Russian on the soil of Muscovy.

The many non-assimilating or temporarily resident aliens continued to attract the deep suspicion combined with fascination which foreigners have always stimulated in the Russian. The Russians called them 'dumb ones'; for such is the original meaning of their word for foreigners, *nemtsy*, which now means 'Germans'. They might be permitted to come to Moscow and engage in a trade or profession, but were compulsorily segregated in the so-called Mutes' Ghetto (*nemetskaya sloboda*). Then, suddenly, the bonds of old Muscovy split asunder when the young Peter the Great broke the taboo on intercourse between Muscovite Tsar and foreign devils by penetrating this alien enclave to carouse with its denizens: his German mistress Anna Mons, the Scottish General Patrick Gordon, the Swiss adventurer Franz Lefort. An even grosser breach of apartheid took place in 1699–1700 with Peter's grand tour of Western Europe in a style which might have been expressly designed to confirm the impression, common among pious Muscovites, that he was Antichrist. Returning primed with sufficient European lore to boost the technological revolution which he intended to impose on sleepy Muscovy, he savagely repressed a military mutiny which had broken out in his absence; cut off his boyars' beards; forced them out of their flowing oriental robes into a form of contemporary European dress; forbade them to marry unless they could acquire some knowledge of mathematics; founded a new capital on his far western shores, one expressly chosen to provide him with a 'window on Europe'; set up the Table of Ranks, a new civil and military hierarchy in which were enrolled his newly europeanised Russian officers and officials who fought and administered side by side with Western Europeans attracted to his service. A particularly important reservoir of the Empire's generals and high officials was to be provided over the next two centuries by the German gentry of the Baltic lands conquered by Peter.

On the desirability of Peter's europeanising programme Russians have been debating ever since. One unfortunate by-product was the creation of a social and cultural gap between the small minority of newly westernised officers, gentlemen and officials on the one hand, and the grey mass of the population on the other: benighted, bearded, illiterate muzhiks together with the similarly garbed and culturally akin merchants and priests. But these members of the thronging lower orders at least were, and knew themselves to be, Russians; whereas members of the gentry as remodelled by Peter were neither one thing nor the other. 'Foreigners at home and foreigners abroad; idle spectators spoilt for Russia by their Western prejudices, spoilt for the West by their Russian habits—they represented a kind of intelligent superfluity floundering in artificiality, sensual pleasures and intolerable egoism.'[2]

However numerous europeanised Russians might become, non-assimilating foreigners continued to initiate Russian enterprises. The country's first factory, the Tula iron works, was built in 1632 by a Dutch concessionaire. Over two hundred years later the coal-mining industry of the Donbass was founded by a Welshman, John Hughes. Italian or Scottish architects planned the walls of the Moscow Kremlin, the St Petersburg Winter Palace, and many another notable edifice in and outside the 'two capitals'. Nineteenth-century Englishmen were to achieve the first ascent of many a mountain peak of the far-flung Russian Empire. Then again, in yet another field, a succession of distinguished Scottish doctors served as personal physicians to the eighteenth-century Russian emperors and empresses. Catherine the Great had herself inoculated against smallpox by one of these, a Dr Dimsdale; and she is said to have kept a carriage and post-horses available so that he could flee the country in the event of some medical disaster, which, fortunately for both of them, did not occur.[3] On a humbler level, Catherine also persuaded numerous European artisans and peasants to settle in Russia, her aim being to populate the vast, sparsely inhabited territories of her realm while civilising its more boorish indigenous inhabitants.

The scale of foreigners' assimilation to Russianness admitted infinite gradations. The beginning might be to learn a little of the language, but the crucial stage was conversion to Orthodoxy. Of the country's capacity to assimilate aliens an American scholar quotes an impressive catalogue of examples. They include the Italian eighteenth-century architect Francesco Bartolomeo Rastrelli; the Scottish General Barclay de Tolly; the playwright Fonvizin and the poet Delvig, both German; the octoroon Pushkin, partly Ethiopian; the Danish lexicographer Vladimir Dal; the Swedish poetess Zinaida Gippius; and the Ukrainian-Polish author Vladimir Korolenko.[4] Gogol, who wrote in Russian, was yet a Ukrainian. Even Chekhov, coming as he did from the south, could jokingly refer to himself as a 'lazy Ukrainian', and was once censured by a Ukrainian actress for not writing in his 'native' language.[5] Alexander Nikitenko was unambiguously Ukrainian in origin, yet became a militant Great Russian nationalist by conviction, for it was often such adoptive Russians who, feeling the convert's compulsion to display extra zeal, became the most rabid patriots of all. The Empire had no more zealous defenders than the Baltic German nobles who commanded so many armies and headed so many ministries. Nor have there been many Russian patriots so extreme and persistent, if the extension of national power is an acceptable criterion, as the Georgian Stalin, though the guttural speech of that multiple slaughterer of Russians always remained alien enough to identify him at once as a foreigner.

Half German and one-quarter Kalmuck by birth, Lenin was more secure in his status as a Russian; and also more apt to denigrate the Russians than his wholly foreign disciple Stalin could afford to be in pre-revolutionary days. Lenin repeatedly castigated the chauvinism of the Great Russians, as revealed in their oppressions of the minority populations of their Empire—in which they formed no majority, but merely a large minority of some forty-three per cent.[6]

However sincere Lenin's pre-revolutionary defence of Russia's non-Russian minorities may have been in intent, the consolidation of power by the Bolsheviks, under Stalin's domination and later dictatorial monopoly of power, signally failed to confer independence on the various nationalities, great and small, of what had now become the Soviet Union. Subjected to continuing Great Russian domination under a different name, the non-Russian nationalities now had the extra burden of being compelled to assert in public that no such domination existed, and to affirm the officially promulgated fiction that each of the Union's republics was *de facto* free—as it is and has been *de jure*—to secede from the USSR. On pain of disgrace and worse for 'bourgeois nationalism', members of minority nationalities have been required to express gratitude to the Russian people for annexing them in the first place, and then for helping them to establish Communism. That the Caucasian, the Central Asian, the Baltic and many other peoples had been wholly or partly incorporated in imperial Russia by military conquest is glossed over. Their territories, including those acquired in Tsarist times, are said to have accrued by *attachment* rather than by violent *seizure*, the term which is regularly applied to the annexationist activities of non-Russian colonial powers. Meanwhile a drive towards greater cultural and administrative autonomy, if not towards total independence, remains a live issue among dissidents in the non-Russian Union Republics, including the most populous of all, that of the Ukraine. On the other hand, all these fourteen non-Russian republics, together with the various autonomous republics and other, smaller non-Russian national units, have produced their quota of russophiliac Uncle Toms. Whether actuated by conviction, foolishness, fear, careerism or a desire to seem important, these are often pathetic as they repeat the solemn litany of gratitude to the Great Russians for having enslaved them so effectively. In such a context it is not fanciful to describe modern totalitarian Russia as the most successful colonial and imperialist power of the twentieth century. Yet the Russians by no means look down on their colonial peoples as mere 'natives'. They have considerable respect for Georgian commercial acumen; for Baltic skill in design and architecture; and in general for the superior *savoir-vivre*, as they are apt to feel it, of their more advanced subject nations.

Does the Russian consider himself to belong to the East or to the West?

Once again there is no lack of witness to each of two mutually exclusive propositions. Is one to believe the poet Alexander Blok when, in a famous couplet from his poem *Scythians* (1918), he truculently describes himself and his fellow countrymen as 'Asiatics with slanted, greedy eyes'? Or does one rather accept the statement made in the opening paragraph of a recent study, *Russia and Europe*, by the German scholar Reinhard Wittram, who claims that 'It goes without saying . . . the Russians have always been a European people'?[7]

Goes without saying? That, with respect, it does not. On the contrary, many billions of words have been spilled on variations of these two contrary propositions. The truth lies somewhere between them. Neither wholly oriental nor yet wholly occidental, Russia partakes of both elements. How little educated Russians of the last century regarded themselves as belonging exclusively to either camp is shown by certain speech conventions then common. *Yevropeytsy*, 'Europeans', was frequently used in a sense specifically excluding Russia: it embraced all the other, non-Russian, lands of the continent, despite the fact that Russia itself occupies a far larger area of Europe than does any other nation. On the other hand, the Russians certainly did not think of themselves as Asians; indeed, the common, highly pejorative, use of the word *aziatchina*, 'Asian-ness', to denote 'squalor', suggests that they wished to dissociate themselves even more from the East than from the West.

Opinions granting Russia intermediate status between East and West are, happily, more common than those which admit of no compromise. Pushkin evidently thought of Russia as part of Europe when he contrasted it with 'the rest' of that continent. But he then went on to claim, in effect, that never the twain should meet. 'Russia never had anything in common with the rest of Europe . . . her history requires ideas and formulas that are different from the ideas and formulas deduced . . . from the history of the Christian West.' Another compromise view loaded in favour of the Eastern solution was that of Custine, who claimed that Russia represented 'a terrible combination of Europe's intelligence and science with Asiatic genius'; but who also believed that Russia would always be more Asian than European.[8]

To the problem of whether Russians think that they *are* more Eastern or more Western, another closely linked question is often appended. *Should* Russia be, or should it become more Eastern or more Western? The latter view was taken by those nineteenth-century thinkers who came to be called westernist. The pioneer westernist, Chaadayev, would not commit himself on Russia's existing position: 'We are neither of the West nor of the East, and we have not the traditions of either.'[9] But when Chaadayev turned from what Russia was—a country of which, he said, both the past and present simply lacked all significance—to what it should be, he showed himself uncompromising in his westernism, claiming that the only possible future lay in adherence not only to European civilisation but even to the Catholic Church.

An opposing, russocentric, view was adopted by those left-wing thinkers who saw their country's guarantee of political salvation in its village commune, claiming it to be an essentially socialist institution unknown to the West. That Russia often had gone, and always should go, its own way was also the contention of the Slavophiles—not least of Dostoyevsky. Hating the westernist doctrine—not that any such doctrine existed in cohesive form—and particularly exasperated by the westernising Turgenev, Dostoyevsky created a vicious caricature of that unfortunate fellow novelist in the novel *Devils*. Here 'Karmazinov' (Turgenev) proclaims a keener interest in the sewage system of his foreign city of residence, Karlsruhe, than in the entire destiny of his mother country. Yet even Dostoyevsky, Europe-hater though he might seem, could claim that the whole of Russian progress, learning, art, civic virtue and humanitarianism proceeded from Europe. Conversely the greatest westernist of all, Peter the Great, that wholesale quarrier and adapter of European technology, never regarded europeanisation as an end in itself; he is reported as stating that 'We need Europe for a few decades, and then we must turn our back on it.'[10]

East–West polarisation, as present in Russian minds, has been fostered in more recent times by the political split between the Communist Orient and the 'capitalist' Occident. Originally Western in basing its creed on the German political thinkers Marx and Engels, the Russian Communist movement was most powerfully promoted in its early stages by revolutionaries operating in Western European emigration. Such were the two prime movers of the Bolshevik October Revolution of 1917, Lenin and Trotsky, both of whom had lived abroad for many years, as had many of their closest associates. This occidentalising phase began to recede when it became increasingly clear in the early 1920s that no Western European revolution, such as the Bolsheviks had long expected and relied upon, was likely to occur in the foreseeable future. The realisation coincided with the acquisition of dictatorial power by a colonial, Stalin—a native, albeit a non-Russian native, of the Empire. Stalin had spent only a few weeks abroad, and was far less of a European than most other influential allies of Lenin. Moreover, he pursued the avowedly insular and thus less occidental policy of socialism in one country, besides projecting in his personal style the image of an Eastern despot. Even at the present day, despite the guarded opening of East–West communications since Stalin's death, Russia is in some ways more Eastern in character than in the half century preceding the revolutions. But it must also be conceded that the terms *Eastern, oriental, Western* and *occidental* are less precise than their users are often betrayed into implying.

However these concepts may be defined, the problem of the country's Western or Eastern affiliations is surely less important to an understanding of the Russian mentality than the problem of Russia's obsession with that problem.

That the West is and has been no less fascinated by Russia than Russia by the West—this emerges from much of the preceding argument, not least from the existence of so many published analyses and descriptions of the country by Western citizens from the sixteenth century onwards. And yet, granted a roughly equal intensity of mutual East–West obsession, one is immediately struck by a difference in quality and attitude. Tending to regard Russia as an enigma or sphinx, the Western citizen instinctively seeks hard information about the country; he hopes to solve its riddles. But the Russian attitude to the West, in so far as it can be summed up, has a strikingly different bias. It is not understanding of, it is *recognition by*, the West that Russians crave. 'Though they do take some interest in what is happening in foreign parts,' wrote André Gide in 1936, 'they are far more concerned about what the foreigner thinks of them. What really interests them is to know whether we admire them enough. What they are afraid of is that we should be ill-informed as to their merits. What they want from us is not information but praise.'[11]

This desire is set in context by a more recent witness who claims that converse between present-day Russians and foreigners tends to provoke a clash between the Russian's outward self-confidence and inner uncertainty. It produces, in other words, 'a compulsion in them to elicit from the foreigner an assurance that all is well in the Soviet Union'.[12] It is this compulsion, for example, which drives them to expressions of tedious self-congratulation—over, say, the building of apartment blocks—so exaggerated as to suggest that such achievements are unique to their civilisation, which in fact has no claim whatever to pre-eminence in housing its citizens. To this evidence may be added the contrary urge which one encounters among those Russians who hold politically dissident views, and who express these to foreigners with the exactly contrary aim of eliciting an assurance that all is *not* well in the USSR: that all is, indeed, the worst in the worst of all possible worlds. Such denouncers of the totalitarian ambience have, in many cases, no sooner concluded their 'frank' exchanges of views with some sympathetic alien than off they run, by previous arrangement, to an agency of their political police with a detailed account of the transaction. And yet these 'spies' are often perfectly sincere, decent people, who had spoken all along from the heart on a matter of intimate concern. Here, perhaps, is the phenomenon most difficult of all for the inquiring foreigner to accept and digest, even though he may suspect the intensity of the pressures which have been developed to produce so unnerving a manifestation.

Whether it is praise or condemnation of Russian dispensations which is elicited, the important point is that the foreigner is in either case regarded as an arbiter of ultimate reality—a status which few Russians would be accorded during their excursions to alien lands. The average Western citizen would, one hopes, always be prepared to receive a USSR-domiciled Russian with courtesy. If the guest should comment on the 'achievements' or non-achievements, the national mentality, or any other aspect of his host's country, such representations will (one again hopes) usually be received with every show of serious concern. But most Western citizens, outside the fortunately restricted Russia-fancying camp, are not sufficiently insecure to feel passionately involved in their hearts with what such a visitor may think of them—not, at least, unless and until he provides evidence of possessing a mature judgement. Such inner aloofness was once particularly prominent, perhaps too prominent, in England. The Englishman in his days of glory never cared tuppence what any 'bloody foreigner' thought about him or his country. How different from the Russian, who can seem obsessed with what foreigners think about Russia to the exclusion of everything else.

A significant gloss on this topic is provided by Valentin Kiparsky in his careful study of English and American characters in Russian fiction. Invoking the Russian practice of regularly introducing foreigners in works of fiction as a foil to the natives, he adds that 'A Russian novel without a West European or, at least, a Polish, Ukrainian, Jewish or Caucasian character, is almost as rare as a West European novel containing a Russian character.'[13] And yet, when one moves from the fictional sphere of imagination, romance and emotion to the world of factual information, the balance is in the opposite direction. Western 'books on Russia' are extremely numerous, and are usually inspired by inquisitiveness, whereas Russians' discourses on the West are relatively few, and are often preoccupied with ventilating emotional and nationalistic issues relevant to their own country rather than with conveying information or sober understanding of someone else's.

Simultaneously or by turns xenophiliac and xenophobiac, Russians have tended to react most strongly to Western nationalities in proportion to their geographical proximity to Russian territory. For example, the writings of that dedicated xenophobe Dostoyevsky maintain a fairly consistent hate-hate, rather than love-hate, relationship with Russia's immediate Western neighbours. His most virulent contempt is reserved for the Poles: topographically adjacent, Catholics, rebels against Russian rule in 1863, and damned in all three capacities. In the various *skandal* scenes of his novels a 'wretched little Pole' usually figures among the minor characters who contribute an atmosphere of absurdity to these fiascos; so too, to be fair, does the odd 'wretched little German'.

Relations with Germany probably cut deeper than those with any other major Central or Western European power. It is with Germany that Russia and later the USSR has fought the two most massive and bloody wars in history. For a century and a half preceding 1917 Russia was, as indicated above, ruled by autocrats of wholly or preponderantly German extraction. Before that a much-hated German, Biron, had in effect controlled policy as a favourite of the Empress Anne in the early eighteenth century. Another German, Count Benckendorff, headed the political police of Nicholas I a century later, being charged with the leading role in the harassment of Pushkin. As Benckendorff's case illustrates, administrative or managerial positions, high and low, were commonly assigned to Germans on the by no means fanciful ground that the organising Teuton tended to conceive more clear-cut and efficiently pursued goals than could be expected from a Slav administrator or overseer. To this belief or prejudice Russian writers commonly deferred when seeking to create 'strong men' or 'men of action': an aim often pursued, though rarely successfully brought off, in Russian literature of both the imperial and the totalitarian periods. These militantly un-Russian characters are apt to bear such names as Stolz (in Goncharov's *Oblomov*) and von Koren (in Chekhov's *Duel*) on the apparent assumption that qualities of determination and effectiveness would never be credited by any Russian reader if attributed to someone with a name ending in -ovsky or -ishchev.

This perennial contrast between the sober, dependable German and the casual, slovenly Russian has struck many observers. Travelling to Samarkand in 1888, Lord Curzon noted the 'overwhelming antithesis between the German and Russian character, the one vigilant, uncompromising, stiff, precise; the other sleepy, nonchalant, wasteful and lax'.[14] The same contrast had impressed Nikitenko during his visit to the northern port of Archangel in 1834. The city's German ghetto was distinguished by its neat, attractive cottages, whereas its Russians 'live in filth and trade like swindlers'. So widespread was the national vice of drunkenness that no one would ever inquire of a stranger whether he drank, but rather 'What's he like when he's tipsy?'[15]

A similar contrast might be observed between disorderly, unkempt typical Russian villages and the neat, well-organised settlements of the many German peasant communities originally attracted to Russia by the immigration policies of Catherine the Great. Yet, far from regarding German efficiency and order as a standing reproach, the muzhik remained content with his own way of life. He was not inspired to imitate these mysterious foreigners; for though Russia's gentry '. . . are singularly prone to adopt foreign manners, customs and institutions; the peasants, on the contrary, are as a rule decidedly conservative'.[16] If there was little co-operation between the Orthodox and these alien infidels, there was also remarkably little friction. German peasants settled contentedly in Russia, retaining their own language and religion while shunning avoidable contact with imperial officialdom. There were also many German traders and businessmen—so many by the mid-nineteenth century that Custine could say, greatly exaggerating, that 'The manufacturers, businessmen and merchants are almost all German.'[17]

Foreigners, especially Germans, were prominent in Russian academic life. University professors, and also academicians—members of the Academy of Sciences founded in 1725—were often Germans who could not speak, and did not wish to speak, a word of Russian. There were also many Russian citizens of German descent who might retain their German surname, but who, like Chekhov's Baron Tuzenbakh in *Three Sisters*, proclaimed themselves culturally and linguistically Russian. How thoroughly a woman of German origin—Chekhov's wife Olga Knipper—could absorb a characteristic Russian tonality from her Russian education and environment, her voluminous correspondence with her husband demonstrates; it is the thoroughly Russian Chekhov who emerges from their exchanges as the less 'Russian', in the vulgar sense.

Not always, either in literature or in life, has the practical, efficient, punctual, businesslike German triumphed over the drunken, carefree, casual Russian. Leskov's story *An Iron Will* depicts a German engineer, Hugo Pektoralis, who possesses all the national attributes in excess. But the dedicated Hugo is no match for his sloppy, vodka-swilling Russian opponent Safronych, who outwits him at every turn, as if to confirm the answer implied in a rhetorical question asked on an early page of the story: 'Can anyone really hope to conquer a people capable of producing such a rogue as Chichikov [the hero of Gogol's *Dead Souls*]?'

Better known to the Western reader is a similar contrast in Tolstoy's *War and Peace*, between the efficient, determined, rational, somewhat unreal Napoleon and his lackadaisical military opposite number, Field-Marshal Kutuzov. In his archetypal wisdom as a Russian, Tolstoy's Kutuzov knows that a commander-in-chief cannot influence the course of a battle, and he therefore feels free to fall asleep during a council of war. As for the real-life Russians of the Napoleonic period, creatively casual or not, they survived the French invasion and pursued the defeated enemy back to his home territory. When Alexander I triumphantly rode into Paris on 19 March 1814, while Parisiennes asked his Cossacks to hoist them on the cruppers of their horses so that they could admire the handsome Tsar, the Russian Empire attained its symbolic zenith. Far from interrupting French–Russian contacts, the war only strengthened them. First-hand observation of France, as of Central and Western Europe in general, helped to stimulate in the Russian army a desire for fundamental reform at home, an experience which caused many army officers to join the Decembrist conspiracy of 1825.

Meanwhile French refugees had fled to Russia and been received in a fluent, yet far from Parisian, version of their own language, at this period the common medium of communication between upper-class Russians, as Tolstoy's *War and Peace*, much of it in French, reminds one. Herzen's father was more at home in French than Russian and disdained the major Russian historico-literary monument of his age, Karamzin's *History of the Russian State*, out of high-bred distaste for the vulgarities of the subject. 'All these Izyaslaviches and Olgoviches—what a bore!'[18] Pushkin, Russia's greatest poet, was sometimes known as 'the Frenchman' because he seemed so well-versed in his second language—in which, incidentally, he habitually wrote letters to his no-less-Russian wife. As these details suggest, the Russian literary language was by no means fully formed at the beginning of the nineteenth century; indeed it was Pushkin himself who played the major role in completing the process of fitting it for flexible and sophisticated utterance. To compare the evolution of such major European tongues as French and English is, therefore, to note yet another area in which Russia was a late developer.

As time wore on, the use of French in Russian mouths acquired different resonances. To Dostoyevsky it was a sign of not being a proper Russian, and he several times attributes a French accent or knowledge of French to such characters as the murderer Smerdyakov, ideologically disparaged for having rejected traditional Muscovite values. To Chekhov, a generation later, the use of—sometimes inaccurate—French was an index of pseudo-genteel vulgarity. By the time of the First World War French had sunk still further, the word *merci* being 'used by nearly all the town population (particularly so by the half-educated ones)'.[19] In more recent times Russian knowledge of French has sunk to the point where the word *merci*, occurring in a printed text, must be translated in a footnote.

The British (or English, for the Russian rarely draws any distinction) have also incurred their share of Russian love and hatred, but on the lower scale which greater distance and inaccessibility dictate. After an anglomaniac phase undergone by some of the Russian gentry in the early nineteenth century and recorded, for example, in Pushkin's story *Lady into Peasant*, English tourists came to be strongly disliked. Turgenev has referred to their glassy eyes, their long, rabbit-like teeth and their droopy whiskers. They are suspicious, rude, haughty; they disdain everything foreign. Still, Englishmen made better managers than Frenchmen or Germans, even if they did exploit Russian workers. Above all the English impressed by displaying, in those far-off days, the psychological security which Russians themselves so often lacked, particularly in their dealings with the West. Tolstoy once called the typical Englishman 'self-assured as being a citizen of the best-organised state in the world', one who 'as an Englishman, always knows what he should do and knows that all he does as an Englishman is undoubtedly correct'. There are many similar tributes of grudging admiration in Dostoyevsky's *Diary of a Writer*. However, self-assurance could be close to arrogance, as Dostoyevsky often complains: 'I am an Englishman, and you are only Russians [one of his typical Britons muses] . . . I, as a son of Old England (at this point his heart quivers with pride), am nevertheless the first man in the world, and you are only people of the second grade.'[20]

The view of the English in the present century has tended to concentrate on their inhibitedness, stiff upper lip, reserve, strait-lacedness. Here is the opposite of that jolly expansiveness which forms so basic an ingredient in a Russian's ideal vision of himself, so that the English may in a sense seem to him inverted Russians. An Englishman visiting Russia can find himself accused of emotional atrophy, in extreme cases by a total stranger in the first two seconds of encounter. 'Who enjoys, who really enjoys life most [as between Englishman and Russian]?' The rhetorical question is posed by Madame Jarintzov and answered over several score pages in the Russian's favour. With the Russian, spoiled by an overflow of happiness, she contrasts the dour Englishman whose highest form of joy occurs at the moment when he can describe himself by the mundane phrase 'full of beans'.[21] This is one possible view. Another is that of Mackenzie Wallace, who describes a Russian village fête as 'one of the most saddening spectacles I have ever witnessed'. Contrasting France and Italy, he laments that all northern nations, the Russians not least, are incapable of amusing themselves, that they 'do not know how to enjoy themselves in a harmless, rational way, and seek a refuge in intoxication'.[22] Without necessarily accepting either of these extreme statements, we may tentatively identify one typical specific in the Russian's attitude to enjoyment. He does not seem capable of absorbing satisfaction unless he is simultaneously awarding himself credit marks for doing so. He will seek out someone else and explain that he, the disadvantaged foreigner, on whom the Russian may never previously have set eyes, is by definition precluded from true happiness —another variant on the familiar 'just-watch-me-being-spontaneous' theme, and another reminder of the Russian's acute sensitivity to audience reaction.

Despite claims that the English and the Russians may be at opposite poles owing to their respective cultivation of reserve and exuberance, the feeling has often been expressed that the two peoples are especially close to each other. Nicholas Khomyakov, a Russian politician of the late Empire, once stated that 'Every Russian when he is among Englishmen at once feels at home, though he may not be like them in character, beliefs, or education. And you will be told of corresponding feelings by every Englishman who has lived in Russia, but not by the Frenchman, the German, or the Italian.' Endorsing this view, Wright Miller claims that, in personal relationships and general attitude to life, 'The English have more in common with the Russians than with many nations nearer home.' He specifies these common areas as 'ways of avoiding social friction, the Russian sense of humour, the Russian attitude to women, and that recent development, Russian sportsmanship'.[23] One senses what he means without feeling impelled to accept his thesis. The trouble is that Russians, not necessarily uninspired by a love of *vranyo*, are apt to seek out representatives of a given nationality and expatiate on the special rapport (or, depending on mood, lack of rapport) allegedly existing between Russia and the nationality in question. It is not surprising, then, to find the fact that Russia and Germany *had not fought on the same side in World War Two* deplored, in conversation with a German, by a Russian war veteran who had conveniently forgotten that they most certainly had done so: in their joint successful campaign of 1939 against Poland. 'We have a great respect for the Germans,' continued this expert on international affairs. 'They're a . . . people with principles, like the Russians, not a lot of sloppy compromisers like the British and the French.'[24]

Nor is it surprising to find an American writing that the Russians in many ways resemble the Americans more than any other people in their eagerness to ask questions and learn new things; in not being afraid to make mistakes. 'They have an attitude of breezy but not annoying self-confidence, born of the knowledge that they have vast spaces and great material resources at their disposal; and they adapt themselves readily to new and entirely untried conditions.'[25] Always impressed by American technical and economic achievements, and often as unstinting in praising Americans to Americans as in abusing Americans to non-Americans, the Russian is also constantly seeking some defect which will balance American superiority. Materialism, the desire to 'make a fast buck', an alleged lack of intellectualism and culture—such are the common accusations.[26] As for another charge, that 'Americans have no music in their souls'—here one recognises a routine item in the Russian litany of implied self-praise, that of disparaging others for lacking attributes which possess the convenient property of being wholly unquantifiable.

As the fourth quarter of the twentieth century began, both the British and the Americans seemed to have entered phases of collective insecurity and self-denigration contrasting sharply with their former self-confidence. Meanwhile the Russians continued as ever to combine, fuguelike, the melody of self-denigration far more intense than that of the Anglo-American with the counterpoint of nationalist bombast.

PATRIOT

In any survey of a people's mind, that people's attitude to itself—its patriotism or lack of patriotism—must loom large, and in Russia's case the topic is particularly obtrusive. That Russian love of country tends to excess has been argued again and again. Even in the bleak days of Muscovy, according to a recent observer, Tibor Szamuely, the Russian people 'regarded their national state and their social system with a feeling of pious reverence and blind faith that went beyond simple patriotism'. Listing the symptoms as ecstatic rapture, exaltation bordering on idolatry, insufferable self-righteousness, unshakeable conviction of moral superiority and self-glorification carried to ridiculous lengths, he adds that 'Instead of "my country right or wrong", it 'was 'my country—never wrong".'

Illustrations of such excessive patriotism are not hard to find. One thinks of Dostoyevsky's journalistic writings, and especially of *The Diary of a Writer*, where his countrymen are credited with such virtues as 'eternal service to common human ideals'. Then there is their superior tolerance—and from Dostoyevsky, that hounder of Catholics and Jews. He claims Russia's as the most democratic social structure in the world, and that under the autocracy. He lauds its lack of territorial designs on any other country, and that hard on the annexation of Central Asia and the Far Eastern provinces, not to mention his own cherished dream of seizing Constantinople. The Russian was, to Dostoyevsky, an exponent of 'human universality'; was free from 'European stiffness, imperviousness, intractability'; sympathised 'with everything human irrespective of nationality, blood and soil'; was even—*horresco referens*—uniquely gifted in speaking foreign languages.[2]

That Dostoyevsky should pause, as he does, while projecting such national narcissism to praise the Russian's 'sober view of himself and absence of any sort of self-elevation'—this, too, is fully in the spirit of such harangues. Launched on a similar hymn to unique Russian virtues, a more recent superpatriot inserts into these splendid fanfaronades the similar claim that 'Self-advertising is not a Russian feature'.[3] But one has heard such boasts from other source too; for example, 'We British don't go round blowing our own trumpets.' Typically Russian though the practice of praising oneself for not praising oneself may seem, it is not unique.

Russian ultra-patriotism may be less prevalent than Szamuely pretends, but he is surely right in claiming special status for it as an emotion unconnected with the wearisome world of reason, evidence and fact. The Russian love of country is more akin to a religious faith, as is emphasised in a famous quatrain by Fyodor Tyutchev. Roughly translated into dull prose, it reads, 'Russia can neither be grasped by the mind, nor measured by any common yardstick. Russia's status is special: no attitude to her other than one of blind faith is admissible.'[4] Such fanatical devotion has always tended to remain unshaken by the persecutions, including long-term imprisonment and exile, which authority has so often inflicted on the individual citizen, not uncommonly through whim, accident or mere clerical error. Hardship, poverty and other evils not wholly attributable to authority have made little difference either—rather the contrary. Pushkin, himself during his entire adult life a victim of official persecution, once called his fellow citizens orang-utans, even asserting that to inhabit Russia was 'like living in a privy'. But though 'far from admiring all that I see around me', he went on to swear that not for anything would he have consented to change his fatherland.[5] A similar attitude was expressed by Boris Pasternak, that renowned dissident and object of prolonged nerve warfare by the Kremlin, who, had he wished, could have left his country in 1958 at the time when he was awarded the Nobel Prize for Literature. Had he done so he would have been able to lead a dignified life abroad, well provided for by his literary earnings. In fact he regarded such a prospect, which he succeeded in avoiding, as an utter calamity, and told me so during a long discussion which I was privileged to have with him at the time. Yet he was living under considerable strain, as he explained, and under a system of government which, though he insisted on regarding it as comic, he had good reason to fear. Similarly, many a humbler citizen has suffered arbitrary arrest followed by years or decades in Stalin's concentration camps—yet has retained his patriotism untarnished.

The Russian calls his country 'Mother' Russia, attaching much significance to the maternal symbol. 'It was remarkable how often ... interviewees [defectors of the totalitarian period] expressed the post-war state of Russia in terms of their "starving, neglected mother".'[6] The poorer the mother and the harsher her conditions of life, the greater the devotion of her sons.

That the Russian should sometimes adopt a truculent, challenging mien when expressing his patriotism is also characteristic, though it is also typical of nationalists everywhere. 'Already in the reign of Ivan the Terrible the incipient megalomania had reached a stage where not only the monarchs of Poland, Sweden, England and France, but even the German Emperor, were, one by one, declared unfit to be treated as equals by the ruler of Muscovy.' In the end even the Turkish Sultan was deposed from the isolated peak which he had been allowed to share with the Tsar, the last remaining sovereign treated as that ruler's co-equal in diplomatic traffic. This same megalomaniac Tsar once wrote to Queen Elizabeth of England accusing her of yielding power to 'clodhopping tradesmen'; and of being no true monarch, but just an 'ordinary spinster'.[7]

In the light of traditional chauvinist idiom, the Georgian Stalin was not using an un-Russian turn of phrase when he warned foreigners against 'sticking their pigs' snouts into our Soviet kitchen-garden'.[8] Nor was the undeniably Russian Khrushchev departing from accepted usage when he issued his famous warning, 'We shall bury you,' to Western diplomats at a Moscow gathering. He was also known to invoke the special nature of Russian-Soviet 'achievements' less distastefully, by citing Leskov's famous story *The Left-handed Man*. Here a cross-eyed, left-handed joiner from Tula demonstrates the superiority of Russian craftsmanship by taking an ingeniously wrought steel flea, presented to the Tsar by English metal workers, and fitting it with microscopic shoes. By this striking feat of one-upmanship is the Russian's edge over the foreigner asserted with delightful humour and irony—elements by no means uncommon in the Russian litany of self-admiration. They are, however, wholly absent from the powerful but distasteful ode *To Russia's Slanderers* in which Pushkin asserts his country's right to crush the Polish rebellion of 1830-1, promising any foreign interventionists in this domestic quarrel of Slavs that they will receive the treatment previously meted out to Napoleon. Nor has this 'our-side-your-side distinction', as it has been well called, been confined to Tsars, statesmen and poets.[9] It can form a barrier to civilised communication between the present-day Westerner and any unduly 'typical' Russian.

The replacement of the Russian Empire by the Soviet Union has made fewer inroads on Russian patriotism than might have been expected from the adoption of a creed as avowedly global in its pretensions as Marxism. An internationalist phase did indeed follow the Bolshevik takeover of 1917—a period when the use of the words *Russian* and *Russia* was officially discouraged or penalised, while the regime yet drew on reserves of patriotism, especially as aroused by foreign intervention during the Civil War of 1918–21. By 1934 Stalin was overtly reviving Russian nationalism, and the word *Soviet* was tending more and more to become a rough code equivalent for *Russian*. Russian nationalism was more prominent than political fervour in bringing victory over Germany in the Second World War, after which it was artificially nurtured by the nationalist campaign sponsored by Zhdanov. It was the period during which all major inventions of the past, including radio and the steam engine, were, correctly or incorrectly, attributed to Russians. This later-modified propaganda campaign has never been entirely relaxed, and users of recent Russian encyclopedias will still find much evidence of it. In particular, wherever foreigners have played a significant role in Russian history, as did the Vikings and Greeks in the Kiev period, their importance tends to be played down, while more emphasis is given to native Russian initiatives than un-Kremlinised scholars will allow. This policy derives from a realisation by the Kremlin 'that the success of its programme of world expansion, and also its ability to maintain its power at home, depend upon securing the maximum possible support from the Great Russian people'.[10]

Despite this cultivation of intense Russian nationalism, recent Muscovite statesmen have not usually indulged in the kind of bellicose, flamboyant utterance associated with Hitler, Mussolini and the heads of other totalitarian regimes. Khrushchev's occasional lapses into drunken abuse, noted above, were happily exceptional.

The adoption of Russian nationalism by Marxist-Leninist

revolutionaries does not mark as sharp a break with tradition as might be supposed. Though pre-1917 Russian revolutionaries often opposed the expansionist policies of their government—they did so, for example, during the Russo-Japanese War of 1904-5—they were also liable to rally to the imperial cause. Decidedly exceptional among his contemporaries was Herzen when he came out against the crushing of the Polish rebellion of 1863, for most other domestic opponents of the Russian government saw no reason why the ancestral enemy should not be suppressed. Even so extreme a radical as Chernyshevsky was intensely patriotic: 'Not to put too fine a point on it . . . there was a good deal of unconscious nationalism in the psychological make-up of the Russian revolutionary.'[11] Even the more internationalist Herzen could occasionally utter the language—admittedly somewhat muted by Dostoyevskian standards—of nationalist bombast. Herzen spoke, for example, of the Russians as 'that people which, by some miracle, has contrived to preserve itself under the yoke of Mongol hordes and German bureaucrats, under the corporal's stick of barrack discipline and the shameful Tatar knout; has preserved its majestic features, its lively intelligence, the broad exuberance of its rich nature under the oppression of serfdom; and which has responded to a Tsar's call to educate itself with that titanic phenomenon Pushkin. Let Europe know her neighbour. So far she only fears him. Let her find out what it is she fears.'[12]

It is a short step from some of the preoccupations mentioned above to the assumption, commonly made over the centuries by Russians in all walks of life, that they constitute a Chosen People, the elect of destiny, who have performed a special role in the past and are fated to perform a still more special role in the future.

So far as the past is concerned, there is the oft-repeated claim to have 'saved Europe' from various threats. By absorbing the shock of Mongol-Tatar onslaughts in the early thirteenth century, by later active campaigning against the Tatars until their expulsion from the Crimea in 1783, Russia arguably rescued Western civilisation. 'Held a shield between the two hostile races of the Mongols and of Europe' is how Blok puts it in his poem *Scythians*. In language only slightly less poetic the historian Klyuchevsky speaks of carefree Europe entranced by its dreams of colonies with their spices and recking little of the East while the infant state of Muscovy still held the pass against the barbarian, '. . . saving European culture from Tatar onslaughts. Thus we found ourselves in Europe's rearguard and defended the rear of European civilisation.'[13] Without denying all force to these considerations, one may yet argue that national survival played a greater role, and an altruistic mission to save European culture a lesser role, than Russian historians and poets will commonly allow.

That Russia again saved Europe or the world—from Napoleon in 1812; from the Kaiser in 1914-17; from Hitler in 1940-5—here are further claims characteristic of Russian-Soviet historians. They will not concede, on an official level, that any nation other than those ruled from Moscow contributed substantially to the defeat of Hitler and his allies, though the Anglo-American invasion of Europe in June 1944 did evoke warm praise from Stalin in the immediate aftermath. To this day the old boasts about medieval Russia saving Europe from the Tatars, so commonly heard from imperial Russian historians, continue to be made the basis for claiming, as it were, good conduct marks from history.[14]

As for Russia's role in the future, the prospect has alarmed Western travellers since the sixteenth century, when Richard Chancellor wrote that 'if they knew their strength, no man were able to make match with them, nor they that dwell near them should have any rest of them . . . I may compare them to a young horse that knoweth not his strength.' Three hundred years later the Frenchman Custine received a similar impression, and concluded that Russia's destiny was world conquest. He even regarded the awesome and magnificent city of St Petersburg as a trophy erected by the Russians to their future power. Such ideas were not only voiced by Frenchmen in the Russia of Custine's day. One native philosopher of the period, Prince Vladimir Odoyevsky, claimed that 'A Russified Europe, as a new force, will bring life to senile and decrepit Europe.' Another, Michael Pogodin, expressed similar ambitions more effusively: 'My heart trembles with joy, O Russia, O my Fatherland . . . You, you are chosen to consummate, to crown the development of humanity, to embody all the various human achievements . . . in one great synthesis, to bring to harmony the ancient and modern civilisations, to reconcile heart with reason, to establish true justice and peace.'[15]

Nor has this sense of Russia's mission disappeared now that its people are ruled in the name of a political doctrine, Marxism-Leninism, for which universal applicability is claimed, combined with the assertion that it is destined eventually to triumph over all other creeds on a worldwide scale. Marxism is remote indeed from any New Word which Dostoyevsky might have had in mind when claiming that such a pronouncement would one day sound forth for the first time in Russia, thereby transforming the general human condition in some manner unspecified. Disqualified by its foreign origin, the atheist socialist creed evolved by two German thinkers would not have suited the conservative and patriot Dostoyevsky, who believed that religion was the very stuff of life, not the opium of the people.

Nevertheless, the emotional force of Great Russian messianism, of which Dostoyevsky reflected one facet only, has clearly been incorporated—to a degree which cannot be determined—in the doctrines of Marxism as preached from the Kremlin. But though comparable urges may be found in the teachings of many another pre-revolutionary Russian thinker besides Dostoyevsky, the Russian government of those days lagged far behind. Compared with a Lenin, a Stalin, a Khrushchev or a Brezhnev, the last Romanov emperors were mercifully parochial in their ambitions. They might annex vast areas of the Far East and Central Asia, they might hold down the Poles and bully the Finns. But they never claimed or implied that they should or would transform the entire inhabited globe in the Russian image. Nor, by contrast with certain Russian philosophers of that day and their revolutionary successors, did the imperial Russian government propagate as a dogma 'the uniqueness, superiority and universal applicability' of the Russian way of life.[16] Even in the 1890s, the period of take-off in the Russian industrial revolution, the Russian government was not in the habit of pointing to this spectacular economic growth rate, unparalleled in the contemporary world, as proof that every other country should be ruled by an autocratic absolute sprig of the House of Romanov. But comparable suggestions, allegedly proving the superior viability of the Muscovite system on the basis of—highly suspect—economic growth-rate statistics, have been not uncommon under the successor regime, particularly in the mouth of the supreme *vranyo*-monger Khrushchev.

DOMESTIC PET

So much for Russia and the world. What of the world and Russia?

One remarkable phenomenon of the last hundred years is the foreign enthusiast who refers to the Russians as if they were endearing but imperfectly house-trained domestic animals.

Indoctrinated by Russians with the patter characteristic of the subject, Russia-fanciers return home to repeat it, acting in effect as unpaid public relations officers. This practice is particularly common in the political area, and has led to the emergence of the fellow traveller, on which little will be said here since politics is not a direct concern of this study. The manifestation can perhaps best be invoked by a brief reference to a single spectacular example of political Russia-fancying. During a visit to the Far Eastern Soviet concentration camp empire in 1944, the American Vice-President Henry A. Wallace was induced to treat the warder-in-chief of this prison province as an 'industrial boss'; and made a speech in Irkutsk, on the very threshold of the world's largest slave empire, to the effect that 'men born in wide, free spaces will not brook injustice and tyranny. They will not even temporarily live in slavery.'[1] As this example shows, political fanciers are by no means confined to those who necessarily wish to see the Russian system adopted on a worldwide scale. They extend to foreign conservatives and businessmen: to anyone, whatever his views, who is sufficiently gullible and unobservant. Such fanciers will, while repeating the prescribed patter, simultaneously appear to congratulate themselves on their broadmindedness and originality in taking a viewpoint so contrary, they wrongly suppose, to that which might be expected of them. The prevalence of this habit among foreigners is a corrective to any tendency to censure as an exclusively Russian vice the practice of awarding oneself implied credit marks during conversation. It also bears out another contention of the present study: that exposure to Russia tends to provoke Russian-type behaviour in even the most stolid alien.

The practice is admirably illustrated by Maurice Baring's recycling of Dostoyevsky's views on Pushkin: 'There was nothing which he [Pushkin] could not understand. Dostoyevsky called him πανάνθρωπος [omnihuman], and it is this capacity for understanding everything and everybody, for being able to assimilate anything, however alien, that makes him so profoundly Russian.'[2] Seldom in the field of human communication can so much empty pretentiousness have been so expertly transferred from one cultural climate to another. A less absurd, though no less disputable, assertion is that of another witness: that the Russian 'poetical achievement is of unique magnificence'.[3] I prefer to regard this as pardonable exaggeration rather than fancying; but still wonder whether Russia's admittedly fine poetry is best praised by such an extreme claim. *Unique* magnificence? But what of Greek, Latin, French, English, Italian poetry? All poetry is unique, of course, but it needs a Russian context to provoke the suggestion that one corpus is more unique than others.

Another feature of cultural fancying is the idealisation of Russia's pre-1917 intelligentsia, that amalgam of muddle-headed and often murderous idealists so often apostrophised by journalists and scholars of the present day as 'superb', 'magnificent', 'uniquely gifted', 'noble' and the like. The intelligentsia has been defined as a 'milieu of earnest, dedicated, passionately honest, fiercely principled scientists and thinkers, writers and philosophers'—which is not altogether misleading, especially the 'passionately' and the 'fiercely'. But is all intellectual effort to be disparaged unless conducted in this frenzied spirit? And is it really true that 'like a phoenix' the unique spirit of the *intelligent* [member of the pre-revolutionary Russian intelligentsia] has survived the purges and repressions of the police state?[4] Even if it were true, would it be a subject for congratulation? These problems are complex and will be considered in detail below.

The religious sphere is perhaps the most characteristic arena for fancying. Many foreign witnesses have expounded the special spiritual significance of Russian Easter celebrations; the peculiar gift for 'participating in the passion of their God'; the sense of universal *agape* and the like. It is not the assertions themselves that one wishes to contradict so much as the implied assumption which often seems to underlie them, and which seems to flourish in the Russian context: that matters of ultimate belief and spiritual intensity can be assessed at a sniff or a glance, as by a housewife buying fish. On the other hand, not all diviners of spiritual sensibility lack professional credentials. They have included, for example, the nineteenth-century canon, quoted above as claiming special spiritual attributes for the Russians, who possessed the technical qualification of field rank in the Church of England. Nor need the Russians necessarily be denied the superior spirituality so often claimed for them, provided that this is not asserted with an off-hand lack of sensitivity so blatant as to disqualify a given observer from claiming competence in this delicate area. Such assertions can be sadly unconvincing, especially when accompanied by reproaches against those who do not repeat this section of the patter for inability to 'see below the surface'.[5]

To induce the English to join in a lamentation on their own inhibitedness, excessive reserve, hypocrisy and the like—this represents the kind of target which the Russian indoctrinator of fanciers has set himself. Yet one knows from experience that such missionaries often prefer to see their evangelising efforts fail. Indeed, they often seem to enjoy the joke, to savour the fellow-feeling which can be promoted when the bluff of nationalist self-praise is called. The Russian is no less sensitive by nature than anyone else, nor can he fail to notice the strong element of condescension so commonly present in the mind of a foreign fancier even as he patronisingly abases himself to what he regards as the Russian level. To read the embarrassingly naïve utterances of that English pioneer of Russian studies, that fancier-of-fanciers Sir Bernard Pares, is to feel an urge to protest on behalf of the vast nation which he has so complacently taken under his wing.

Extreme nationalism has been evoked above as a typical Russian trait. But the suggestion has never been made that it was universal, or that it was cultivated by that vast section (surely the majority) among Russians which does not qualify as typical. Even if Russians err in boasting about their own country, it must not be forgotten that they can also show themselves acutely conscious of its faults, and castigate these with greater force and subtlety than any hostile foreign witness. It is also to their credit that even the most boastful individuals are rarely so in their individual capacity. The Russian will not obsessively seek to demonstrate that he is a better man than you are. Rather will he, if he is of the boastful variety, say or 'tactfully' imply: 'I belong to Category A which is superior in the following respects to Category B, that to which you have the misfortune to belong.' In this sense the 'typical' Russian does indeed manifest a collective rather than an individualist psychology.

There is also this to be said in the Russians' favour: that, though many of them show a keen affection for foreign countries, they have not themselves bred fanciers as the term has been qualified above. They have often felt strong emotions for and against alien cultures. They have sometimes felt impelled to deride or to imitate the English, the Americans, the Germans, the French and other breeds. But from the fancier's prime characteristic of smug condescension they have remained comparatively immune.

THE CLASS STRUGGLE

To what extent has Russian society fallen, to what extent does it still fall, into different social classes?

One view is that, by contrast with England of the same period, the Russian community of the eighteenth and nineteenth centuries was a simple two-tier affair.[1] By the ignorant and by those who accept the thesis that Russians are instinctively democratic and egalitarian in the ultimate degree, they are sometimes credited with total classlessness. Bewailing the constant pressures on English fiction writers to respond to their own complex class system, an English novelist contrasts Dostoyevsky's advantages. 'It is all the same to him,' writes Virginia Woolf, 'whether you are noble or simple, a tramp or a great lady.'[2] That social standing was one of Dostoyevsky's major concerns as a writer, particularly in his early career, escaped this witness. But though she is wrong in suggesting that Russia knew or knows no class differentiation at all, it may yet be that the Russian system, albeit permitting a yawning gap between privileged and unprivileged, is relatively simple. On the whole a given Russian has tended and still tends to belong to one of two basic categories, sometimes known as 'we' and 'they'. 'We' are the vast majority of the people, the receivers and evaders of orders, passive, sporadically obedient and inwardly resentful or resigned. 'They' are the givers of orders, a relatively small group who stand towards 'us' as exploiter to exploited or officer to private soldier.

The further back one goes to the beginning of the nineteenth century, the more closely may the elite 'they' be equated with a specific social class or estate: that of the gentry, numbering about one per cent of the total population. The elite may also be crudely equated with two other categories, those of landowners and officials, which both overlapped with the gentry in that all landowners and higher officials belonged to the gentry estate. To the peasantry, approximately eighty times as large, four-fifths of the population belonged, and this estate corresponded fairly closely with the exploited 'us'. That there were many rich peasants, that there were also many desperately poor and downtrodden gentlemen and officials—these undoubted facts do not invalidate the general thesis. As for intermediate categories, consisting of clergy, merchants, lower townsfolk and others, these tended to remain culturally akin to the peasants whom they resembled in speech and dress.

That every Russian citizen, up to 1917, was formally assigned to one of these or similar categories, which were entered in his 'passport'—an identity card required for internal travel—is a significant detail. But though the number of estates was considerable, and though the refinements of the structure brought in categories which have not been mentioned here, the essential two-tier division into elite and non-elite remained valid. Historically speaking, the elite and non-elite of the imperial period correspond respectively to the Tsar's higher and lower underlings of the Muscovite period. The former were the heirs of the administrators compulsorily shaved, educated and put into European dress by Peter the Great, while the vastly more numerous peasantry together with the associated lower townspeople, merchants and priests continued to shamble about in their beards and caftans or sheepskins. No late nineteenth-century traveller could miss the difference. 'He easily recognises the French-speaking nobles [gentry] in West-European costume; the burly, bearded merchant in black cloth cap and long, shiny, double-breasted coat; the priest with his uncut hair and flowing robes; the peasant with his full, fair beard and unsavoury, greasy sheep-skin.'[3] Meanwhile the same visitor's Russian friends might be assuring him in all sincerity that there were no social classes at all in this supremely democratic society, and never had been—a characteristic *vranyo*-type statement.

That Russia was behindhand in certain kinds of social snobbery is nevertheless true. For instance, relatively slight importance was attached to such titles as prince, count and baron. Where all a nobleman's children, not merely the eldest son, inherited his title, princes were no rarity: there are said to have been about two thousand of them in 1917.[4] By the title-conscious English an *émigré* Russian prince has accordingly tended to be treated as a person of more social consequence than he may possess. This being so, there was little place in Russia for the obsession with pedigree which was once so noticeable a feature of Western European society. Imperial Russia also enjoyed no small degree of social mobility. Lomonosov, the eighteenth-century fisherman's son who became a leading poet, grammarian and academician, is the example most commonly quoted. To him may be added such nineteenth-century figures as Michael Pogodin, the serf's son who became a professor of history and prominent publicist; Alexander Nikitenko, born a serf, who rose to high rank in government and academic service; Anton Chekhov, the provincial grocer's son who became the world's leading short-story writer. Herzen, himself the son of a Russian gentleman, has noted and perhaps exaggerated the ease with which a peasant of his day could enter the gentry, or a gentleman descend to the peasantry.[5]

Another witness goes too far when he virtually discounts any ill feeling between social classes.[6] There may have been less than in many another country, but it was by no means lacking. For example, many peasants spoke with satisfaction of the hanging of the five Decembrist gentlemen-conspirators in 1826, as of the sentencing of others to Siberian hard labour, also expressing the wish that members of the elite could be given a taste of the knout;[7] for gentlemen were traditionally exempt from corporal punishment as inflicted, often with extreme brutality, on the peasantry. Another tradition of the resentful muzhik was 'loosing the red cock'—that is, burning down the local manor house. Nor was there anything in village tradition to prevent him shortly afterwards bowing to the ground and imploring forgiveness from the squire and his family, assuming that they had survived. Other aspects of resentment from below may be freely observed in Russian folk poetry, as also in the epilogue to Dostoyevsky's *Crime and Punishment*. Here convicts from the peasantry object to the presence among them of the convicted gentlemen axe-murderer Raskolnikov. They complain of his *modus operandi* as breaching class copyright. 'It's not a gent's place to bash folks with a hatchet.'

Whatever else may be urged about imperial Russia's class structure, acute sensitivity to social gradations was certainly not lacking. Where a Frenchman or German would tend (Gogol unconvincingly asserts in his *Dead Souls*) to address a millionaire or tobacconist in much the same terms, Russia had her 'experts in sophistry'. These connoisseurs of status could grade their manner with a niceness of nuance according to whether the landowner whom they might be addressing owned one hundred, three hundred, five hundred, eight hundred or, as the case might be, a thousand souls. 'In short, you could go up to a million without running out of nuances.'[8] A coarser sample of the same phenomenon is found in Chekhov's well-known story *Fat and Thin*, where two old schoolfriends meet accidentally, after many years, in a flurry of hearty and intimate effusions. But these are hurriedly cut off when it turns out that the fat one has reached the higher echelons of the Table of Ranks, while his thin friend has failed to achieve promotion. When this becomes evident friendly communion abruptly gives way to condescension on one side and awed sycophancy on the other.

It is against such indications, for and against, that the many claims attributing to the Russian either an exceptionally egalitarian or an exceptionally class-conscious response must be tested. And while, as usual, the assertions of Russians and their observers tend to one extreme or the other, the customary tame conclusion—that the truth tends to hover between opposed poles—will be found most helpful to those who probe these arcana in a spirit of genuine inquiry.

The elaborate formal categories of the imperial period were already falling apart, though still theoretically operative, when the whole structure was swept away by the 1917 October Revolution. That the successor society is by no means classless does not require labouring to anyone familiar with it. The country now has two classes, according to its own official doctrine: those of peasants and workers, besides which the 'toiling intelligentsia' is officially regarded as a separate category (not a class), being termed a stratum.[9] But behind this formal structure a two-tier division into upper and lower servitors is still, broadly speaking, operative. The upper servitors are those who have geared their careers to making the system work. By no means can elite status be exactly equated with membership of the Communist Party, with the possession of high professional qualifications or with having undergone higher education; but it tends to be associated with all these features. As for the non-elite—that, as ever, constitutes the majority of the population: those who are set in motion, presided over, manipulated and otherwise supervised by their betters. After a brief post-revolutionary phase during which it was thought appropriate for all, high and low, to receive or appear to receive pay and material rewards on the same scale as everyone else, this levelling policy was explicitly repudiated by Stalin. The system which he introduced, and which still operates, is one of extremely wide but deliberately camouflaged pay differentials accentuated by a tax system free of the progressive element which tends to level out net incomes in many un-Kremlinised countries. Privileged access to such amenities as housing, special shops, theatre tickets and the like has also helped to create the 'new class' of Soviet bourgeois. They figure in the comments of foreign observers such as the Yugoslav political dissident Milovan Djilas, who first publicised the term 'new class', and also in occasional critical works of Soviet-published Russian fiction, of which the best-known is Vladimir Dudintsev's novel *Not by Bread Alone*. Members of this 'new class' often dispose of vast sums in roubles which they may have difficulty in spending, for it is only in the West that money, in adequate quantity, can buy practically anything.

A foreigner may easily be taken for a member of this totalitarian bourgeoisie. I was once walking absent-mindedly up Gorky Street in Moscow, swinging that hated symbol of unmerited privilege, a leather briefcase, when an intense-looking, strikingly handsome young woman advanced on me—like the would-be assassin Vera Zasulich on the hated General Trepov in 1878—and hissed the accusation 'Soviet bourgeois' through her elegant teeth. (But so complicated have Russian *mœurs* now become that I was later on the same day, without briefcase, refused admittance to an outdoor dance floor on the grounds that my somewhat casual attire—no tie —was considered insufficiently 'cultured'.) A similar experience was related to me by a foreign diplomat who once chanced to be waiting for a train in an almost deserted suburban station. Hearing angry tones from across the rails, he observed what seemed to be, in the real rather than the symbolic sense, an 'ordinary Soviet worker' voicing a reproach from the relative safety of the other side of the track. 'How long are you bastards going to go on sucking our blood?' It was not in my informant's capacity as capitalist lackey, but as one mistaken for a member of the native oppressing class, that he received—or believed he received—this incorrectly addressed but all too natural abuse.

Officials, according to the popular view, have been sucking the blood of the Russian common man since time immemorial, and especially since the institution of the Table of Ranks by Peter the Great in 1722 put officialdom, so to speak, on an official basis. The official was known as a *chinovnik* until the abolition of the Table in 1917. *Chinovnik* still remains in use, but only as an abusive equivalent for the post-revolutionary term *sluzhashchy*, which has officially superseded it. Under the pre-1917 regimen official rank, based on automatic promotions in conformity with a pre-arranged timetable rather than on zeal or merit, secured the status of hereditary gentleman for those who progressed as far as the eighth grade (later raised to fifth grade); and was therefore a powerful agent of social mobility. 'Russia was the only country except China in which the status of noble or gentleman was conferred by education. The high-school ... passing-out examination turned the muzhik into a lord.'[10] This helps to explain nineteenth-century officials' obsessive attitude to their rank and its appurtenances, which included medals and orders also awarded on a more or less automatic scale. 'These people,' says Nikitenko, 'are right in wanting a cross or rank—without it, who would recognise them as people? ... Charming female company ... respect, popularity: all must be purchased by parading your dignities.' A contemporary of Nikitenko's, the Decembrist Nicholas Turgenev, even claimed that Russians lacking rank were 'completely outside the pale, officially and legally speaking'.[11]

This 'gigantic administrative machine which holds together all the various parts of the vast Empire' seemed to penetrate every nook and cranny of Russian life.[12] Everywhere, and especially in the capital, St Petersburg, one seemed to see nothing but uniforms. These were all the more obtrusive in constituting no monopoly of the armed services, being also worn by civil servants, schoolboys,

students, professors—and even by merchants wishing to present
the world with outward evidence of their inner worth. The prevalence of uniforms helps to explain the common impression that
officials were more numerous than was in fact the case. It also helps
to show how the *chinovnik* became one of those 'typical' Russian
phenomena, such as drunkenness, which caught the attention of
observers to a greater extent than appears justified by statistics.
With only a dozen civil servants, approximately, for each ten
thousand of the population, the Russian Empire was happily
understaffed in the mid-nineteenth century by comparison with
Western Europe, where the proportion of officials was three or
four times as great.[13]

And yet, small though it was, the official class somehow seemed
to dominate the country and to make nineteenth-century Russia a
pioneer in developing an oppressive bureaucracy such as has since
become the curse of the civilised world. Russian officials early
evolved that spirit of ill-placed administrative zeal, that passion for
useless formalities, that intoxication with petty power which per-
meated all fourteen grades of the Table of Ranks; as also did a
preoccupation with trivialities—a preoccupation which did not,
according to one masterly understatement, preclude disorder.[14]
Above all it helped to generate *chinopochitaniye*: 'rank sycophancy',
as it can be punningly translated, whenever a person of junior rank
such as a Titular Councillor, a mere 'Your Honour', encountered
a personage of senior rank such as a State Councillor entitled to be
addressed as 'Your Excellency'.

The *chinovnik* evoked widely different reactions in the elite and
non-elite. He was feared by the peasantry, but despised or mocked
by the gentry and intelligentsia; being described, for example, as
'*un espèce de canaille qu'on appelle chinovnik*'. The title 'general',
which was held by all officials, civilian as well as military, of the
fifth grade and above, became the rough equivalent for 'pompous
blockhead' to the nineteenth-century younger generation. Nor was
there any lack of *chinovnik*-baiting by *chinovniki* themselves. One
such civilian 'general', himself anything but pompous, regarded
his fellow officials as wretched individuals: 'the worst natural
enemy of the people's welfare'.[15]

The widespread low opinion of civil servants was not exclusively
based on the obsession with hierarchy which so many observers

have noted. There was also the *chinovnik*'s practice of requiring bribes from his clients, a routine dating from the Muscovite period, when senior provincial administrators had received no salary, but had been expected to 'live off the country' like members of an occupying army. Inadequately paid, nineteenth-century officials tended to be classified as honest if they confined the taking of bribes to an informal tariff. The dishonest were those whose greed exceeded this norm, like the official in Gogol's *Inspector General* who was accused of accepting bribes 'above his rank'. Some of the more unscrupulous officials, and especially those stationed furthest from the capital, practised the grossest forms of extortion. They were fully capable of accusing some rich person in their locality of an imaginary crime, and of holding him in prison until he paid a required sum.

Far from disappearing with the October Revolution of 1917 and associated abolition of the Table of Ranks, bureaucratic practices have only proliferated during the ensuing sixty years. But that is only to be expected, since proliferating bureaucracy is so common a feature of modern society in general. In totalitarian Russia the process has been accentuated through the incidence of state interference on a scale far exceeding that of any Tsar or Tsar-Emperor. To this must be added that the most successful power-seeker of modern times, Stalin, made inspired use of bureaucratic methods in a rise to power which depended not only on violence and the threat of violence, but also on card indexes, record files, dossiers and interlocking committees—all packed with the dictator's nominees and all watching over each other to an extent of which no individual member, and perhaps not even the dictator himself, could ever be certain. With the death of Stalin, and consequent abandonment of large-scale arbitrary arrest and imprisonment as a control technique, the essential structure yet remains, with the result that a key organisation such as the Soviet Army is inter-penetrated with Party, police and special political controls of phenomenal intricacy. As for the bureaucratic presence, after a period under Khrushchev when this was somewhat mitigated by the influence conceded to specialist and technical advisers, the top structure has probably become more bureaucratised than ever since 1964.[16] And yet the curse of bureaucracy has been vigorously condemned by modern Russia's successive rulers from Lenin onwards. Energetic attempts have been made to curb the evil; but have been no more successful in the Kremlin's orbit than anywhere else.

As for bribery, corruption and gross inefficiency, no statistics are available on the comparative incidence of these phenomena in imperial and totalitarian Russia. That they have by no means died out the modern periodical press abundantly testifies. Here one may read of such minor idiocies as the bulk freighting of bathing costumes to the Arctic Circle, or of snow ploughs to the Black Sea coast, all freely admitted under the heading of 'self-criticism'. One may also read so many press denunciations of blackmailing, extortionate, venal officials that a recent, by no means hostile, foreign observer can refer to the 'bribery, corruption and knavery which are so widespread and which nowadays constitute the chief internal "enemy" of the Soviet state'.[17] The system of illicit deals and under-the-counter arrangements known as *blat* or *kombinatsiya* flourishes widely. It is frequently used, for example, by factory managers who seek to fulfil the norms imposed by the economic plans without necessarily pursuing direct personal gain; indeed, the obtaining of spare parts by *blat* has long been an integral part of an economic structure which would surely collapse if such special arrangements were suddenly to be abandoned. Nor has excessive deference to rank passed away, though its methods have changed and it may have decreased somewhat since the days of Gogol and Saltykov.

Among other social groups the peasantry has frequently been invoked above on account of its numerical importance and a special evasive attitude to authority evolved over the centuries in response to oppression. Having thus developed by the mid-nineteenth century 'a power of continued, dogged, passive resistance such as is possessed . . . by no other class of men in Europe',[18] the peasantry was to see its numerical superiority of more than four to one slowly but inexorably eroded. Not until the 1960s did the USSR cease to be a preponderantly rural country, if judged by the place of residence of the larger number of citizens. The drift to the towns had been constant throughout the nineteenth century, had accelerated with the industrial revolution of the 1890s, and had then further accelerated with Stalin's Five Years Plans from 1929 onwards. But though town dwellers have now outnumbered country dwellers for nearly twenty years, and though urbanisation still proceeds apace, the peasantry remains a numerically significant force, and to a far greater degree than any corresponding rural element in Britain or the United States. Even in the towns—in Moscow or Tula, for instance—a Russian crowd seems to react in a more peasantlike manner, however defined, than would be the case in Rome, Munich or Pittsburgh.

Nor is the significance of the present-day peasantry confined to the many scores of millions officially categorised as peasants. In his book *The Taproot of Soviet Society* (1961) an American observer, Nicholas P. Vakar, argues that Soviet leaders have modelled their politics less on the precepts of Marx and Lenin than on the parish pump mentality which they or their fathers originally absorbed in their native villages. In 1967 a consulting psychiatrist, Henry V. Dicks, could make a similar claim the basis for constructing certain helpful *Notes on the Russian National Character*, in which he writes that 'Bearers of power in the Soviet Union are largely the children of Great Russian peasants, or the urban working class, many of whom have retained a close connection with their peasant background.'[19]

Though Russians' and Russia-watchers' statements on the muzhik exhibit their usual polarity, it is rare to find a denunciation of the class as violent as that of Maxim Gorky in his essay 'On the Russian Peasantry'. To peasant collective sadism, on which his views have already been quoted, may be added many other charges levelled against the muzhik, including that of exploiting his neighbours. For the lot of his fellow peasants the peasant cares nothing, according to Gorky: 'No one in Ryazan weeps over a bad harvest in Pskov.' Gorky's peasant is equally unconcerned about famine in the towns, exploiting his position as food grower to extort the very boots and shirt off the unhappy, hungry city-dweller's feet and back.[20] These views on peasant callousness accord with such rustic proverbs as 'My hut is at the end': in other words, '*I*, whose home is not endangered, am damned if I will help *you* put out the fire which is consuming *your* hut.' Once again a non-Russian equivalent ('I'm all right, Jack') indicates that certain vices are not exclusively Russian. Moreover, Gorky was grossly unfair to the terrorised peasant of the early Soviet years—so often compelled to disgorge his stocks, including even seed corn, for no return whatever by armed requisitioners from the towns; and often lucky if he escaped such clashes with his life.

Such outspoken denunciations of the peasantry as that launched by Gorky, in the aftermath of the civil war of 1917–21, can be balanced by innumerable tributes to peasant virtues expressed by peasant-fanciers, who include such major figures as Leo Tolstoy and Dostoyevsky in addition to those whose love of the Russian common people (*narod*) earned them the name of *narodniki*, 'populists'. Alas, persons of this type were commonly town-dwellers who barely knew one end of a peasant from the other. Yet they idealised the muzhik, as some have since come to idealise the —once no less oppressed—black people of America: out of a guilty conscience rather than from intimate knowledge. For centuries the Russian peasant had carried the weight of the country on his back, as ploughman, labourer and soldier. Might he not, then, be compensated for expending so much blood, toil and sweat over the ages by a little condescending praise, which, after all, costs nothing? Another common element in populist dithyrambs to the peasantry is the built-in self-congratulatory tone of the speaker: 'Watch me being magnanimous towards our poor muzhik.' Here, once again, Russian hyper-consciousness of audience reaction frequently seems to be present, and it is the audience's reaction to himself, not to the peasant, which seems to take precedence in the fancier's mind. Some of these points are made in an unjustly neglected early story of Chekhov's, *Good-for-Nothings*. Here a condescending landowner displays the labourers on his estate to his visiting brother as if they were animals in a zoo. He rhapsodises about the muzhik's instinctual wisdom, natural sense of justice and innate strength, as contrasted with the speaker's own class. 'We're all skin and bone ... outsiders, rejects—how dare *we* consider ourselves *their* betters?' The muzhik-fancying squire interrupts a peasant meal, compelling the picturesque bumpkins to sing folk songs while their buckwheat gruel congeals on the table, and eventually gives instructions for two of their lustier womenfolk to be sent up to the manor for his and his brother's after-dinner delectation; the girls are required to give a folk-dancing exhibition and, it is implied, more intimate entertainment as well.[21]

Himself for many years a country squire with an excellent record as a good neighbour to the local peasants, on whom he bestowed free medical care and three village schools, largely planned and financed by himself, Chekhov could feel justified in expressing his acute exasperation with the spurious element in much intellectual peasant-fancying. Concerned to help the peasants in a practical way, and also to describe them accurately and unsentimentally in his most famous story, *Peasants* (1897), he was so repelled by the trendy folkniks of his day that he rarely uttered a generalisation on the Russian muzhik. He was disgusted by those fanciers with whom he found himself unwillingly celebrating the thirty-sixth anniversary of the Emancipation of the Serfs on 19 February 1897 at the Continental Hotel in Moscow. 'Boring and silly. To dine, to drink champagne, to make a great fuss, to give speeches on peasant consciousness, on the peasant conscience, freedom and so on, while all the time tail-coated slaves [the waiters] scurry about the tables, as much serfs as ever they were: and while coachmen wait out in the freezing air of the streets. This is to lie to the Holy Spirit.'[22]

Discounting the statements of many peasant-fanciers as belonging to the language of mysticism or metaphysics, one can yet collect from a host of less biased and patronising witnesses a mass of testimony which more than counter balances the claims of Gorky. The late nineteenth-century French journalist Victor Tissot stated, for instance, that 'There is nothing more gentle, more humane than the Russian peasant.' When a witness as hostile to Russian society as Custine pauses to comment on the peasants' freedom from moral degradation (in contrast to their degrading surroundings) together with their wit and their pride, he deserves to be heeded. So too does Nikitenko, who expressly dissociates himself from trendy peasant-fancying as much as any Chekhov. The man who is prepared to denounce the romanticising of the peasant, and who does not hesitate on occasion to call the peasant a drunken savage, may be listened to when he praises the same peasant's sincerity and superiority to his educated fellow-countrymen. Pushkin has written a very paean to the muzhik: to his independence, boldness, cleverness, enterprise, dexterity, honesty, industry and tolerance. These, and many other judicious witnesses, must not be ignored.[23]

In peasant communities, as they have stabilised themselves in state and collective farms from the collectivisation campaign of 1929 onwards, the ancestral disadvantages of the muzhik have to some extent been institutionalised. Where other citizens are issued with a 'passport' enabling them to travel inside the country, peasants have been denied this privilege, though they are now said to be on the point of receiving it. The result has been to restrict and hamper their movements, and in effect to bind them to the land, so that foreign observers have compared collectivisation with serfdom. In earnings, welfare, pensions and educational activities, too, the modern peasant has lagged behind his urban brothers. Nor has he been relieved from the odious patronage of peasant-fancying non-peasants, who are as ready as ever to dilate on his sterling qualities as unacknowledged compensation for the disadvantages under which he labours.

Meanwhile the peasant continues whenever possible to protect himself by traditional methods against the exactions of the state. 'The struggle between state edicts and peasant cunning is unending.'[24]

INTIMACY

Now that the Russian's wider affiliations as a social being have been reviewed it remains to examine him as a member of his smallest unit, the family. This is in a sense his most important relationship, yet does not call for extensive treatment, since the Russian family has never differed strikingly—if so gross a generalisation may be permitted—from the Western family. Both have tended to become progressively smaller, less cohesive, less patriarchal and less closely united by religious belief and observances.

Though the family has not played an overwhelming role in expressing or stimulating any differentiation between the Russian and the Western mind, certain significant features must be recorded. In particular, the Russian family has tended to be less united than its Western counterpart. This is an inevitable outcome of the greater degree of intervention in personal relationships practised by a state so authoritarian in its manifestations: Muscovite, imperial and totalitarian. In the days of serfdom peasant families could be split at the whim of individual landowners empowered to draft them into the army, and even to nominate them for Siberian imprisonment and exile. The most feared of these fates was selective drafting into the army, a function assumed after emancipation by the village commune. Conscription was for twenty-five years in the first half of the nineteenth century, and was mourned in the villages as a calamity. The recruit might never reappear in his native village, being almost lost to domestic life on induction into the forces, while his abandoned wife, if he had one, tended to be considered half-widow, half-whore. Even more disruptive was sentence for a criminal offence to a prison term in Siberia, which involved the loss of civil rights and was followed by permanent exile even when the sentence had been served in full.

After reforms enacted in the middle of the nineteenth century by Alexander II to mitigate recruitment and certain penal procedures, official assaults on the peasant family decreased. But centrifugal tendencies remained. It was still common for a peasant to remove himself permanently from his village, yet without severing legal ties with his commune, and to take up work in a distant town as labourer, craftsman, waiter or domestic servant. However, as a nineteenth-century observer has noted, 'The artisan who goes to work in a distant town never takes his wife and family with him.'[1]

Despite such reservations family ties remained close, surviving the 1917 revolutions, the ensuing civil war, and also the following period, up to the mid-1930s, when the newly totalitarian state sought to dissolve domestic bonds on general principle. Divorce and abortion became readily available, while free love was extensively preached and ostentatiously practised, parental control over children being eroded and undermined. Yet the Russian family retained sufficient cohesion to be easily reinstated when Stalin decided to do so by rendering divorce and abortion difficult or impossible, and by re-establishing parental control over children.

It is through domestic conservatism, fostered by official policy, that marriage and family life in present-day Russia more closely reproduce the Western pattern than might be expected in view of totalitarian rigours and official claims to have pioneered a new, revolutionary way of life. But a marginally smaller degree of family cohesiveness still remains a characteristic Russian feature. Since most wives and husbands are in employment, but not necessarily in the same enterprise, and since both are at the disposal of authority to a greater extent than their Western counterparts, one or other may suddenly receive a posting to a distant part of the country on orders not necessarily compulsory in the strictest sense, but difficult to evade in practice. For husbands and wives to take their holidays separately, and at different times of the year, almost seems the norm; it is far more common than in the West. Another distinction is that, in this land of restricted privacy, the domestic hearth is more vulnerable to licensed or self-appointed snoopers in accordance with the assumption, characteristic of totalitarian *mœurs*, that everybody's affairs except the state's are everybody else's business.

Another feature is the prevalence of marriages of convenience based on the shortage of living space. Whereas, in the West, an individual may be suspected of marrying for money, in Russia he or she will more probably be suspected of embracing wedlock for a half share in a room or small flat. Another motive for marriage may be that it can convey the coveted and elusive Moscow residence permit. Cases are reported of men who, for a consideration, will marry and divorce in rapid succession a series of provincial girls thereby enabled to reside in the metropolis of which they would otherwise have seen as little as Chekhov's Three Sisters.

Less cohesive in the sense that family ties can more easily be loosed, the modern Russian family tends to be closer than that of the more advanced Western nations in a purely physical sense: if its members live together, they do so in the extreme proximity imposed by dearth of space. That the people actually prefers this huddling and bundling is, as indicated above, the contention of Russia-fancying witnesses rather than of those directly concerned.

To turn from the family to the role of women, inside and outside the family, is to be struck by a significant improvement in female status after centuries of male dominance. 'If the [Russian] woman be not beaten with the whip once a week she will not be good,' reports the sixteenth-century English witness Antony Jenkinson. 'And the women say if their husbands did not beat them they would not love them.' Meanwhile a contemporary manual of etiquette, the *Domostroy*, was instructing the Muscovite husband in the technique of beating his wife: this must be done courteously, lovingly, and in such a way as neither to blind her nor render her permanently deaf; the possibility of a husband not beating his wife seems to be discounted. Two centuries later a French monk, the

Abbé Chappe d'Auteroche, denounces Russia's barbarous provinces where 'men tyrannise over their wives, whom they treat as their slaves, requiring of them the most servile offices', such as pulling off their boots. A twentieth-century authority laments that nowhere have women been more cruelly beaten than in the Russian village, and instances a significant peasant proverb, 'The harder you beat a woman the tastier the cabbage soup.' Such homely anti-feminist tags are legion, from the notorious 'Woman is long on hair but short on brain' to such collectors' pieces as 'A mare ain't a horse, a hen ain't a bird, a woman ain't a person'; 'Seven women have only one soul between them'; 'Woman has no soul, only a vapour.'[2]

So much for the status of the pre-revolutionary peasant woman at its lowest. Her more privileged sisters also suffered disabilities in imperial times. Subjected to legally imposed male tutelage, they were permitted the 'passport' required for internal travel purposes only by consent of a father or husband, who thus almost had the right to keep a daughter or wife under house arrest. Women could own property. But they found access to careers difficult apart from a few special areas such as governess-ship, prostitution and the stage, being debarred in varying degrees from access to higher education. For these reasons feminism became a burning issue with the radical movement, reformist or revolutionary, which first acquired significant momentum in the 1860s. So dedicated was the pioneer radical Chernyshevsky to female liberation that he went beyond the goal of mere equality between the sexes; women had been so long under-privileged, in his view, that they were now due for a spell of over-privilege. Hitherto a man had been able to consort with mistresses without incurring social censure, whereas his wife had found it difficult or impossible to maintain a lover. Now, in all fairness, so inequitable an arrangement must be reversed. Chernyshevsky insisted on his own wife conforming to his programme, also illustrating its implications in his influential novel *What Is To Be Done?* 'My dear, hitherto I have only loved you. Now I respect you.' Such, according to that scourge of radicals Dostoyevsky, was the reaction prescribed for a Chernyshevsky-indoctrinated husband at the happy moment when he should receive the news that his wife had asserted her integrity by embracing adultery.[3]

In present-day Russia the old male-dominated marriage is no longer the norm. No statistics are to be had on wife-beating through the ages, but one may safely claim that this barbarous practice has ceased to be as widespread as many nineteenth-century and earlier observers have reported. In any case the modern Russian woman seems both morally and physically equipped to defend herself. She often looks capable of husband-beating if necessary. Even if physically weaker than the male, she is likely to possess greater stamina and force of character. Thus has the new Russia evolved a corps of formidable, energetic, self-confident matrons. Transferring to the low-level or middling political sphere, to which they are confined, woman's traditional role as guardian of tradition, these now constitute a bulwark of a system which might fall apart were it left in the exclusive custodianship of the easy-going Russian male. Nor is this impressive breed of woman exclusively a product of totalitarianism. The Russian peasant, a pre-revolutionary authority notes, 'rather admires vigour and strength in his mate';[4] and had long ago invented the term *boy-baba* as a term of praise—meaning, as near as one may translate, a 'woman embattled'.

Russian literature again and again invokes a situation particularly familiar to Turgenev's readers: a beautiful, strong, well-integrated, decisive woman becomes erotically implicated with some spineless, dithering pipsqueak of a man who invariably emerges discredited from the involvement. In fiction of the totalitarian period the clash between strong female and weak male is more than ever in vogue, and has been well analysed in terms which recall the life-cycle of the spider. In Russian fiction, pre-revolutionary and post-revolutionary alike, a feeble, vacillating hero is again and again 'contrasted with a young woman of unusual strength and integrity of character' who shows 'more purity and dedication and also more practical common sense than the man'.[5] Thus do firmness of purpose and strength of character tend, in Russian fiction through the ages, to be confined to the female sex.

Despite the Russian female's strength of character and physique, and despite progress in establishing equality between the sexes, some officially unavowed male domination continues. No woman has yet attained a truly influential position in the post-revolutionary political world, which may be scanned in vain for Catherine the

Greats. The most eminent, to date, has been Catherine Furtsev, who was appointed to the Party Presidium in 1956, but lost this position in 1961. Nor is this discrimination at the higher levels confined to Communist Party organisation. Despite the prominence of women in medicine, teaching and cultural work, few indeed are appointed to the most senior posts in these or other areas.

On a humbler level, too, the modern Russian woman is at a disadvantage when compared to her male partner. Her equality is enshrined in law, and she receives equal pay for equal work. But her 'right to work' has become blurred with something less desirable: a *de facto* obligation to work outside the home, even if she is a wife and mother, since the low standard of living makes it impossible for most husbands to support a full-time housewife. Women have constituted about half the total labour force for some years now.[6] But this is no unmixed gain for the feminist cause owing to the common domestic arrangement, not enshrined in law, whereby—in addition to full-time outside employment—the Russian housewife may be faced with the daily martyrdom of queueing for food and other household necessities, besides having to do housework, and to feed and clothe her family. Meanwhile her allegedly equal spouse is playing dominoes or drinking with his friends.

In their attitude to divorce, as to parenthood, present-day Russians again tend to be marginally less addicted than their Western counterparts to maintaining the family as a cohesive institution. Divorce is now easily obtained in Russia, and its incidence has recently been recorded as exceeding the notoriously high level found in the United States. There are even districts of Moscow where the number of divorces in a given year is in excess of the number of marriages. As for children, they tend—in view of the desperate economic strain imposed by the burden of feeding and housing extra dependants—to be regarded as a nuisance. Wide use is made of abortion, legalised in 1955, to limit their numbers: a procedure all the more crucial in view of the poor quality or unavailability of contraceptives. Abortion thus seems to constitute, both inside and outside marriage, almost the main method of birth control—an increasingly effective method, to judge from the fall in the birth rate from 2·7 per cent in 1950 to 1·8 per cent in 1973.[7]

Turning to the sexual activities and preoccupations of Russians, and the extent to which these may differ from Western practice, one generalises with reluctance in an area so private. One point may, however, be made with confidence. So far as public utterance is concerned—whether in posters, in films, or in the printed word —there is no pornography as extensively cultivated in the West. Rather is prudishness the fault. Here, too, the usual double standard seems to operate. For instance, the Russian visitor to a foreign country may, in his official persona, high-mindedly condemn such manifestations of capitalist decadence as placards advertising striptease joints, or—in one bizarre instance which I recall—female dummies standing undraped in a dress-shop window. Yet the same puritan scourge of capitalist immorality may later be heard retailing 'locker-room' stories on a level of obscenity and tastelessness almost passing belief. May one relate the observance of this double standard to the peasant custom of veiling the holy icon with a curtain, or removing the cross from one's neck, before engaging in sexual intercourse?

On sexual morals it is impossible to achieve statistically valid conclusions. That casual promiscuity is cultivated by some sections of the community is beyond doubt. Having investigated this problem in the field, one American journalist judges that seven out of ten of Moscow's young women are instantly available to any presentable male.[8] These are respectable girls seeking relief from everyday routine: enthusiastic amateurs, not the professionals who may also be found and who are less moved by the spirit of adventure.

Reticent or even priggish in public utterance on sexual matters, Russians—at least their less cultured representatives—can be free in informal contexts with their use of equivalents for English 'four-letter words'. A Russian will unhesitatingly consign someone else's mother to an incestuous form of what used to be called a fate worse than death. So flexionally rich is the language, such its wealth of affixes, such its facility in forming derivatives, that the creatively inspired need not confine themselves to such crudities as the form *yob*, 'fuck'. They can add a further dimension by uttering the compound imprecation *yob tebya pereyob*, 'Fuck you in the *n*th degree'. Or they can refer to someone as a *nedoyobysh*: for which the nearest English equivalent may be 'one scraped off the sheets with a spoon', like the luckless young man of Dunoon in the limerick. Meanwhile, though pornography may be officially prohibited, just as the existence of prostitution may be officially denied, foreign visitors to the Soviet Union continue to observe both manifestations, though they are less openly paraded than in more permissive societies.

A foreign witness has told me of a visit made some time ago to the provincial city of Astrakhan, where he chanced to meet the town's chief pimp. This organiser of Caspian call girls explained the local tariff and other technicalities of his profession in an earthy idiom which other languages might envy. He remarked that it might be necessary to pay a hundred roubles for a *baba s bagazhom* (roughly translated into American English as 'prime ass'); but that a mere twenty would be enough for *kakoye-nibud nikudyshnoye vyyebannoye barakhlo*, 'some useless piece of clapped out junk'. He also remarked of one of his 'hotter' items that *ona sovershenno syeblas*, of which the kindest rendering might be 'had been overdoing things'.

Bawdy verse has a tradition long antedating the revolutions. The classic, somewhat overrated tragi-comic ballad *Luka Mudishchev*, Russia's equivalent of *Eskimo Nell* and often mistakenly attributed to the minor eighteenth-century poet Barkov, has recently been published (in Russian) in the West. Pushkin's long outlawed bawdy ballad *Tsar Nikita and his Forty Daughters* has even been found to possess sufficient literary merit to receive publication in English translation by the American magazine *Playboy*, in December 1965.[9] Author of many such sallies, Russia's greatest poet often found himself in trouble through offending the prudish standards of his day. A grave *skandal* was created by his mock-heroic *Gabrieliad*, in which Lucifer and the Archangel Gabriel compete for the favours of the Virgin Mary, thereby casting doubt on the paternity of Jesus Christ.

IV
Regimentation
and Resistance

AUTHORITY AND SUBMISSION

Techniques of imposing central authority throughout the ages are
now to be reviewed, together with the responses which these have
evoked in conformists.

That the Russians were 'born for slavery', that they actively preferred enslavement to freedom, that they would happily exhibit
the bumps on their foreheads raised through zeal in executing the
kowtow—such claims are common in Western travellers' tales of
the sixteenth century.[1] Three hundred years later a Russia-
domiciled Englishwoman, a Mrs Smith, saw a serf thank his master
for a beating, and concluded that such a people would take centuries
to appreciate the blessings of freedom. 'Perhaps they are too Asiatic
ever properly to do so.' Meanwhile her French contemporary
Custine was accusing the whole nation of being intoxicated with
servility, and commenting on the general atmosphere of sycophancy; of which, incidentally, one seems to detect not a little
in that French marquis's own attitude to the all-powerful Nicholas I.[2]

Despite the changes since Custine's day, traces of what might
seem a slave mentality have not disappeared from Muscovite
psychology. 'Their long history of subservience makes it easy for
the Russian people to slip back into the habits of servility when the
occasion demands it.' For freedom and civil liberties as understood
elsewhere the average citizen seems to have little desire, especially
among the lowest social groups.[3] Should his views on freedom be
solicited, the Russian is liable—if in patriotic and *vranyo*-
intoxicated mood—to claim that his country already has far more
of it than any other. 'I know no other land where man breathes so
freely,' a well-known Russian song unconvincingly asserts. No
less common is a contrary statement: an admission that the country
lacks freedom altogether, and this combined with the hope that

such a curse may never alight. 'Heaven forbid that we should have freedom here.'

Poised, as he so often seems, to carry any idea to its logical extreme, the Russian is apt to equate freedom with anarchic licence. To him freedom 'means making mischief', according to the nineteenth-century critic Belinsky. He claims that the Russian nation would not, if liberated, move towards a parliament; it would rush off to the pot-house to drink spirits, smash glasses and hang members of the gentry, those beard-shavers who wear frock-coats instead of homespun smocks.[4] The modern *émigré* philosopher Fedotov reckons the following items as prominent in the national conception of liberty: 'the wide open spaces, vagabondage, the gipsy ethos, hard liquor, orgies of debauchery, blind sensualism, highway robbery, rioting, despotism'.[5] But though some may revel in anarchic violence, they are not the majority. 'If we ever have freedom here I shall be hanged from the first lamp post,' is an opinion sometimes expressed. Orgiastic outbursts, wild excesses are not to every individual's taste, and there still seems to lurk in the popular consciousness a fear of the licence of the Time of Troubles, of the revolts of Razin and Pugachov and of all three twentieth-century revolutions. So starved of liberty, moreover, has the people been, especially under Stalin, that many a defector or refugee has experienced great difficulty in adjusting to American, British, French, Israeli or other foreign life; to one regimented from the cradle such alien environments can present the spectacle of utter chaos.

If the nation's attitude to freedom and authority exhibits these features, an explanation may be sought in the evolution of regimentation during the last half-millennium. A force overwhelming and arbitrarily imposed, commanding total obedience except on the occasions when deceit and trickery allow loop-holes for evasion, a force feared but not respected—such has been authority to the Russian throughout the ages. There is, surely, no other feature which more sharply differentiates the generalised Russian experience from that of the West. This is partly due to the shattering impact which Russian authority has traditionally made, especially in view of its capricious nature. Furthermore, authority has not only tended to bear down more severely on the Russian; it has also tended (as already noted) to do so progressively. In other words, it has grown ever more rigorous over the centuries, by contrast with the West, where the exactions of centralised power have tended to decline.

The onward march of authoritarianism has been no smooth, orderly progression. Bouts of intense governmental oppression have alternated with periods of relaxation. The graph of oppressiveness is no steadily rising straight line, but an ascending meander.

Kievan society presents few features indicating a penchant for regimentation outstripping that of other medieval states. It is Tatar influence from 1240 onwards that seems to have given disciplinary trends their initial impetus, imparting despotic and traditionally 'oriental' features. Without keeping the country under permanent occupation, the Tatars instituted in effect a comprehensive 'protection racket'. They took a census of the subjugated Russian population, and imposed a quota of recruits and tribute; then retreated to a distance, swooping to conduct reprisals when their demands were not met. Before a Russian prince could ascend his throne he was compelled to journey to Tatar headquarters at Saray on the lower Volga, there to make obeisance to the Khan and to undergo various humiliations before receiving, if he found favour, a patent to rule. The system put a premium on sycophancy towards the Khan, combined with treachery towards competing princelings—a process of unnatural selection which only the most cunning, ambitious and obsequious could survive. In the end it was the princes of Moscow, eventually promoted to Grand Princes, who revealed the greatest pertinacity in ingratiating themselves with their masters and betraying their fellows. The Tatars accordingly allowed them to operate as enforcers empowered to collect tribute from lesser princelings, who thus fell under Muscovite rule, at first within the framework of the Tatar Empire known as the Golden Horde. When the Golden Horde declined, and Moscow became strong enough to withhold tribute, no change was necessary: exactions previously passed on by Moscow to Saray now stayed in Moscow, while Muscovite Grand Princes continued to rule on principles absorbed from the Tatars: arbitrary despotic violence and indifference to the welfare of the subject.

How deep an imprint did the Tatars leave? One extreme view is that of Karl Marx. 'The bloody mire of Mongol [Tatar] slavery ... forms the cradle of Muscovy, and modern Russia is but a

metamorphosis of Muscovy.' Referring to the principle, introduced by the Tatars, whereby unlimited service obligations were
placed on the entire population, the historian George Vernadsky
has called the Tatar-imposed administration 'a peculiar system of
state socialism'. In keeping with this suggestion Belinsky, himself
an early Russian Socialist, has referred to the centuries of the Tatar
Yoke with approval as forging the scattered parts of the country
into unity. So great a boon did he rate this contribution that it
outweighed for him many less desirable legacies: the seclusion of
women, a slavish mentality, the knout, corruption in justice,
squalid habits, mental laziness, ignorance and self-contempt.[6]
Belinsky thus ascribes traditional Russian slovenliness to Tatar
influence. It may be added that certain significant words—*kabala*,
'bondage'; *nagayka*, 'whip'; *kandaly*, 'fetters'—came into Russian
from Tatar together with terms reflecting administrative practices:
those describing the postal and customs services; the word for
money.

Emerging from the Tatar Yoke, the Grand Princes—soon to call
themselves Tsars—of Moscow already seemed to enjoy absolute
power. He 'holds unlimited control over the lives and property of
all his subjects',[7] said Herberstein of Grand Prince Basil III in
the early sixteenth century. Linking lives and property in this way,
the ambassador shows how keenly he appreciated the authoritarian
nature of Muscovite rule, which went beyond mere sovereignty.
The monarch was considered literally to own, as his personal property, everything within his realm, including his subjects' persons
as well as their possessions, a principle sometimes called patri-
monial. He was thus more than a mere despot who infringes the
rights of his subjects; to do that was beyond even his unlimited
power, since they possessed no rights.

'In the sway which he [the Tsar] holds over his people, he sur-
passes all the monarchs of the whole world.' 'The state and
forme of their government is plaine tyrannicall.' 'No Master hath
more power over his slaves than the Great Duke [Grand Prince]
hath over his subjects.' Such was the verdict on Muscovy delivered
by its sixteenth- and seventeenth-century foreign visitors Herberstein, Fletcher and Olearius respectively.[8] They unite in portraying
a simply structured society. First there is, alone in all his glory, the
ruler himself, absolute master of all he surveys. Then come his

higher slaves—princelings, boyars and other upper servitors, the predecessors of the later *dvoryanstvo*, 'gentry'—whose function it is to transmit or issue instructions. Their recipients form the third and lowest level of the underslaves who constitute the vast majority of the population, whether peasants or inhabitants of the sparse and not very numerous towns. 'All the classes of the nation from top to bottom . . . were bound to the service of the state,' Vernadsky has asserted. The philosopher Berdyayev claims that 'the Moscow Orthodox Kingdom was a totalitarian state'. I do not agree, for reasons to be given below, but it is not hard to see how such an impression could arise. Nor is a similar thesis—that all Russian land had already been fully nationalised by the late fifteenth century—difficult to sustain if one calls to mind the forcible transplantation of populations from one part of the country to another for administrative convenience.[9]

Yet the authority, already seemingly absolute, which Muscovy's rulers had inherited from the Tatars, appeared to possess the logic-defying property already noted: that of becoming progressively more absolute as the decades rolled by. Successive rulers extended their power and territory in all directions. They also exerted irresistible pressure to erode the right of free movement whereby virtually all citizens, whether princes, boyars or mere peasants, had been permitted to transfer allegiance from one master to another. The process of bonding all lower servitors to higher, and all higher servitors to the sovereign, was long and bloody. One of its episodes was Ivan the Terrible's onslaught on his boyars and princes. In this sanguinary campaign he was prepared to risk destroying his country, provided that his personal power could be made to predominate ever more. He thus anticipated Stalin's seemingly wanton liquidation of *his* higher servitors—his managers, his officer corps, his senior Party officials—in the purge years 1936–8. Both these orgies of destruction, Ivan's and Stalin's, took place at times of national peril: from Poland and Livonia in the sixteenth century, from Hitler nearly four hundred years later. One is also reminded that Stalin once praised Ivan's methods to a well-known film star, but criticised the dread Tsar for wasting on his prayers time better spent on killing more boyars.[10]

Did the Russians feel an irresistible inner drive to submit to absolute rule? Their seventeenth-century evolution suggests as much. The period began with that decade of chaos, starvation, civil strife, plunder, confusion and despair termed the Time of Troubles (1604–13). Muscovy was now partially ruled, misruled and competed for by various pretenders to the throne; also suffering attack by Swedes and occupation by Poles, not to mention famines and peasant revolts. Here was the first occasion on which regimentation broke down so calamitously, giving way to anarchy. From this the election of a boy Tsar, Michael, by a kind of national assembly, brought relief in 1613, instituting the new dynasty of the Romanovs which was to rule until 1917.

Michael Romanov and his two immediate successors were comparative mediocrities, even Alexis—the second and least feeble of the trio—being nicknamed the Most Gentle Tsar. But though the relaxation of authoritarianism might have been expected to take place under such rule, this did not occur. In 1649 a new, rigorous law code completed the bondage of all citizens. The peasants' reaction was to stage revolts which evoked memories of the Time of Troubles before they were suppressed. Was it the recollection of that decade of anarchy which chiefly reconciled the people to slavery under a single all-powerful master who, though passive, was capable of maintaining or restoring civil peace, even if it seemed like the peace of near-stagnation?

With the advent of Peter the Great at the end of the seventeenth century, authoritarianism was still further reinforced—not because the ruler's notional powers, assumed to be unlimited all along, had increased, but because the new sovereign was able to use those powers more aggressively than his three Romanov predecessors could have contrived. Peter transformed Russia by ruthless measures, all ultimately designed to improve his military effectiveness. Not least among his achievements was the invention of two discipline-enhancing institutions destined to flourish on a global scale after his death: military conscription and a political police force. But the many atrocities inflicted on his subjects differed from the cruelties of Ivan the Terrible in being more rationally conceived. Torturings and executions were part of Peter's method, but were imposed on a smaller scale, serving the rational purpose of increasing his power and that of the Russian state. Peter differed from Ivan in being less concerned to appease the demons within his own soul. Yet, paradoxical though it may seem, Ivan had a stronger hold on his subjects' affections than Peter could command. Russians like a touch of magic or even madness in their rulers. To be forced to obey another in the name of logic and expediency is, in the last resort, a deadly insult—what self-respecting man can, in his heart, feel it reasonable for another to be his master? But to be forced to obey in defiance of sense and reason by the black magic of an Ivan—this was a more tolerable alternative than the bleakness of Peter's authority purportedly based on rationality. No wonder the muzhiks were so convinced that he was Antichrist. Similarly, to invoke a parallel from modern times, Stalin—an outstandingly harsh ruler who had the happy instinct of investing his person with an aura of myth, cult and absurdity—was probably less unpopular than Khrushchev, who was far more concerned to explain his frequently grotesque manoeuvres in terms of rational motivation.

In the middle and late eighteenth century the character of Russian authoritarianism was modified through a major social change: the gentry acquired its freedom from all service obligations. Once liberated, Russian gentlemen exploited their new opportunities to bring about several palace revolutions resulting on three occasions in the slaughter of a sovereign. Yet the gentry's new freedoms remained precarious; just how precarious the mentally unbalanced Emperor Paul abundantly demonstrated, during his brief reign of 1796–1801, by a series of eccentric oppressions. That these provoked his assassination by a group of intoxicated officers and gentlemen shows how vulnerable both sides were in the unofficial alliance between sovereign and gentry created in the late eighteenth century.

Between 1801 and 1855 two successive Tsars fought a rearguard action in defence of Russian absolutism, now menaced by libertarian urges. Alexander I paid lip service to liberty and equality, but only provided that there was no question of implementing these notions associated with the French Revolution. French political thinkers, German philosophers—ideas emanating from these Western sources already seemed to threaten Russian authoritarian government. Alexander's successor, Nicholas I, therefore took steps to check the influx of alien concepts, asserting the autocratic principle so rigorously that he has been accused of inventing the police state. Yet even Nicholas failed to silence the press, that vehicle for Russian literature at the beginning of its greatest age: a literature remarkable both for artistic originality and for a prominent element of political protest.

The years 1855 to 1917 see Russian authoritarianism on the defensive. Alexander II made a determined attempt to reform institutions and democratise society. After his assassination in 1881 his successor Alexander III enacted much reactionary legislation, yet by no means destroyed the new atmosphere of relative freedom. The last Tsar, Nicholas II, made the same attempt with even less success; and felt compelled, in 1906, to grant an embryonic parliament, the State Duma. Though its powers were limited indeed, the concession marks the abandonment, in however small a degree, of the principle of absolute rule.

The establishment of Bolshevik rule in 1917 sees a dramatic upsurge in authoritarianism. This increase in rigour derived partly from the adoption of a political programme with claims to universal applicability such as no Romanov emperor had ever put forward. To this must be added the benefits of modern technology permitting the establishment of a totalitarian terrorist bureaucracy such as could not be created even by a Peter the Great before the days of the radio, the telegraph, typewriters, general literacy—and, finally, computers. Yet the graph of Russian authoritarianism did not proceed in a smooth and orderly line after 1917. Governmental violence reached its peak during the quarter century of Stalin's supreme power, from 1929 to 1953. Compared with that period the preceding years, those of Lenin and the struggle for Lenin's succession, were marked by greater restraint, as were the following eras, those of Khrushchev and Brezhnev. But the totalitarian apparatus—the rigorous censorship, the travel restrictions, the thought control, the conscription and browbeating of the citizenry —all remains intact. One new feature distinguishing the totalitarian from the imperial period has been the obligation to pretend that no such controls exist, and even that the modern Russian citizen is more free than his Western counterpart. With this one may contrast the blunt admission of the bluff Nicholas I that the Russian system was an outright despotism and that such a system accorded with the genius of his people.[11]

Seen from below, Russian state power has always worn an awesome, crushing aspect, while presenting a very different vista when viewed from above. It is the precariousness, the vulnerability, of the supreme ruler's position which is apt to strike him as its dominant feature. Never in Russian history has there been any accepted procedure for transferring power from one potentate to another. Khrushchev's removal by the Party Central Committee in October 1964 has been called the first occasion 'in the entire history of Russia since Riurik [in the ninth century] that the established leader of the country was removed by the rules of representative procedure'.[12] Though a sitting ruler might be thought to gain additional security through the lack of any means providing for his dismissal, in fact the opposite was often the case, since he could be ousted by one means only: a *coup d'état*, usually accompanied by assassination. Hence Madame de Staël's well-known quip, that Russia was a despotism mitigated by strangulation.

It is from his immediate entourage, not from the masses of his humbler subjects, that the Russian ruler has usually had most to fear. In such an atmosphere despotic urges at the summit begin to seem, if not excusable, at least human, natural and intelligible. Nor is it merely fear for his personal safety which has bred in the Russian ruler the instinct to quell his subjects before they quell him. If, like an Ivan the Terrible, a Peter the Great or a Stalin, he has conceived the ambition not merely of staying alive, but also of strengthening his fief economically, militarily and culturally—a by no means eccentric or insane ambition—he is apt to become frustrated by certain mental habits of the Russian people, that instrument through which he is obliged to operate. Seen from outside, they may indeed seem exceedingly docile. But why has it so often been necessary to discipline them into docility so extreme? Surely because many of them are the reverse of regimentation-prone in their souls? Their charmingly evasive tactics, their disarming unreliability, their delightful unpunctuality—these qualities may well enchant the casual observer as much or more than the Russia-fancier. But what of the man in charge with a practical task to perform? To him these same endearing features can assume a different aspect.

Many years ago in London I chanced to set up and head a sizeable teaching institution which employed about a score of Russians over a period of years. That they cheerfully co-operated and efficiently discharged their duties I can testify, while adding, however, that this satisfactory consummation was preceded by a difficult phase in which they virtually compelled me (by persistent unpunctuality and so on) to adopt the methods of an Ivan, a Peter or a Stalin writ exceeding small. Either the institution was to dissolve in hopeless *bezalabershchina*, or the supreme overlord had to develop the instincts of a petty tyrant. Once the second option had been grasped—which was what my colleagues evidently wished—no further difficulties occurred. The experience did not reconcile me to the methods of an Ivan the Terrible, a Peter the Great or a Stalin. But it made it possible, as nothing else could, to understand that neither elemental perversity nor an evil-be-thou-my-good philosophy need be invoked to explain the proceedings of the Russians' many despotic masters. Perhaps there was simply no other way of achieving results: of bringing about that happy transition from the imperfective to the perfective aspect which, as the strict compartmentalisation of these two Russian verbal categories suggests, can be difficult to accomplish in the land where they hold sway.

The mailed fist or total anarchy: here is the choice with which subordinate Russians tend to face those responsible for their collective efforts. Must one then conclude that it was the Russian mind which moulded the authoritarian state? Or is the Russian mind rather the outcome of that authoritarian state? All one can assert with confidence is that the two phenomena have interacted for at least half a millennium.

TSARISM AND ANTI-TSARISM

Having considered submission to authority, the argument turns to the equally crucial theme of resistance to authority.

That the Russian is not genetically precluded from grasping the concept of freedom under the law; that he can enjoy and intelligently use liberty when available; that he can hanker after freedom in a sober and dignified spirit when it is not available—of these propositions abundant evidence can be adduced. It is also true that many neither accept nor respect in their hearts the all-powerful authority which so often compels their obedience. Even under totalitarian regimentation they are careful to distinguish those ordinances, usually with political implications, which it is prudent to obey, from other regulations which may safely be flouted. Traffic codes, injunctions against poaching, the requirement to show one's ticket to a train conductor, whistles blown by official beach-masters to command holiday-making sunbathers to turn over and thus avoid undue exposure—all these things can be and are blatantly ignored. Obliged, as part of his university course, to take instruction in dialectical materialism, a student will chatter loudly to his neighbour during lectures on the subject—and in a manner which few Western citizens would think legitimate when absorbing divine revelation in church, their nearest equivalent to such a devotional context. But then the Russian Orthodox always did converse with each other during church services, even in the days when their now dethroned church represented authority—just as they have long tended to ignore No Smoking notices in public places. Such was firmly established practice in the universities of the nineteenth century, when 'no law was firmly enforced': an exaggeration, but an understandable one. It is for punctilio in obeying such regulations that the Russian tends to despise the Germans, whom he considers regimented in their souls. And not only Germans. 'We [Russians] never see English people lying on the grass for hours, and missing their meals for the pure pleasure of it ... *We* do not give up our afternoons to enjoy Nature in a decent, organised way by means of out-door games.' Such a contrast has also been drawn (by an American) with Americans, who allegedly conform with society's taboos because they wish to conform; how much more slavish an attitude, it might seem, than that of the Russian conformist, who conforms because he has to.[1]

Here is another paradox: members of a strictly regimented society despise others for being over-regimented. Once again the familiar concept of polarisation seems relevant. At any given moment the Russian tends to be highly conscious either of being or of not being in a hierarchic relationship. He is apt to make the most of such a context, playing to the limit one of two contrary roles: giving and receiving orders. But outside that context he has a keen sense of equality. 'In all relations which are not defined as leader and led, superordinate and subordinate ... Russians demand the most absolute equality in their personal relationships. It would appear that Russians do not conceive of any intermediate positions: there is either complete equality, or complete superordination and subordination.'[2] They thus tend to seem doubly polarised: first, between wholly authority-free and wholly authority-dominated relationships; secondly, within the latter only, between total domination and total submissiveness.

With this twin, double-pronged attitude to freedom and authority is linked—whether as cause or effect or both—one striking feature of Russia throughout the ages: the absence of institutional-ised means for registering political opposition. There is nothing which more sharply distinguishes the country's evolution from that of the major Western European countries. Lacking until the last years of the Empire even the semblance of a parliament, of political parties and of effective corporate pressure groups, the Russians long ago developed techniques of resistance based on flight, peasant revolt, pretenders to the throne and palace revolutions.

Flight from the service of an oppressive central or local overlord has already been mentioned as a traditional right of peasants and princelings in the centuries preceding the consolidation of auto-cratic power by Moscow's Grand Princes, later Tsars. The aboli-tion of this right, through enserfment and the binding of the gentry to lifelong service, has been noted as one of the means whereby Muscovy rose to dominion over other principalities. But flight from the centre did not end simply because it had become illegal and hazardous. On the contrary, it became the main process where-by the peasant masses expressed their opposition to authority. 'Opposition to the state did exist among the lower orders, but owing to the super-abundance of physical space it expressed itself in running away, in removing oneself from the burdens which the state placed on the people, and not in active resistance or struggle.'[3]

There thus arose on the southern and south-eastern periphery of Russia, and also in Siberia, communities of rough frontiersmen known as Cossacks. They fought against each other and their neighbours—Poles, Tatars, Turks, Caucasian tribesmen—siding now with, now against the centrally controlled Russian state in which most of them had originated. The milieu has been com-pared to the American Wild West, with the Tatar as Red Indian, the Russian army as the US cavalry, and the Cossack as pioneering frontiersman vaguely owing allegiance to his ataman or sheriff. Nor was there any lack of hard liquor, cattle rustling, lynching, punch-ups, posses chasing badmen and so on. The claim has even been

made that the Cossack—with his high spirits, comic humour, booz-
ing, brigandage and brawling—was 'in many ways closer to the
popular idea of the cowboy than was the cowboy himself'.[4] Meanwhile the expanding central state was progressively re-embracing
its prodigal Cossack sons until the drilled and militarised descendants of swaggering frontiersmen became the government's most
reliable riot police, and could be depended upon literally to whip
protesting students into a semblance of submission.

On three major occasions earlier Cossacks had allied themselves
with disaffected peasantry—the distinction between a Cossack and
a disaffected peasant not being always easy to draw—and had promoted upheavals which overthrew or severely threatened the
central power. In the early seventeenth century they helped to set
a pretender, False Dmitry, on the throne of Moscow, thus beginning the Time of Troubles. They were also prominent in the many
other peasant revolts of the period. These established the new
tradition of a devastating but fortunately rare class war in which
rampaging peasants and Cossacks massacred the rich and shared
out their wives and property. The same simple ideology also helped
to inspire the Cossack-peasant revolts of Stenka Razin in 1670-1,
and of Pugachov over a century later. In these conflicts Russian
anarchy, a phenomenon no less extreme than Russian regimentation,
ran riot; but with one curious reservation. In all such upheavals,
and in many a minor revolt, a pretender or false Tsar—either the
rebel leader himself, as with Pugachov, or a puppet figure—remained an indispensable item in the equipment of the mutineers.
They thus clearly signified, while attempting to unseat an individual monarch, their loyalty to the monarchy as an institution.
Even the most disaffected were not yet trying to overthrow their
system of government.

The same claim can be made for rebellions at the other end of
the social scale: the palace revolutions carried out, mainly in the
eighteenth century, by guards officers of St Petersburg. These conspirators tended to install ladies on the throne: the Empresses
Catherine I, Elizabeth and Catherine the Great. The fourth and
last notable palace revolution occurred with the strangling of the
eccentric Emperor Paul by a posse of drunken officers and achieved
the accession of his son Alexander I, in some degree an accom-
plice, on 12 March 1801. Far removed though these high-level

conspiracies were from the peasant and Cossack risings invoked above, they too were similarly concerned to replace an uncongenial with a congenial absolute monarch—not to replace absolute monarchy with another kind of government.

On these primitive forms of opposition the Decembrist Revolt of 1825 represented a considerable advance. It was at once repressed, but the aspirations behind it were not so easily quelled. On this occasion a change of system, not simply a change of rulers, had been the goal. Thus, though the Decembrists had no common programme—some aiming at a constitutional monarchy while others hankered after a republic—their motives were more political, and hence more modern, than the dynastic urges which had fired Russia's previous peasant and palace revolutionaries. The Decembrist movement also brought in the common people as rank-and-file mutineers, if only because they were ordered to take part by their revolutionary officers.

The accession of Alexander II in 1855 began a new chapter in the saga of Russian political dissent. Hitherto the resistance movement had worn as primitive an air as had the autocratic power. Still, to the extent that the political *coup*, particularly if mounted by serving officers, has become so prominent a global institution in the late twentieth century, even eighteenth-century Russia now seems to have marched in the very van of modernity and progress. Of developments from 1855 onwards this claim may be made more confidently.

After beginning his reign by relaxing the harsher measures of his predecessor, Alexander II discovered that to dismantle a tyranny may be to invite reprisals which might with greater justice have been undertaken against the earlier dispensation. Finding it safe to express oppositionist views long banned as seditious, disaffected citizens hastened to denounce and attack the new administration. Thus the adoption of liberal measures, including the emancipation of the serfs, came to coincide with the development of the country's first serious revolutionary movement. So far, however, the number of active conspirators was small: a few score, perhaps, in the 1860s, and a few hundred in the 1870s. Nor did they subscribe to any common doctrine or programme. Their impact derived rather from the scandalous nature of their methods, especially political assassination. A political police chief, General Mezentsov, was fatally stabbed on a main street in St Petersburg; Prince Dmitry Kropotkin, a provincial governor-general, was shot dead in his carriage. Eventually, on 1 March 1881, the Emperor himself was slaughtered by a home-made hand grenade on a St Petersburg quayside.

Other oppositionist practices were the distribution of blood-curdling manifestos and the attempted manipulation of the down-trodden peasantry which should have been, but so infuriatingly was not, ripe for revolt. Efforts to educate, agitate or otherwise activate the muzhik by peaceful persuasion took on a widespread character in 1873-4, when hundreds of young intellectuals went into the villages, seeking contact with the 'dark masses', but seeking it with conspicuous lack of success. Still loyal to the Tsar, still infuriatingly non-militant despite his dire poverty, the Russian villager was more likely to denounce these touring student agitators to the police than to turn revolutionary himself. On the one notable occasion when urban revolutionaries contrived to stir up a genuine village revolt, at Chigirin in southern Russia in 1877, they could do so only by issuing a forged manifesto—and that in the name of the Tsar—calling on the peasants to rise against the landlords and officials. That the rising was harshly suppressed, that the peasants were flogged, that the intellectual instigators were not flogged but briefly imprisoned, and then staged a daring escape—all was, once again, very much in the spirit of the age.

Throughout Alexander II's reign the conflict between government and revolutionaries had remained a small-scale duel which intrigued the population at large while failing to enlist broadly based sympathies on either the governmental or the revolutionary side. While the general attitude remained that of apathetic political voyeurism, the imperial administration proved incompetent to quell the handful of terrorists who threatened the throne and virtually imprisoned the monarch in his palace during his last years. But the Tsar's assassination, followed by the accession of the tough-minded Alexander III, drove the terrorists on to the defensive—as they remained until the accession of Nicholas II in 1894. Then the resistance movement began to acquire new strength and confidence. Political parties—illegal, legal and semi-legal—were founded: those of the (Marxist) Social Democrats, later to split into Bolsheviks and Mensheviks; of the peasant-fancying Socialist Revolutionaries; of the liberal Kadets.

The 1905 revolution was the first mass explosion of popular discontent since the Pugachov revolt of 1773–4 had menaced the throne of Catherine the Great. Once again, in the later rising as in the earlier, masses of the common people threw off restraint with vigour corresponding to the degree of regimentation under which they had laboured so long. Here was no co-ordinated upheaval—rather a series of widespread sporadic strikes and rural riots coinciding with mutinies among uniformed peasant conscripts returning from recent defeat in the Russo-Japanese War, which had begun in the previous year. The revolution was provoked by the massacre, in St Petersburg on 9 January 1905, of peacefully demonstrating workers by imperial troops. That 9 January came to be known as Bloody Sunday, as the result of these events, is less significant than that the Emperor had begun to acquire, among the common people, the nickname Bloody Nicholas. Here was the writing on the wall for the Romanov dynasty, long protected by the almost mystical reverence in which Russian peasants had held their Tsar. Moreover, however closely the riots, assassinations and lynchings of the revolutionary year might echo earlier peasant upheavals, the significant fact is that the days of pretenders to the throne were long gone.

Now that the throne itself was beginning to incur disrepute, the common people could at last begin to contemplate the possibility of a Tsarless Russia. Moreover, an alliance now seemed at last to be operating between the disaffected popular masses and the disaffected professional classes. Teachers and even ballet dancers came out on strike in 1905 along with railwaymen and factory workers; they marched in the streets carrying red flags; they attended inflammatory political meetings. Stressing that all earlier Russian revolutionary movements had been confined to members of the educated and privileged classes, the influential liberal thinker Peter Struve emphasises the novelty of the 1905 affair, in which 'the ideas of the intelligentsia made contact with the ideas of the common people—for the first time in Russian history in this sense and form'.[5] There is also the point that violence had now much increased by comparison with Alexander II's reign, during which a mere half-dozen assassinations had been enough to panic the administration. Now political murders were numbered by hundreds or thousands. So too were the executions of the period.

The 1905 revolution was suppressed by armed force; but, as noted, the Emperor bowed to the call for democratic reform sufficiently to institute the elective assembly, called the State Duma, which continued to meet in four successively elected incarnations from its establishment in 1906 until it was overthrown in 1917. Meanwhile Nicholas II still retained, and exercised with alarming frequency, the right to dismiss and appoint ministers who were obliged to execute his policy of pious but vacillating conservatism. The Duma continued to deliberate during the years of the First World War—that calamity which undermined popular confidence in the imperial regime more drastically than any Bloody Sunday.

PSYCHOPATHOLITICS

To turn from oppositionist activities of 1855–1917 to the mentality of the individuals concerned is to enter an area of confused terminology. In the 1860s there 'arose', as is commonly said, Russians of a hitherto unfamiliar brand. Some called themselves 'new men'; and also, being little troubled by doubts about their own moral probity, 'honest' or 'decent' people. They figure additionally as men of the sixties, as progressives and as radicals, besides being further described on occasion as dissidents, revolutionaries, Socialists, Communists, Jacobins, liberals, terrorists, anarchists, Reds—not to mention Nihilists, *narodniki* and members of the intelligentsia. Too easily does one receive from the literature of the subject the impression that these hazy terms possessed a more precise connotation than they had or could have. Too easily, also, may it seem that these same terms are mutually exclusive, whereas they considerably overlap. Few indeed were the Russian oppositionists of the nineteenth century who could not be described by several of them at the same time.

As this plethora of categories suggests, the spectrum of political opposition in the late Empire admitted infinite gradations between infra-red and pale pink. At the extreme end of the band, resistance to the Tsars was sometimes embraced by persons who, outside the political context which seems to excuse everything, might have been more appropriately located in a ward for the criminally insane than among harbingers of rationally based social justice. Even in Russia, however, the tally of political psychopaths was smaller than that of those who tended towards the central bands of the spectrum: liberals, whose approach did not exclude compromise and practical common sense.

As is no secret, Russian oppositionists of the more restrained type lost the day ultimately, and were swept away by the events of 1917. But the liberals' signal failure to achieve the peaceful transformation of their country was arguably due to historical accident rather than to any lack of persistence or intelligence. The fact that they eventually failed so catastrophically does not prove that they were foredoomed.

Russian liberalism has received comparatively little attention from Western historians. This neglect derives partly from a tendency to ignore political losers, and partly from the failure of the tamer brand of oppositionist to project those exotic qualities which the outside world has come to expect from a Russian. What, compared to the gibbering anarchist Bakunin and the murderous fanatic Nechayev, were such humdrum figures as a Shipov, a Chicherin, a Maklakov, a Milyukov—or hundreds of others who have failed to attract posterity's attention outside specialist ranks owing to their incompatibility with the stereotype of the wild, arm-flailing, inspired, bomb-throwing Russian? But though such figures have been comparatively neglected in the West, they have not been passed over in silence. One modern authority, George Fischer, has treated the phenomenon extensively in his *Russian Liberalism*, while another recent historian, Richard Pipes, has embarked on a full-scale biography of an outstanding representative of the type, Peter Struve. The former study stresses the patient work carried on by Russian liberals in their main areas of endeavour. These included the universities and influential professional associations as well as the periodical press—censored by the government, as has been seen, but far from censored out of existence. Then there were the elective organs of local government instituted by the central government from 1864 onwards. In them all social classes were represented, but on a franchise weighted in favour of gentlemen and property owners. Though these bodies were subject to governmental interference, they yet offered considerable scope for altruistic Russians who found their vocation in practical service to their fellows. Many of these modest persons preferred to practise medicine, to build roads, to teach and to administer on a local level, rather than to throw bombs or redefine for the *n*th time the term *intelligentsia*.

In the light of such considerations one may understand Michael Karpovich's contention that the feebleness of the Russian liberal movement has 'too often ... been asserted as something self-evident, and thus not in need of further investigation'. The same point is made in a different way by Pipes when he claims that, during the fifty years preceding the downfall of the old regime, 'liberalism was the dominating philosophy of Russia's educated classes ... the force behind all the major constructive changes carried out by the imperial government'.[1]

Turning from moderate to extremist oppositionists, one is once more reminded of the pioneering function performed by Russian society of the late imperial period. To notable progress, as indicated above, in the field of assassination and assault by high explosive, must now be added the triumphant breaching of any tendency towards male monopoly in these crucial areas. Delicately nurtured bomb-throwing girls with nerves of steel—Russia pioneered the evolution of this type, which has since become a commonplace throughout the world.

Among the female pioneers of Russian terrorism was Vera Zasulich, would-be assassin of the St Petersburg City Prefect, General Trepov, on 24 January 1878. Obtaining audience, she drew a revolver and fired, but succeeded only in wounding him, to the regret of his many ill-wishers, before standing trial and escaping to foreign parts. In the following generation another woman terrorist, a high official's daughter called Tatyana Leontyev, kept a secret dynamite store in her family home, also planning to shoot the Emperor Nicholas II through a bouquet of flowers. Abandoning this project, she went abroad and assassinated, at Interlaken, an unfortunate Frenchman whom she had mistaken for the unpopular Russian Home Secretary, P. N. Durnovo—a reminder that no less than three Russian Home Secretaries were assassinated in the brief period 1902–11. But the most illustrious of Russia's lady killers was Sophia Perovsky, the former schoolmistress and provincial governor's daughter who led the victorious bomb squad into action against Alexander II on the Catherine Quay on 1

March 1881. The tenacity of the *skandal* as an institution may be illustrated by the lamentable circumstances of her public execution, together with that of her four accomplices. The affair was outrageously bungled, though eventually brought off successfully, by an incompetent hangman who drowned the protests of the attendant medical officer with drunken abuse. One is reminded of a comment made many years earlier, during the execution of the five Decembrist leaders in 1826, an affair managed with even greater *bezalabershchina*. 'My God, they can't even hang a man decently in Russia,' one of the temporarily reprieved victims was moved to remark.[2]

Male assassins and would-be assassins were also legion, and included such psychotic personalities as Dmitry Karakozov, the twice-expelled university student who attempted to shoot Alexander II in 1866. His frequent suicide attempts, a pilgrimage which he made to the Monastery of the Trinity and St Sergius shortly before the attempt, the manifesto which he circulated announcing his intentions in advance, and which chanced to come into the possession of the authorities, too sunk in complacent incompetence to take the appropriate steps—all these features mark Karakozov as a representative of the resistance movement's lunatic fringe. Another assassin was Sergey Kravchinsky, author of Chief of Gendarmes Mezentsov's death by stabbing on a St Petersburg street in 1878, but only after being with difficulty dissuaded from attempting literally to decapitate that inoffensive high functionary with a heavy sabre.

The most grotesque figure of the political resistance movement was, by common consent, Sergey Nechayev: apostle of wholesale destruction for its own sake, dedicated extortioner, blackmailer, confidence trickster and murderer. Nechayev was also an enthusiastic recruiter to political secret societies dominated by himself—units which he contrived to represent to their few members as part of a non-existent world-wide conspiratorial network. One of his many feats was the slaughter of a backsliding comrade, the absurdly named student Ivan Ivanovich Ivanov. This murder, accomplished collectively by a group of dupes under Nechayev's supervision, was designed to assert his personal authority while binding his associates together in common guilt. But the episode was sffiuciently unusual, despite the Russian context, to cause considerable scandal when the facts emerged. Not least through its very sordidness, it seemed so symbolic of extremist political opposition as to obsess Dostoyevsky, stimulating him to write the novel *Devils*. Here Nechayev himself, his dupes and his victim all figure under other names. *Devils* is surely the greatest political novel ever written—perhaps the greatest novel ever written. It analyses with superb insight the phenomenon of political psychopathology, here termed *psychopatholitics*, of which Nechayev was so outstanding an exemplar. Even as a prisoner in the St Petersburg Peter and Paul Fortress this demoniac revolutionary contrived, long after *Devils* had been published, to suborn his warders and smuggle out of his dungeon with their aid a correspondence course in assassination for the edification of fellow terrorists who were then plotting the death of Alexander II.

Another oppositionist activity, the dissemination of bloodcurdling revolutionary manifestos, received particularly exuberant expression on the occasion when a daring horseman careered down St Petersburg's Nevsky Prospekt on a galloping charger, scattering subversive literature in all directions. A further, even more notorious, example of oppositionist publishing enterprise occurred when another terrorist composed a bloodthirsty revolutionary proclamation in a cell in a Moscow jail and smuggled it out with the aid of a complaisant or bribed warder. As many similar episodes also illustrate, the imperial government's security measures were remarkably lax; they fell short of the 'Tsarist reign of terror' which the successor regime has contrived to present to posterity.

If the Russian revolutionary movement still arouses confusion, the cause may be sought in its muddled development. As the Empire drew towards its close, oppositionists increasingly tended to confuse their roles, and even to interchange them with those of police agents. A revolutionary infiltrates the police, who (not necessarily unaware of his original affiliations) then instruct him to infiltrate the revolutionary organisation to which he already belongs even as he pretends to betray it—or genuinely betrays it? He thus becomes a double agent, only a preliminary to further refinements whereby his oscillating and simultaneously dwindling loyalties turn him into a treble, quadruple and so on agent. In the end the unfortunate man confronts both himself and his historian with the impossibility of deciding just how, at any stage of his career, he conceived his aims. The prince of these multiple agents was Yevno Azef, who headed the most dangerous group of political assassins of the early 1900s while simultaneously working or pretending to work in close collusion with, and in violent opposition to, the general in charge of political security. Then there was Dmitry Bogrov, the secret police agent who assassinated his ultimate employer, Prime Minister and Home Secretary Stolypin, in the Kiev opera theatre in 1911, and whose motives—never elucidated—were, again, possibly unclear to himself. There was also Roman Malinovsky, the police agent who infiltrated the Bolsheviks so successfully that he became their leader in the State Duma; he was later executed by Lenin for being too effective a policeman. Or too embarrassing a Bolshevik?

Among many similarly ambivalent role-players of the period was Sergey Zubatov, a schoolboy revolutionary who later rose high in the political police. In his capacity as police officer he established special trade unions designed to wean disaffected workers from revolutionary leadership by securing tangible economic benefits calculated to reduce their interest in causing merely political unrest. With this in view Zubatov organised widespread strikes aimed at extorting extensive concessions from employers. But so successful were these stoppages as to threaten public order and eventually cause Zubatov's dismissal, either for excess of zeal or because, in this treacherous and ambivalent context, no one could be sure where such a person stood. Though Zubatov was presumably no oppositionist, but rather a bulwark of authority, 'The suspicion inevitably arose that he was a crypto-revolutionary exploiting police techniques to further the cause of subversion.'[3] A still more ambiguous trade-union organiser of the period was Father George Gapon, leader of the massacred demonstrating workers of Bloody Sunday, 9 January 1905. Gapon too combined leadership of organised labour with other functions: those of police collaborator, minister of religion and international playboy. It was in the first of these capacities that he was eventually assassinated by an ex-comrade who had, incidentally, saved his life on Bloody Sunday.

Nothing, perhaps, will ever fully explain this policeman-revolutionary symbiosis which so sapped the morale of the late Russian Empire. Even among revolutionaries who were not also police spies, many actively supported the less liberal policies of the authorities whom they were trying to overthrow—by directly advocating extreme reactionary measures. Wishing to demolish the political system entirely, they were reluctant to see it introduce reforms which might prolong its life by rendering it more acceptable to the population. Chernyshevsky, for example, would have liked to see Russia's serfs emancipated *without land*, and hence without any means of livelihood: this harsh provision would have inflamed their grievances, thus increasing the chance of transforming them into a revolutionary force.[4] Similarly, a high official, who considered himself a moderate progressive, could incur rebukes from more militant progressives for his fight against extreme conservative trends in the Tsar's administration. He was reproached, he wrote, for delaying a crisis by opposing the kind of reactionary measures which he should have been supporting as likely to expose the absurdity of a doomed regime more effectively than any arguments.[5] The more tyrannically the Russian government could be induced to behave, the greater the likelihood of it being overthrown by bloody revolution. For this reason the assassination of Alexander II, though a tactical failure—since it led to the effective suppression of opposition for a decade and a half—was yet a strategic success since it diverted the government from reform, thus making its violent overthrow more likely in the end. That bloody revolution was a self-justifying activity; that it could in some mysterious sense be equated with the true interests of humanity, irrespective of any context in which it might occur; even that the more people killed the greater the benefit to the human race—such were the calculations of a section of the opposition.

However seriously one may attempt to do justice to Russia's moderate oppositionists, who outnumbered the wilder specimens of the tribe, the latter have exercised a greater spell over posterity because they pioneered a more distinctive national style. Liberals such as Turgenev or Nikitenko could be found almost anywhere in the civilised world, but one had to go to St Petersburg or points east to be sure of meeting a Nechayev or a Sophia Perovsky. Not that all extremists were assassins or psychopaths, for many a less violent dissenter was to be found among those who, too far to the left in their views to be termed liberals, were for a time categorised by their critics as Nihilists. That there were also extremists of the right, for example in the ranks of the nationalist and anti-Semitic Black Hundreds, is also true. But here, least of all, can Russia claim any monopoly. It was its leftist, not rightist, fanatics who typified the broader streak in the national mentality.

The term Nihilist, as applied to politically disaffected Russians, was introduced by Turgenev in his novel *Fathers and Children* (1862) to denote one who 'does not bow down before any authority, and accepts no principles on trust, however much respect they may enjoy'. The Nihilist was or pretended to be a stern, matter-of-fact individual judging objects in terms of their practical utility, and assessing art from an anti-aesthetic angle: 'A decent chemist is twenty times more useful than any poet.' Nor, according to another saying of the period, were the entire works of Pushkin worth a single well-made pair of boots. Atheism; egalitarianism; feminism; a general contempt for property, as for the state and all its works— these too were features of Nihilist belief. But it was less Nihilist philosophy which caught the attention of non-Nihilists than certain externals foreshadowing the 'hippie' or 'beatnik' of the mid-twentieth century. Loud voices, loutish manners, aggressively untidy clothing, dirty chewed fingernails, an unwashed appearance: such was the uniform of the tribe. Straggly beards and long hair were cultivated by the male, as was bobbed hair by the female of the species—who was equally prominent in the movement. Blue-tinted spectacles, high boots, walking sticks, a rug flung over the shoulder were also part of the style, as was chain-smoking and the renunciation of such frivolities as combs, soap, crinolines and the practice of men kissing women's hands by way of greeting. Above all, extreme youth was characteristic of the Nihilist, who naturally added contempt for parental authority to contempt for every other form of authority—yet while simultaneously accepting the sanction of his own elaborate taboos, among which the simulation of nonconformism was the most rigorously conformist feature of all.

Most Nihilists had been touched or lightly brushed at some stage by higher education. Indeed, the classic Nihilist had been expelled from at least one university, preferably for hounding a 'reactionary' professor. No less typical, though, was having attended—and again, preferably, having been expelled from—one of the many theological seminaries designed for the training of future clerics, but now informally doubling as breeding grounds for future revolutionaries. The nation's high schools were hotbeds of Nihilism, too.

Nihilism could never have flourished without the connivance of older people, and this took two diametrically opposed forms. There were, on the one hand, members of the older generation who greeted these juvenile aberrations with gratifying and undignified displays of indignation, an encouragement to the young to intensify their provocations and grow their hair even longer. Equally characteristic were those senior citizens who pandered to the young through feebleness of spirit or a desire to court popularity. The novelist Turgenev was given to these postures—one of the many points made against him by his ideological enemy Dostoyevsky in the novel *Devils*. Here the 'great writer' Karmazinov is pilloried as, Turgenev-like, pathologically scared of modern revolutionary youth. 'Imagining from ignorance that they held in their hands the keys of Russia's future, [he] ingratiated himself with them in a humiliating way, mainly because they paid no attention to him whatever.'[6]

However witty the folk-fancier Dostoyevsky might be at the expense of Turgenev the Nihilist-fancier, it was neither Dostoyevsky nor Turgenev to whom Nihilist youth turned for lessons in the art of living. That function was chiefly performed by Nicholas Chernyshevsky, whose novel *What Is To Be Done?* (1863) has been described again and again as the worst work of fiction ever written. Aesthetic values had, however, been explicitly renounced by those who accepted this document as their Bible and guide to etiquette. From Chernyshevsky's book young people could learn how to regulate their relations with the opposite sex; but not on the basis of equality, for the author had gone beyond that—asserting, as has been noted above, the need to grant women superior privileges sufficient to compensate them for centuries of male domination. More important as a guide to conduct was the dynamic and dedicated asceticism of the novel's main hero, the herculean revolutionary saint Rakhmetov. Not that Chernyshevsky could directly describe his weird superman as a revolutionary, for censorship made it impossible to do so. But Rakhmetov's contempt for money, his cult of physical hardship, his sexual and alcoholic abstinence, his habit of eating raw beef, combined with an occasional excursion into outright masochism (such as a night spent on a bed of nails)—

all combined to suggest a very monster of militancy who might, through witchcraft if not through sheer will power, succeed in toppling the massive battlements of the Tsarist state.

THE INTELLIGENTSIA

To turn from Nihilism to the intelligentsia—another term which gained currency in the 1860s—is, in a sense, not to change the subject, since many an individual Nihilist could equally well be classed as an *intelligent*, 'member of the intelligentsia'. *Intelligent*, intelligentsia—the terms lacked the pejorative implications of Nihilism. They suggested neither extreme youth nor dirty finger-nails; and have continued in use long after Nihilism began to seem dated, possessing the advantage of greater elusiveness. Everyone could recognise a Nihilist. But how did one detect an *intelligent*? The notion more or less embraced Nihilism, but it also seemed capable of more or less embracing many other schools of thought as well. The concept could also be invoked disparagingly, by use of the contemptuous derivative *intelligentik*, 'egghead'.

In its broadest sense 'intelligentsia' is still used in the USSR as a rough equivalent for white-collar workers. The Soviet intelligentsia has been officially identified as a 'social stratum consisting of persons professionally employed in mental labour. Included in it are scientists and artists, engineers, technicians, agronomists, doctors, lawyers, teachers, and the great majority of office workers.' In this sense the word has an admirable clarity, and has been further refined to cover all who have received or engaged in higher education, and who occupy posts normally requiring a higher educational qualification. One advantage of this definition is its precision: the individuals concerned can be counted: there were 10,676,000 of them in 1967, according to a recent historian.[1]

In the last six decades of the monarchy, too, the term could carry exactly the same sense: for example, when a nineteenth-century novelist writes of a ball in a provincial capital being attended by 'all the local intelligentsia'. The difficulty was, though, that the word also possessed an infinite range of narrower meanings, as has been well expressed by the literary historian D. S. Mirsky. First equating the intelligentsia with the educated and professional classes as a whole, he goes on to attribute to the term a second, more restricted sense, confining it to that section of the educated and professional classes which was intensely and actively interested in political and social issues. He then notes a third, still narrower usage, whereby the word was applied only to 'those groups which were more or less radically inclined'.[2]

As Mirsky's explanation suggests, most historians of pre-1917 Russian culture have been apt to locate the intelligentsia at some purportedly specific point between its narrowest and broadest poles, as specified above, with the unspoken implication that those who place it anywhere else have failed through lack of sensitivity to perceive the true nature of the phenomenon as apprehended by the speaker. Hence the innumerable definitions of the intelligentsia, of which a whole anthology could be collected. It is not enough to say, as one authority does, that 'Each generation of the intelligentsia has defined itself in its own way, renouncing its ancestors and beginning—for a decade—a new era.' Rather does it begin to seem as if every individual potential *intelligent* was principally or even exclusively engaged in the narcissistic process of defining and re-defining the category. 'One of the favourite occupations of the Russian intelligentsia had always been the absorbed study of itself.'[3]

As emerges from the above, the chief criterion distinguishing one man's conception of the intelligentsia from an infinitude of others is the degree—ranging from nil to infinity—of political radicalism which is regarded as mandatory. According to the early twentieth-century thinker Sergey Bulgakov, the 1905 revolution was 'the spiritual offspring of the intelligentsia'. The same claim has been made for the 1917 revolutions, of which the intelligentsia has been described as constituting the general staff. Yet the claim is explicitly denied by a post-revolutionary Russian *émigré* authority, Fedotov, as emanating from the intelligentsia's enemies: 'A significant section of the intelligentsia—the liberals—never thought of revolution, and there are names in the pantheon of the movement's saints which have nothing in common with political struggle.'[4] Fedotov instances the Slavophiles—a category explicitly excluded by Mirsky from the intelligentsia in one of his narrower senses.

Unfortunately this and many other such disquisitions on the

intelligentsia serve only to demonstrate yet again the folly of attributing cohesiveness to that which will not cohere.

However defined and classified, a significant and obtrusive section of educated or semi-educated Russians continued, long after Nihilism had become obsolete, to hold ideas commonly associated with that movement: opposition to state, church and property; positivism, utilitarianism, feminism, egalitarianism, an obsession with the importance of science. So tenacious did the cult of youth remain that Bulgakov, writing in 1909, could call spiritual paedocracy (toddler power) the greatest evil of Russian society. It was also 'a symptomatic feature of the heroic style cultivated by the intelligentsia, of its basic traits, but in . . . exaggerated form. This grotesque interrelationship, whereby the assessments and views of schoolchildren and students function as guide-lines for their elders—it inverts the natural state of affairs and is equally detrimental to both parties.'[5] A desire among older people to stand high, at whatever cost, in the estimation of the young—a desire which the sneering contempt of the young only inflamed and reinforced—also remained a prominent feature of Russian intellectual society.

Another legacy of the 1860s was a tendency to embrace social and political betterment with wholehearted abandon. The crusading spirit, altruism, idealism, dogmatism, intolerance, rancour, censoriousness, masochism, a compulsion towards self-martyrdom —these features tend to recur in the evolution of Russian intellectuals in the last decades of the Empire. They help to explain certain well-known descriptions of the intelligentsia: 'a sect, almost an order of knighthood'; 'something like medieval knights'; 'a monastic order or sect, with its own very intolerant ethics, its obligatory outlook on life, with its own manners and customs and even its own particular physical appearance'.[6]

Such comparisons are helpful in emphasising the missionary spirit, but are misleading in suggesting so extreme a degree of cohesiveness. Monasticism and knighthood have this in common, that an individual either joins or does not join these orders, and that an exact tally of their adherents could, at least in principle, be produced at any given moment by reference to the relevant authorities. But the Russian intelligentsia, however defined, had no register of members, no formal oath of allegiance, no records, no files, no offices, and thus no clear distinction between members and non-members. Potential adherents therefore found it impossible to compute their own numbers, much as they wished to do so. One method—counting the signatures collected, at the turn of the century, to honour a jubilee of the radical journalist N. K. Mikhaylovsky—gave a total of 20,000.[7] The figure at least underlines the vast numerical difference between repeatedly redefined nineteenth-century intelligentsia and the very differently, far more explicitly defined Soviet intelligentsia of the 1960s with its ten million-odd members, as noted above.

Since the pre-1914 intelligentsia, however categorised, was nothing as precise as a club, political party, religious sect or order of knighthood, but rather a fluid and amorphous grouping, individuals might seem to enter and leave the category with considerable ease. Chekhov, in no sense a member of it as commonly conceived, once wrote that he distrusted 'our hypocritical, bogus, hysterical, uneducated, lazy intelligentsia' because it regularly bred its own oppressors: former young rebels or liberals who, in later life, would join the conservative establishment as reactionary officials, editors and the like.[8] Even to abuse the intelligentsia effectively seemed to require an intelligentsia apprenticeship. One of the most scathing denunciations of the Russian intelligentsia—the symposium *Landmarks* (1909)—is the work of members of (or former members of) the category, however conceived. These were all intellectuals whose argumentative methodology, vocabulary and general style of thought still remains that of those whom they denounce. Might their denunciations have been still more effective had they wielded a less cumbrous tool than the language of the intelligentsia? Similarly—to compare small things with great while invoking a parallel from a remote discipline—the poet Homer probably wished, in Book Nine of the *Iliad*, to cause Achilles to express disillusionment with the heroic ethos of the Greek epic tradition, but found himself in a linguistic quandary. 'Homer in fact has no language, no terms, in which to express this kind of basic disillusionment with society and the external world.'[9] Where Homer nods, what can be expected from a Berdyayev, a Bulgakov or any lesser *intelligentik*?

A further demonstration of the fluidity of the concept is the frequency with which philosophers of the subject parade outstanding exemplars of Russian culture in order to decide whether they do—or more usually do not—'belong'. Peter Struve excludes Push-kin, Lermontov, Gogol, Turgenev, Chekhov, Vladimir Solovyov, Saltykov. He is doubtful even about Belinsky and Herzen; and seems to accept only Bakunin and Chernyshevsky. A similar review by Fedotov excludes such leading minds as Samarin, Ostrovsky, Pisemsky, Leskov, Klyuchevsky—and, of course, Tolstoy and Dostoyevsky.[10] Here is the remarkable picture of a Russian intelligentsia from which virtually all the most prominent Russian intellectuals have been rigorously banished.

One striking feature often associated with the intelligentsia was a failure to register solid achievement in any field. Intellectual work, in the sense of systematically accumulating knowledge; of writing and completing a competent novel; of painting an adequate picture; composing a technically competent symphony; compiling a reputable dictionary, grammar or edition—work in that sense, if representing achievement spread over several years and carried to a successful conclusion, tended to seem incompatible with membership of the intelligentsia. An individual *intelligent* might be a power-house of cerebral activity; his collected writings might total many volumes. But the activity must be essentially narcissistic or masturbatory, confined to the sterile world of political and social theorising, to the juggling, rehashing and general jactitation of 'ideas', and those often ill-digested second-hand concepts borrowed from abroad.

That Dostoyevsky and Tolstoy, for example, could not rate as members of the intelligentsia was chiefly due to the monumental size of their achievement, and only secondarily to the unsuitability of their ideas. An idle, ungifted Tolstoy would have been a fully acceptable representative of the type; to which a Chernyshevsky, for instance, could gain entrance partly through his status as a prophet and pioneer of certain notions, but even more so (one suspects) through his proven incompetence in the area of creative craftsmanship, as revealed in his atrocious fiction. Competence of any kind could not easily be reconciled with adherence to the intelligentsia. Even to have assembled a systematic stamp collection would have been to dissociate oneself from that elusive grouping as commonly conceived. 'We snatch up any old ideas and bits of knowledge, any old convictions without the solid and profound foundation of stout-hearted, sober labour.' Ignorance also tended to accompany this lack of industry, 'a lack of serious knowledge and historical experience'.[11]

Together with an incapacity for serious intellectual labour went contempt for the labours of others and for their fruits, whether intellectual or material. This approach, which so destructively tends to unite the idle rich with the idle poor—both categories being well represented among Russian intellectuals—was partly the outcome of a rigid egalitarianism, of an obsession with the fair redistribution of wealth so extreme that the question of creating wealth was pushed into the background. The attitude helps to explain the militant lack of creativity so easily associated with the *intelligentik*. 'The interests of distribution and egalitarianism always preponderated over those of production and creativity in the mind and emotions of the Russian intelligentsia.'[12]

Uncreative and incapable of sustained labour, the typical representative of the intelligentsia was not intellectually lazy. On the contrary: his mental cogwheels, not being engaged in driving anything, could idly revolve with awesome celerity. Never wearing out his brain in any sustained and serious inquiry, he was free to talk, talk, talk. Garrulity is thus a characteristic of the type. Such was the heated atmosphere of Golushkin's dining room as described in Turgenev's novel *Virgin Soil*. 'Words of all sorts—progress, government, literature; the taxation question, the church question, the woman question, the law-court question; classicism, realism, Nihilism, communism; international, clerical, liberal, capital; administration, organisation, association, and even crystalisation: this was what really seemed to rouse Golushkin's enthusiasm, this hubbub. It seemed to be the very essence of everything.'[13]

Another hallmark of the intelligentsia was an extreme degree of intolerance combined with the practice of imposing its taboos by bullying and intimidation. On the methods whereby a senior *intelligent* might seek to whip a deviant juvenile into line, Chekhov's early career provides an instructive example. No sooner had the young man emerged into prominence with his first important story, *The Steppe* (1888), than he found himself called to order by N. K. Mikhaylovsky, the movement's Grand Inquisitor. Hitherto Chekhov had 'sinned', Mikhaylovsky told him, by contributing to the wrong kind of periodical, especially the conservative or reactionary

newspaper *Novoye vremya*. Should he dare continue writing
for such journals after producing *The Steppe*, that sin would
become irredeemable. Chekhov must abandon Evil and espouse
Good. 'God has given you much, Anton Pavlovich, and of you
much shall be required.' Strong-minded behind his courteous
exterior, Chekhov rejected this and further impertinent attempts
to instruct him in his professional duties and groom him for
intelligentik status.[14] But others, less strong-minded, succumbed
and fell into line. In many cases their adherence to the intelligentsia
was a form of inverted, anti-establishmentarian conformism, revealing as little originality as that of their opposites—those
despised contemporaries who had 'sold out' to the imperial state
by seeking careers in the civil service or other branches of the
establishment.

That Mikhaylovsky, a professed agnostic, should have addressed
the young Chekhov like an archbishop haranguing a delinquent
candidate for holy orders—here is a feature typical indeed of the
educated Russian mentality, which has always seemed prone to
religious, especially godlessly religious, postures. 'The religion of
revolution, of a great social transformation—that is the only
religion which I bequeath to you': such was Herzen's legacy to his
son as expressed in his famous treatise of 1850, *From the Other
Shore*. As Berdyayev explains in *Landmarks*, 'Scientific positivism,
and everything else Western, was accepted in its most extreme
form and converted not only into a primitive metaphysic, but even
into a special religion supplanting all previous religions.' The
same point is put more vehemently by another contributor to the
same symposium, Semyon Frank. 'If one understands the essence
of religion as *fanaticism*, as fervent, almost obsessive devotion to a
pet idea, devotion which inspires man not only to self-sacrifice and
heroic deeds but also to the grotesque distortion of all his perspectives in life, to the intolerant destruction of everything inconsistent with the idea in question—then, of course, the Russian
intelligentsia is religious in the highest degree.'[15]

Of the Russian tendency to embrace ideas, including those
militantly and exclusively secular, with religious fervour, Dostoyevsky has much to say. The Russian is, according to him, always
liable to be bowled over in his tracks by an idea which falls on him
'like an enormous rock and half squashes him—and there he is

writhing underneath it and unable to extricate himself'.[16] Chekhov was as immune from this tendency as Dostoyevsky was prone to it, but he recognised its existence. 'If a Russian does not believe in God it means that he believes in something else, and this he does not inactively, not like a German doctor of philosophy, but so that every one of his beliefs bends him into a hoop.'[17] The urge may be related to a general tendency noted above. 'This Slavonic capacity of yielding oneself wholly to one's ideas and emotions,' is how Madame Jarintzov puts it, predictably contrasting the stolid Englishman, who could never be swept off his feet by an idea or by anything else. Unlike the despised German or Englishman, the typical Russian 'cannot go on doubting for very long; his inclination is to make a dogma for himself quickly, and to surrender himself to it wholeheartedly and entirely'.[18] The nineteenth-century Russian thus tended to be intellectually out of tune with the sceptical West, seeming a throwback to the days of the medieval Church and, simultaneously, a pioneer of the conformism-imposing totalitarian, terrorist bureaucracies of a later age. 'The pre-Revolutionary Russian *intelligent* was in many ways a precursor of that phenomenon of our time known to the social scientist as *Twentieth-century mass man*.'[19]

Dedicated, totally committed, many Russian oppositionist intellectuals courted martyrdom by challenging the cumbrous embattled might of the imperial state. A few suffered capital punishment in the nineteenth century—but only for complicity in terrorist acts, not for their beliefs as such. A larger number underwent imprisonment and exile, Chernyshevsky's long Siberian ordeal being one of the most severe on record. For these reasons such renegades or partial renegades from the intelligentsia as the authors of *Landmarks* can allude to the self-victimisation of the group's 'martyrs'. Sergey Bulgakov, for instance, praises the 'unwavering readiness for all sacrifices of the intelligentsia's best representatives . . . The Russian intelligentsia has evolved and developed in an atmosphere of constant martyrdom. It is impossible not to bow down before the shrine of the Russian intelligentsia's sufferings.'[20] On the last point one may differ on two counts. First, the degree of persecution mobilised by the imperial authorities, though not negligible, seems almost insignificant if compared with that of the post-imperial twentieth century. As a Russian gentleman, the imprisoned intellectual received from his goalers and from interrogating gendarmes courtesy and consideration which somewhat mitigated the hardships of imprisonment and exile. And he was, as has been noted, generally immune from the floggings not uncommonly meted out to those peasants whom he had manoeuvred into mutiny. A second consideration is that a readiness to sacrifice one's life, freedom and comfort for a cause need not, surely, be admired without reference to the motives inspiring these sacrifices or the results to which they have contributed.

In analysing the self-sacrificing activities of the Russian oppositionist intellectual—activities which so easily spilled over into sacrificing non-intellectuals—one could stop short at their own professions: that they sought 'the good of the people', 'the common weal', 'freedom', and a revolution sanctified by the struggle against a wicked and doomed regime. But behind all this there often seems to pulsate a more primitive urge towards destructiveness for its own sake, a destructiveness all the more dangerous for the mask of pseudo-creativity with which it tended to be concealed. Such, at least, is the view of many competent witnesses. One speaks of destruction being recognised 'not only as *one* of the techniques of creativity, but as broadly equated with creativity—or rather as entirely taking the place of creativity'. The Russian 1905 revolution, another critic of the intelligentsia has admitted, 'developed vast destructive energy, like a gigantic earthquake, but the creative elements in it turned out much weaker than the destructive'. This recalls the slogan coined by that spokesman of Nihilism Dmitry Pisarev in the year of emancipation, 1861: 'What can be smashed must *be* smashed.' But even Pisarev added that 'whatever will stand the blow is fit to survive'; it needed a Nechayev to concentrate exclusively on the first proposition, wholly neglecting the second.[21]

To consider the intelligentsia's evolution is, according to one school of thought, to contemplate an unending chain of noble self-sacrifices in a great cause. But is it legitimate to ignore the corrupting force of frenzied verbalising, of the mindless espousal of revolution for revolution's sake? Revolution—fostered, planned, endlessly discussed and blessed in advance by the pre-1917 intelligentsia—eventually culminated in the mass liquidation of the survivors of that 'order of knighthood' by a cunning, determined and strikingly unchivalrous non-intellectual, Joseph Stalin. To consider these things is to understand how an acute observer can describe members of the intelligentsia as 'impelled by some strange kind of collective death-wish', and as perhaps unconsciously feeling 'that the sole reason for their existence was their self-destruction'.[22]

Nowhere is the tendency to combine irreconcilable opposites more evident than in the political context, as was recognised by Dostoyevsky when he created Shigalyov, the Nihilist theoretician of *Devils*. 'Proceeding from unlimited freedom, I end with unlimited slavery': such, in a much-quoted phrase, is the essence of Shigalyov's contribution to political theory. He reflects the mentality of many another politically conscious visionary who has consecrated his life to creating a notional heaven on earth, while simultaneously driven by his inner logic towards creating the reality of hell. Fired by 'pure' love for the common people, representatives of this section of the intelligentsia were inspired yet more by even purer hatred for those whom they could conceive as enemies of the common people—including, of course, the common people themselves on the many occasions when they failed to behave as hoped or predicted. Enemies, enemies, enemies—the *intelligent* seemed to see them everywhere. They included all those who, however diverse their views, rejected the dogmas espoused by himself, and were hence hindering the onward march of progress. 'Thus, out of a great love for mankind in the future is born a great hatred for human beings; thus the passion for creating a heaven on earth becomes a drive towards destruction.'[23]

In this paranoid context another feature of the world at large pioneered by Russia—the link between politics and criminality or gangsterism—becomes intelligible. 'The Nihilistic element in the intelligentsia's faith somehow sanctions criminality and hooliganism, giving them the opportunity to clothe themselves in the mantle of idealism and progressiveness.'[24]

Attached though he nominally was to egalitarian beliefs, the typical *intelligent* found it difficult to react to others except as inferiors or superiors—a trait nowhere more exemplified than in his relations with the common people designated as the main victim of his self-sacrificing benefactions. On the one hand the *intelligent* acknowledged his debt to the suffering masses, his duty to help them, and often enough his moral inferiority to them. At the same time he tended to look down on the peasant masses with aristocratic disdain. This attitude may be detected in Belinsky, and above all in Chernyshevsky, who sacrified everything for 'the people' while yet believing that they had no interest outside their own material advantages. 'The mass is simply the raw material for diplomatic and political experiments.'[25]

The intellectual peasant-fancying *narodnik* loved the peasantry, certainly; especially as he rarely met any peasants. But they were, to him, an object for vaguely conceived favours bestowed by their betters rather than individuals who might possess some notion of what help they would prefer to receive. 'Devotion to an idealised concept of "the people" was blended with an almost aristocratic contempt for the actual down-to-earth, prosaic propensities of the real people.'[26] It was the peasant-fancying intelligentsia, never the people themselves, which was to decide where the people's true needs lay. And what a nuisance the confounded peasantry could be —all these ill-treated, poverty-stricken, miserable robots who should have been ready to arise from their slumbers and rally to the revolution at the word of command; but who stolidly refused for decade after decade to see where their duty lay until at last they began to behave in 1905 as it had been their duty to behave in the 1870s, and to start dutifully murdering landlords, officials and other representatives of the oppressing state on an adequate scale.

While, at the turn of the century, the more peasant-fancying section of the intelligentsia was founding its own political party, that of the Socialist Revolutionaries, another section—that of the Marxists—was founding the Social Democractic Party. This soon split into two factions, Bolshevik and Menshevik, of which the former has eventually evolved into the present-day Communist Party of the Soviet Union. Far from expecting revolution to sprout in the countryside, the Social Democrats proclaimed the peasantry stagnant and reactionary, placing their hopes in the political mobilisation of the industrial workers. For a long time these proletariat-fanciers seemed less dangerous to the imperial regime than the peasant-fanciers: first, because Russia's workers were overwhelmingly outnumbered by her peasants; and secondly because the Socialist Revolutionaries were addicted to assassination as a power-seizing tactic, whereas the Social Democrats were not. It was, however, the proletariat-fanciers who eventually triumphed

in October 1917—partly because factory workers could be effectively mobilised under arms in the capital city and other centres
of power; they thus constituted a suitable vehicle for a *coup d'état*
such as the ill-organised peasantry, despite its greater numbers,
could less effectively be provoked into staging.

Another reason for eventual Bolshevik success in 1917 was the
leadership of Lenin, whose sense of timing enabled him to launch
the October Revolution at the moment when Russia's provisional
government, that temporary heir to the Tsars, was most defence-
less. Lenin added determination to seize and hold power, as also
the ability to inspire his associates with similar resolution. His
other talents included a gift for never being bemused by the
intricate ideological signals, couched in relatively abstract terms,
with which he enlisted support and paralysed resistance without
losing sight of the realities of power. This, for him, always grew
out of the barrel of a gun and only secondarily out of the collected
works of Marx and Engels. The master, not the slave, of ideology,
Lenin was to that extent no typical Russian *intelligent*. His chief
value as a reflection of the Russian mentality thus derives less
from any tendency to typify it than from his skill in exploiting its
more vulnerable aspects; these include both the political fanaticism
and the sheer silliness which significant numbers of *intelligenty*
seemed to generate so abundantly. As for his personal attitude to
the tribe, he again and again voiced his contempt for the Russian
intelligentik.

Untypical though Lenin may be of the intelligentsia, his authoritarian temper nevertheless reflects a long-standing Russian intellectual tradition. He was far indeed, as has been seen above, from
being the first Russian radical to believe that social progress can
only be imposed by force, and through a dictatorship exercised by
a person such as himself. This authoritarian drive was truly Russian in tending to submerge the individual in the collective, and
also because it mirrored (in opposition) the authoritarian elements
of the very state which was to be supplanted. Long before Lenin
had been heard of there had come into being, alongside the controls
somewhat laxly imposed by the Russian state, a contrary set of
rigorous taboos imposed by intellectuals opposed to the state. Of
the 1860s, for example, Mackenzie Wallace writes that 'The Press
was able for some time to exercise a "Liberal" tyranny scarcely less

severe than the "Conservative" tyranny of the censors in the preceding reign.' It was the same phenomenon which caused Nikitenko
to report, in his diary for October 1857, that 'In their intolerance
they [the new opposition] are becoming representatives of a new
and almost greater despotism than the previous one.' Herzen went
further still. Writing in 1851, he claimed that 'An opposition which
leads a frontal attack on a government always has itself, in an inverted sense, something of the character of the government
attacked. I believe that there is some justification for the fear of
Communism which the Russian government begins to feel: Communism is the Russian autocracy turned upside down.'[27]

Nearly forty years later Chekhov claimed that the political
despotism of the imperial Ministry of Internal Affairs was at least
equalled by that of the editorial office of *Russkaya mysl*, a Muscovite oppositionist journal.[28] Indeed, the former tyranny may have
been the easier to bear, since it was at least imposed, however half-
heartedly, by the police-backed power of the state, whereas the
other discipline was a matter of social pressure to conform with
certain taboos. Even a nonconformist may bow with dignity to
superior power; there is of course something far more slavish in
the conformism of one who can be made to toe the line by fear of
not being considered a liberal. Mikhaylovsky's unsuccessful
attempt to bully Chekhov in this way has already been recorded.
It was the mentality of such as Mikhaylovsky which later induced
Chekhov to prophesy that 'Under the banner of learning, art and
persecuted freedom of thought Russia will one day be ruled by
such toads and crocodiles as were unknown even in Spain under
the Inquisition. Yes, you just wait. Narrow-mindedness, enormous
pretensions, excessive self-importance, a total absence of any literary or social conscience: these things will do their work ... will
generate an atmosphere so stifling that every healthy person will be
bloody well nauseated.' In the same spirit are the denunciations of
the intelligentsia's 'credulity without faith, struggle without creativity, fanaticism without enthusiasm', of the dogmatism, censoriousness, woolly-mindedness, ignorance and general dottiness so
eloquently expressed in *Landmarks* some twenty years later.[29]

Nikitenko, Mackenzie Wallace, Dostoyevsky, Chekhov, the
authors of *Landmarks*—are these opponents of the intelligentsia to
have the last word? Or should one think of the pre-revolutionary

intelligent as one who 'took up the noble responsibility of fighting for [his] fellow Russians against tyranny and reaction'? Is the intelligentsia more properly regarded as 'this milieu of earnest, dedicated, passionately honest, fiercely principled scientists and thinkers'? 'Dedicated souls, many endowed with wide cultural and personal charm . . . in their intellectual earnestness they present an attractive and even exciting picture.' 'Heroism . . . disinterestedness . . . personal nobility.' From the studies of modern *intelligent*-fancying observers one may multiply such quotations *ad infinitum*.[30] They show, at least, that no unanimous verdict of guilty has been uttered against the pre-revolutionary intelligentsia as a whole. Rather is the opposite the case, and the difference of opinion derives less from the nature of the intelligentsia, however defined, than from the premises with which the problem is approached. 'Intellectual earnestness', as is evident from one of the quotations given above, can be an attractive quality to some, and it is among them that the pre-revolutionary Russian intelligentsia's most fervent posthumous admirers are likely to be found. But if the impression is left that all Russia's intellectuals, as opposed to her *intelligentiki*, were blessed or cursed with the quality of humourless earnestness, the present study has indeed been written in vain.

TOTALITARIANISM
AND ANTI-TOTALITARIANISM

To those who see a characteristic Russian rhythm in the alternation of anarchy and regimentation, the two revolutions of 1917 must seem a striking confirmation of a traditional pattern, now developing on a scale unprecedented in the country's earlier history and carrying new threats or hopes for the future of the world at large.

In the first revolution of that fateful year the anarchic principle was predominant, as also in the ten-month period of 'provisional government' which followed. When, at the end of February, the monarchy suddenly disappeared it was not pushed, but rather fell —even though immediate causes can be traced in a general breakdown of confidence, and especially in conditions in the capital city, then called Petrograd. They included the disaffection of Cossacks and others key military units, local food shortages; and, to an extent difficult to determine, the operations of agents paid by the Berlin government with which Russia was still at war. But there was no concerted *coup d'état*, no organised conspiracy to unseat the government and imperial system. Events seemed rather to take place by accident, surprising not least the very revolutionaries and *intelligentiki* who had for decades been predicting revolution, discussing the form which it would take, and considering the most effective ways in which it could be channelled.

Between March and September 1917 Russia—though still at war —enjoyed the longest period of emancipation from authority in her modern history. But this proved to be the reign of lawlessness, not of freedom under the law. Lack of experience in operating representative institutions, an ineradicable craving for regimentation or anarchy or both, a spirit hostile to the principle of compromise, sheer bad luck—for whatever combination of reasons the provisional government of 1917 was permitted neither to govern nor to complete arrangements for electing a permanent successor under a new constitution. When it disappeared in October it did not collapse, as rule by the Romanov dynasty had collapsed earlier in the year, but was violently ousted. The instrument was a *coup d'état* plotted by the leaders of the small, highly disciplined Bolshevik movement, which combined libertarian professions with an increasing vocation for imposing rigid controls.

Though far indeed from enjoying majority support in the country as a whole, the Bolsheviks were, as already noted, supported by workers and troops in key areas in or near the capital. They derived much of their appeal from their apparent ability to behave decisively in an age of indecision, as also from their skill in harnessing idealistic patter to techniques of conspiracy, intimidation and trickery which, outside the all-sanctioning political context, would have been dismissed as criminal.

To seek features characteristic of the Russian mind among the chaotic events of 1917 and their sequel is to enter a particularly speculative area. But it may not be fanciful to discern already familiar qualities. In launching themselves on the unknown with such ferocious enthusiasm the Russians brought to bear the quality of *razmakh*, 'gusto', which they have already been observed displaying in other areas. This revolutionary dynamism, together with its corollary—the ease with which the masses, so violently

aroused from their slumbers, were so quickly put to sleep again—
reflects the age-old Russian tendency either to embrace or to
eschew action with a totality of commitment alien to other breeds.
However, it must also be remembered that the revolutions were
not the work of Russians alone, but that representatives of the
Empire's other nationalities also played a major part, both as
leaders and as led.

Another outstanding Russian trait is vulnerability to Revolution
as an abstract notion conceived—like History—in personified guise
as an independent agency capable of taking sweeping and inevitably beneficent initiatives in human affairs. On the hypnotic effect
of this pregnant word the memoirist and poet's widow Nadezhda
Mandelstam makes the point that it played a greater part than
terror and bribery ('though, God knows, there was enough of both')
in breaking the resistance of the post-revolutionary intelligentsia.
Revolution was a word 'which none of them could bear to give up
. . . and its force was such that one wonders why our rulers still
needed prisons and capital punishment'. However, as she also
notes, revolution is 'a word to which whole nations have succumbed'.[1] That intellectuals in countries other than Russia can be
manipulated through the threat of being considered inadequately
liberal, revolutionary or left-wing in their views is too widely
observed a phenomenon to require illustration. Here again the
Russian claim to pre-eminence can only be that of early initiators,
not of continuing monopolisers.

On Revolution as a logic-defying concept manifested in Petrograd in early 1917, the historian George Katkov makes a valuable
comment. Quoting a contemporary observation ascribing the sudden death of a counter-revolutionary major to 'a well-aimed stray
bullet', he continues, 'A well-aimed *stray* bullet! When these words
were written the dreamlike logic of revolutionary rhetoric had
already replaced common sense in Russia.'[2]

After their tactical victory and seizure of power in Petrograd in
October 1917 the Bolsheviks remained vulnerable owing to their
lack of support in the country at large, where the Socialist Revolutionaries were known to command far more votes. Since these votes
were likely to prove decisive in overthrowing Bolshevism at the
elections (to which the Bolsheviks were nominally committed) for
a constituent assembly, the new rulers were faced with the

alternative of immediately suppressing opposition by force or being unseated by the inevitable course of events. Lenin, who saw this dilemma with admirable clarity, persuaded wavering colleagues to support the destruction of their political opponents. The campaign of suppression began with right-wing movements, soon moving on to fellow Socialists, and then to fellow Marxists of non-Leninist persuasion. The publications of these rival movements were banned; their spokesmen were imprisoned or executed—a policy to which extra momentum was imparted by a civil war of increasing ferocity. The process of totalitarianisation had not been completed by Lenin's death in 1924, and during the whole of the 1920s considerable freedom of speech still remained. Literary censorship was largely negative at the time, in the sense that writers were forbidden to attack the assumptions of the new state; but were not, as later, required to make positive affirmations in its favour. However, Nadezhda Mandelstam has rightly warned against a common tendency to regard the Soviet 1920s as a golden age. She points out that it too was an age of terror, however effectively the even severer persecutions of the 1930s may blind observers to the realities of the earlier decade. The same point is also made by other present-day observers, figuring prominently for example in Solzhenitsyn's monumental study of Stalinist horrors, *The Gulag Archipelago*. In any case full totalitarianism had been established by the time of Stalin's fiftieth birthday in December 1929, after which he ruled as unchallenged dictator for nearly a quarter of a century.

With the virtual end of the Civil War in 1921, Lenin and his government had found themselves committed to establishing a heaven on earth in a territory which, by no means exclusively through their own operations, had become a fairly near approximation to hell. Such were the devastations, human and material, inflicted by seven years of war, first against Germany and then against the forces of White Russia. No power on earth could have restored so shattered a realm for many years or even decades, and it was therefore necessary to mobilise the weapon of pretence lest the miracle-working claims of the newly triumphant political creed, its assertion that it could create a utopia, be exposed. In a sense, therefore, the whole of Russia together with its surviving empire, soon named the USSR, was converted into a giant simulated prestige project. Or, rather, certain isolated areas were picked out for minor, genuine prestige projects, such as the great Dneprostroy Dam, while a continuing propaganda campaign proclaimed by suggestion that these enterprises were typical, if not of the country's progress as a whole, at least of achievements so imminent that they could be claimed as actual.

Perhaps the most striking example of such an enterprise has been the impressive Exhibition of the Achievements (i.e. non-achievements) of the National Economy in Moscow. Around this foreign tourists are traditionally freighted, and can observe a few spectacularly fecund cows, sheaves of super-corn and gleaming combine-harvesters, the hope being that they will regard these as typical, not as the glaring exceptions which they regrettably constitute. It was a lucky accident for the post-revolutionary government that traditional Russian *vranyo*, together with the age-old training in hieratic speech forms, could be harnessed to such operations.

The government has also exploited the traditional Russian genius for blurring the concept of time. On the one hand both citizenry and foreign visitors are deluged with *vranyo*-infused, self-pitying tirades about the iniquities of the inglorious past: those of the Tsarist regime, of foreign intervention in the Civil War, of the Teuton occupant in 1941-5. On the other hand they are also bemused by ecstatic visions of the glorious future when, in *x* years, America will be overtaken and the problems of providing abundant food, transport, living space and other amenities will have been triumphantly solved in a manner destined to shame every other society on earth. Thus is every attempt made to divert attention from present actualities which, though not necessarily sordid or discreditable in all their aspects, emphatically do not bear out the wonder-working claims of official doctrine. To pretend that a paradise has been (well, is just about to be) triumphantly established on earth, while simultaneously explaining that failure to realise such a goal is due to the machinations of enemies (Tsars, Whites, Hitlerites, Americans, capitalists)—here is one of those splendidly self-contradictory operations which so baffle observers uninitiated into the mysteries of *vranyo*. This sensation of being surrounded by 'enemies', now sedulously inculcated into the Russian masses, has been lifted directly from the paranoid fantasies of the pre-revolutionary Russian *intelligentik*.

So much for the psychology of post-revolutionary official policy. But what of opposition to the new authority? To what extent does that reflect traditional elements in Russian mentality or mark the evolution of new traits? The investigation is hampered by the difficulty of disentangling the Russian mind from its near or not-so-near relative, the Soviet mind.

Since the earliest years of Soviet rule there has been considerably less scope for political opposition than was to be observed even during the severest period of nineteenth-century oppression, that of the later reign of Nicholas I (1848–55). The newly established Bolsheviks had, during the decades preceding their assumption of power, already learned through personal experience how easily an authoritarian state could be undermined and brought to collapse by political disaffection. Conscious that a more ruthless or intelligent exercise of power by the imperial government might have led to the suppression of their own movement, they had been put on the alert in advance. Never were they likely to forget how they themselves had exploited the inefficiency and corruption of the imperial police. They had written inflammatory anti-Tsarist propaganda in jail, they had spirited it out through bribed or duped warders. They had smuggled weapons, explosives and illicit pamphlets into the country. Their spies had infiltrated the imperial political police. They had even benefited in the end, in terms of the corruption of the imperial apparatus, through the infiltration of their own ranks by police spies. And they were determined not to permit such activities now that they themselves were in charge. Hence the immediate establishment of a new political security police (the Cheka) and the appointment, as its head, of a revolutionary with a long record of arrests and escapes under the previous dispensation: Felix Dzerzhinsky. Hence too the vastly more rigorous penal conditions progressively imposed in the prisons and newly instituted concentration camps of the Soviet period, from which escape was rendered far more hazardous than it had been under the Empire. Before 1917 an imprisoned or exiled Bakunin, Kropotkin, Trotsky or Stalin could and did flee from Siberian confinement with what seems ridiculous ease; he could travel about the Empire despite the extensive passport controls notionally in force; he could slip illicitly abroad for a conference with other revolutionaries and return equally easily, equally illicitly. Such activity could not be halted entirely, but was restricted with greater success than the nineteenth-century Romanovs had achieved.

Under these grim conditions post-revolutionary political opposition has rarely attained the panache of imperial times. There were no more dissident broadsheets scattered by galloping riders, no more stabbings of chiefs of police in daylight on the capital's main streets; for though the head of the Petrograd Cheka was fatally shot in August 1918 by a Socialist Revolutionary assassin, such was not to be the pattern of the future. By those citizens who wished to oppose the new government established in Moscow, duller and less exuberant methods had to be adopted; and to this extent the mentality of the Russian in opposition has undergone considerable modification.

So severe was Stalinist oppression from the 1930s onwards that opposition virtually disappeared within a few years. Much of the fundamental resistance had come from the peasants, compelled to enter collective farms *en masse* and driven to such despair that they slaughtered their own livestock. Their opposition was crushed by armed force, mass arrest and wholesale consignment to concentration camps, combined with Stalin's policy of contumaciously failing to relieve, and even of fostering, the great peasant famine of 1931–2. What of resistance to authority at a higher level? Such an episode as the clandestinely circulated Ryutin manifesto of 1932, in which Stalin's removal for incompetence was demanded by a moderately important Party official—this was highly exceptional. By now the dictator had destroyed all serious potential opposition. And yet, wishing to consolidate his rule in the ultimate degree, he adopted from 1934 onwards a policy of pre-emptive overkill directed against all those who, though in practice not pursuing policies disloyal to him, might conceivably have joined a notional opposition under hypothetical circumstances. The dictator thus invented and proceeded to liquidate an impotent or non-existent conspiracy of wreckers, saboteurs, rightists, Trotskyites and the like. It was on faked charges that the victims in Stalin's great show trials perished, as did the myriads of those anonymously liquidated in the concentration camps.

During the Second World War popular opposition to Stalin was expressed by sections of the population which initially welcomed the German invader, only to be repelled later by the infliction of

Hitlerite atrocities on an even greater scale than those previously inflicted by Stalin. On the whole it was the non-Russian peoples of the USSR, and notably the Ukrainians, who initially welcomed the enemy. But many disaffected Russians joined the ill-fated army of General Vlasov, which fought on the German side during the war. These forms of resistance to Russian authority are without parallel in the imperial period, confirming the thesis that opposition is an area in which the traditional Russian mentality has maintained itself less durably than elsewhere.

The same is true of the post-Stalin period. Since the dictator's death in 1953 the political resistance movement has undergone a complex evolution which cannot be described in detail here. As every reader of the Western press knows, dissent has flourished, if that is not too strong a word, in the climate of 'thaw' or comparative relaxation introduced by Stalin's death. Unfortunately the nature and importance of this movement have been distorted in the minds of many Western observers, including not a few specialists as well as those non-specialists who are informed on these matters largely through the 'media'. First, the degree of relaxation permitted since 1953 has tended to be grossly exaggerated. And secondly, the assumption has often been made that the post-Stalin relaxations are progressive: that they have, in other words, gradually increased and are somehow bound to continue increasing until, one day, Russia will have been transformed into a society liberal and democratic in the Western sense. As one who has sought to expose this misconception for at least twenty years, I note with melancholy satisfaction that the realities seem at last, in the late 1970s, to be penetrating the Western folk brain. In the minds of Western politicians, on the other hand, the old heresy of automatic Kremlinite self-liberalisation seems to have been supplanted by a new and no less dangerous illusion: that the Kremlin can be bribed by concessionary shipments of grain, machinery and other tangible inducements to behave itself.

That these misunderstandings should have been fostered by 'capitalist' journalists is probably inevitable in an atmosphere which encourages both editors and readers to demand two features above all in newspaper reports and comments on Russia: novelty and comfort. Alas, the country has rarely justified either requirement. To this atmosphere of unjustified hopes must be added the spectacular but in some ways regrettable newsworthiness of Soviet dissidents. In them the sensation-craving Western newspaper reader can contemplate from a safe distance brave men defying an all-powerful state, which—it has all too easily been inferred—will one day succumb like a blundering Goliath to a very army of Davids, eagerly mend its naughty ways and tamely join the community of free nations.

Despite such comforting illusions, it is now at last dawning on the Western mind that the Brezhnev period is more, not less, oppressive than the preceding Khrushchev era. Nor can it now seem surprising to find the year 1962—in which Alexander Solzhenitsyn's *One Day in the Life of Ivan Denisovich* erupted into a Moscow-published journal—rated as the high-water mark of post-Stalinist liberalisation. A well-qualified British observer of the mid-1970s has described the general intellectual climate in the USSR as 'undoubtedly harsher and less promising than ten to fifteen years ago'.[3] As the example of Solzhenitsyn's story indicates, imaginative literature has continued in the totalitarian period to perform a function analogous to its traditional role in the imperial period: as a vehicle in which material critical of authority can appear more easily than anywhere else, and as a barometer indicating the atmospheric pressure on society at large. But, as the example of Solzhenitsyn also shows, this function has been in decline since 1962.

Aware as they are of Western urges to exaggerate Soviet liberalisation, and realising that it is in their interests to foster the erroneous impression that Russia is moving towards the 'Western way of life' (and is therefore less menacing than might otherwise be supposed), the Moscow authorities have intelligently exploited their own liberals. These are sanctioned to tour foreign countries demonstrating that the Russians, too, are human beings possessing the usual complement of eyes, ears and limbs, and that they are capable of baring their teeth in the rictus of simulated benevolence: all of which purportedly proves that their 'system', contrary to the claims of ill-wishers, does tolerate political opposition. Even in Stalin's day this role could be, and was, performed with no little skill by an Ilya Ehrenburg. Since his time the main liberal, in this rather special sense, seems to have been the poet Yevgeny Yevtushenko. To say this is not to suggest that such licensed liberals are insincere when they express their views, merely that the authorities appear to tolerate or approve their activities as a device for further bemusing the Western brain already so pathetically ill-adapted to assess the non-Western brain. Licensed liberals in the above sense are a relatively new phenomenon, for such refinements in public relations were beyond the range of the imperial Russian government.

Though an Ehrenburg or a Yevtushenko may indeed have been operating under informal license, as indicated here, this is not true of the literary dissidents as a whole. Two in particular have captured the world's imagination through prolonged defiance clearly unwelcome to officialdom: Pasternak and Solzhenitsyn.

Pasternak was the post-Stalinist pioneer of what, for want of a better word, has been called 'smuggled' Soviet literature: smuggled in the sense that works which have either been rejected for publication in Russia, or would be unlikely ever to achieve such publication, have been spirited abroad and issued in foreign translation. Here again a tradition of imperial Russia has been revived, for censorship-menaced works of that period were often first published abroad: some of Pushkin's political and blasphemous verse, for instance, and certain writings of Tolstoy. In the 1920s, too, it was common for USSR-domiciled Russian writers to publish—at first without official disapproval—in Berlin.

Pasternak's novel *Doctor Zhivago* (1957) revived such memories by becoming the first notable post-Stalin work to be spirited abroad for publication. Though denounced by Kremlinised critics as heretical, it is a measured, cool and objectively presented tale. Yet, by assuming the private life of any private individual to be inevitably more important than his function as a collectivised cog, Pasternak implicitly contradicted official dogma. He also did so by implying in private conversation that the premisses of his society were too absurd even to be worth refuting, though no decent man could long refrain from laughing at them. Here Pasternak was rejecting not merely a Soviet but also a common Russian train of thought. In *Doctor Zhivago* he chides Gogol, Tolstoy and Dostoyevsky for excess of portentousness: for 'preparing for death, worrying, looking for meanings, drawing up balance-sheets'. With these philosophically over-committed figures he contrasts Pushkin and Chekhov, praising their 'childlike Russian quality . . . their modest unconcern with such pompous themes as mankind's ultimate destiny and their own salvation ... They lived out their lives unobtrusively in an individual manner personal to themselves.'[4]

In making that distinction, and in inferentially ranging himself with Chekhov and Pushkin, the author of *Doctor Zhivago* was underlining a point which I have hoped to make here in a different way. Not every Russian is permanently obsessed with ultimate profundities. The quieter, the less theatrical approach is not less common on Russian soil than the flamboyancy which has become accepted as typical. Moreover, as the names invoked by Pasternak show, it would be an error to suppose that there was any monopoly in genius on either side of the register.

Pasternak died in 1960, and his place as premier literary dissident was taken by Alexander Solzhenitsyn. The documentary-type story *One Day in the Life of Ivan Denisovich*, with which he first attracted attention, was the first unvarnished account of Stalinist concentration-camp life to appear in any Kremlin-sanctioned publication. The work remains one of the most powerful evocations of the theme on record, and I recall the satisfaction of discovering it in the Moscow literary journal *Novy mir* and of being the first translator to publish an extensive extract in English. Its taut, austere, restrained manner gave no indication that its author was, or was about to become, one of the most prolific and undisciplined scribes on record. He now has to his credit many items of fiction, long and short, together with numerous other works: autobiographical, historical and publicistic. Virtually all his writings, whether nominally fictional or not, bear a documentary character, and all combine to present a panoramic view of twentieth-century Russia. In these wide-ranging works, as in his personal style, Solzhenitsyn does not project himself as one of those modest self-effacing Russian geniuses praised by Pasternak. Here is a former camp victim, sufferer from grave illness and target for official persecution who has mobilised courage and perseverance far exceeding the human norm. Since his expulsion from the Soviet Union in early 1974, Solzhenitsyn has become a notable figure on the world stage. His thunderous manner, his wide range, his moral earnestness, his tendency majestically to ignore or neglect the subtler and more elusive virtues of literary creativity—these traits, all of them traditionally Russian, contrast with the frivolity and facile optimism of much political thinking and literary criticism in the West. It was, therefore, perhaps inevitable that his teachings should evoke a response far from universally sympathetic.

Solzhenitsyn has been said to speak for Russia with as much authority as the very Soviet government.[5] But he is also a major figure in an older Russian tradition. While still resident in his native country he acquired a status similar to that of the later Tolstoy—the Tolstoy who long defied the might of imperial Russia, protected only by his international reputation. Now, in exile, Solzhenitsyn has veered towards the position of Alexander Herzen, who emigrated in 1847, and whose denunciations of Russian tyranny helped to make him the country's leading nineteenth-century political *émigré*.

Among dissidents still resident in the USSR at the time of writing, an outstanding figure is Andrew Sakharov. No author of belles-lettres, he is a leading atomic physicist and has been called 'the father of the Soviet H-bomb', a title which he himself disavows. Once again the dissident movement has thrown up, as it has in the case of others too numerous to mention, a man of remarkable independence and courage. To tag Sakharov as an heir to the pre-revolutionary Russian intelligentsia, as one dissident-fancier has done,[6] is surely to misread his character and achievements. A man of great intellectual distinction in his specialised field, Sakharov has shown in his writings on global politics a degree of sober common sense, personal modesty and lack of narcissism as far removed as possible from the style of the nineteenth-century intelligentsia. He has been involved in controversy with Solzhenitsyn, whose lapses into old-fashioned *narodnik* sentimentality about the 'ordinary' Russian (as in his novel *August 1914*) the more fastidious scientist does not share. Sakharov has preached phased democratisation of the Soviet Union, whereas Solzhenitsyn seems to believe that a period of continuing, albeit dwindling, authoritarianism must be a prelude to progress. But there is more in common between the two men than has sometimes been allowed. Both have taken issue with Western politicians and Western public opinion for ignoring the menace of the USSR as an aggressive terroristic bureaucracy, and for being willing to play the 'peaceful co-existence' game by Russian rules. In particular the policy of *détente*—that whereby Western states make tangible concessions to Moscow in return for meaningless and unenforceable assurances—has incurred the criticism of both.

In personal style Sakharov differs from the flamboyant Solzhenitsyn, belonging rather to the modest and unobtrusive Russian type of which Chekhov, Nikitenko and others have been cited as exemplars. As this reminds one, the ranks of Soviet dissidents have naturally included figures at all points on the spectrum from exuberance to restraint. Of the former, Valery Tarsis seems an outstanding representative, while a more disciplined approach—in his writings as well as in his personal style—has been cultivated by Victor Nekrasov.

As for the rank and file of Soviet-domiciled dissenters, they have inclined to the sober and solid approach of the 'untypical' Russian, if only because official controls render any other posture difficult. They have not, taken as a group, advocated the overthrow of the Soviet system either by force or peaceful means. Rather have they urged that the system should live up to its own liberal pretensions. It is the flouting—through traditional official *proizvol* or arbitrariness—of laws guaranteeing extensive civil rights which the dissidents attack, particularly in their remarkable periodical publication, the *Chronicle of Current Events*. Anonymously published and circulated in typescript, this is a notable example of *samizdat* or 'do-it-yourself' publishing. The practice has flourished since the death of Stalin, again reviving a long-standing tradition. Much of Pushkin's work, for instance, was first read by his fellow-countrymen in privily circulated manuscript copies.

The *Chronicle of Current Events* has been appearing since 1968, with a break of two years in 1972–4 when the authorities contrived to suppress it. It is a sober, restrained publication which details in objective, equable style the abuses to which Soviet citizens are exposed by authority—often, as noted above, in defiance of its own regulations. This impressive publication presents a further demonstration of the abiding truth that to be a Russian is not necessarily to err on the side of over-exuberance. Recent dissidence, as charted in the *Chronicle* and elsewhere, has tended to focus on three issues: on the rights of non-Russian minorities, which are no direct concern of the present study; on the situation of religious believers, a topic discussed above; and, finally, on political freedom in general —a theme comprehending the others.

Why does a state as repressive as the USSR, equipped with a

vast under-employed political police authority, tolerate these heresies? First, despite all controls, the authorities may simply be unable to suppress a movement as broadly based as Soviet political dissent. Secondly, they may not wish to do so. It is, after all, normal police practice in civil as well as political cases to allow the 'criminal' to continue his activities under surveillance rather than to drive him and his associates underground by immediately arresting all concerned. The Okhrana (imperial political police) followed this procedure before 1917 and the KGB does so now. Furthermore, the Soviet authorities derive propaganda advantages from permitting dissidence to continue, for the befogged Western folk brain has long insisted on interpreting the phenomenon as proof of that blessed progressive 'liberalisation' of the USSR which, it is wishfully expected, will one day deliver the world from all its problems. In a sense, then, the West has tended to feel that it can safely relax so long as Russia maintains these dissidents whose 'movement' will one day peacefully transform the Kremlin into a source of international sweetness and light.

In any case by no means all dissenters are left unmolested. Many have been treated with great severity. They have been sentenced to imprisonment for anti-Soviet activity, incarcerated in mental hospitals, harassed in other ways. A dissenter can never know what to expect. The authorities may allow a given individual his head for a while. Or they will bully and intimidate him and his associates as a prelude to arrest, compulsory psychiatric 'treatment' or expulsion from the USSR. Solzhenitsyn, Tarsis and Nekrasov are only a few of the many troublemakers, as the Kremlin sees them, who have been unceremoniously dumped on the world at large either by expulsion or by the withdrawal of a passport after foreign travel has been sanctioned and embarked upon.

Opinions naturally differ on the future of Soviet dissidence. Some of its foremost representatives are also among the most pessimistic. 'If a man does not keep silent it does not mean that he hopes necessarily to achieve something,' Sakharov once stated.[7] He would probably agree in finding Western public opinion tragically mistaken in conceiving the dissidents as capable of miraculously halting Kremlinite expansionism unaided. This is all the less likely to happen in that dissent remains, as for a long time the nineteenth-century *narodnik* movement remained, chiefly a purview of the educated classes. A large percentage of its representatives are academics, and it has few links with workers and peasants. They, too, have occasionally mounted riots or strikes, which have been harshly suppressed, and of which news has often filtered out only after considerable delay. Meanwhile the divorce between educated and less-educated dissent is more remarkable for recalling the dilemmas and exasperations of the 1870s than for offering hope of political change in the immediate future.

In estimating the degree of disaffection, actual and potential, in present-day Russia as a whole, this investigation will maintain a modest reticence. Even in Western societies, where sophisticated opinion-polling techniques are freely and openly operated, the assessment of group political attitudes is notoriously difficult. How much the more so in the closed society of totalitarian Russia, where even the most casual question by an unofficial inquirer can be interpreted as an attempt to subvert the structure of the state. As for the confidence with which foreign Russia-watchers will pronounce on the population's loyalty to the regime, on the attitudes of 'Soviet youth' and so on, I can only marvel once more at the readiness with which, in a Russian context, even level-headed observers will commit themselves to dogmatic assertions about the unknowable. Yet this is a vital matter on which even the following uninspired guess may have some significance. That the general underlying political attitude is profoundly apathetic, despite the nominally enthusiastic ritual affirmations periodically extorted from sections of the community—this at least it seems safe to suggest. The passionate believers and the passionate disbelievers in the totalitarian system are, one may also confidently conjecture, far less numerous than are the internal neutrals. This neutral or apathetic mass would, however, probably rally to the national cause in the event of war, according to a common assumption from which I do not dissent. Nor do I feel that one may build many hopes for constructive change on the undoubted fascination exercised on Russians, especially the young, by almost any manifestation of Western culture, including such books, films, musical recordings and articles of clothing as, in one way or another, reach the Russian consumer.

V
Continuity and Change

To what extent has post-1917 Russia retained and even institutionalised traditional pre-revolutionary features of the national outlook? Conversely, to what extent is one notable Kremlinite claim—that of having evolved, in Soviet Man, a new and superior brand of human being—to be taken seriously?

To the sceptical this last assertion may seem absurd enough to send him to the opposite extreme, inducing him to exaggerate the many elements of permanence in the Russian psyche. From the pages of this book alone much evidence could be adduced to suggest that the Russian, far from being change-prone or revolutionary-minded, is supremely immutable in his mentality and in the various institutions, taboos and customs which that mentality has evolved as appropriate to itself.

Among these is numbered the lavish use of arbitrary government-sponsored terror against wide sections of the citizenry. Governmental terror—whether Muscovite, imperial or totalitarian—has embraced such typically though not exclusively Russian features as mass deportation by ukase; arrest and imprisonment administratively ordained through officials uncontrolled by the judiciary or any *habeas corpus* act; the periodical sacrifice of the country's very terror-purveying high officials as scapegoats for official policy; the victimisation of disgraced persons' relatives and associates; the mass conscription of labour for prestige projects; the pre-emptive punishment of those deemed liable to commit offences which they may not have committed even in imagination; the persecution of those considered guilty of facecrime (failure to simulate adequate political subservience); laws providing harsh penalties for those seeking to change the system of government; laws, no less severe, directed against failure to denounce such persons.

Such are some among many considerations suggesting that, while systems may come and systems may go, perennial Russia rolls on for ever.

In comparatively minor detail, too, one may trace much continuity between pre-1917 and post-1917 punitive practice. There is the tendency to sentence those involved in vehicular accidents, no matter whether traction by Tsarist quadruped or post-Tsarist internal combustion engine is involved, to harsh terms of imprisonment without regard to culpability.[1] And what is there about the Russian climate which has led two leading despots separated by a century—Nicholas I and Stalin—to decree independently of each other that certain political prisoners should be incarcerated in windowless cells? The imposition of compulsory psychiatric or other medical 'treatment' on political offenders is also sometimes invoked as a parallel between Russia old and new. However, the only well-known nineteenth-century victim—Chaadayev—was treated with far less severity than the modern objects of this macabre persecution. Moreover, Nicholas I (in contrast to Stalin) was prevailed upon to restore window privileges to the sentenced political miscreants, the Decembrists, whom he had sought to mew in eyeless dungeons: a reminder that Russian imperial penal procedures, from the early nineteenth century onwards, were milder than those of the succeeding period.

In the area of official propaganda and political myth the gulf between appearance and reality has also been stressed as an abiding feature of Muscovite, imperial and post-imperial Russia. Here too a general proposition seems convincingly reinforced by trivial details. For instance, it was a nineteenth-century custom to make a special point of publishing in Russian translation such foreign books as seemed to reveal particularly discreditable features in other European countries. This policy has, again, been followed in the totalitarian period. It has also embraced films such as the Italian *La Dolce Vita*: sanctioned (one surmises) for distribution less on artistic grounds than because they seem to portray 'capitalist' civilisation as reeling, doomed, into anarchy and chaos. Then again, there is the traditional Russian governmental practice of representing as concessions to popular demand measures and policies imposed by the whim of a single autocrat. The rewriting of history to suit official myth is another procedure common to Tsarist and post-Tsarist Russia alike. To this may be added persisting official secretiveness as expressed in the imposition of unperson status; in the unavailability of such basic reference material as guides, street plans and—later—telephone directories; in the suppression of statistics about suicides, criminal prosecutions and accidents.

Then there is the special place occupied in Russian tradition by imaginative literature as a medium through which opposition to official policies may, despite severe censorship controls, be more effectively expressed than elsewhere. The circulation of banned works in manuscript or typescript (now called *samizdat*), the practice of smuggling these works abroad for publication banned at home (now called *tamizdat*)—these are features common to the evolution of a Pushkin and a Solzhenitsyn. No less common to the nineteenth and twentieth centuries is the practice of disciplining imaginative authors through literary bureaucrats: themselves often mediocre or failed writers. 'Official optimism'—the obligation placed upon authors of belles-lettres to present Russian conditions in an unreal and cheerful light—had influenced the processing of a Pushkin and a Chekhov long before it was enshrined in the government-imposed literary method evolved in the 1930s, and known as Socialist Realism. 'Russia's past has been admirable. Her present is more than magnificent. As to the future, it is beyond the power of the most daring imagination to portray it.' This homily to historians was formulated by the nineteenth-century chief of political police General Count Benckendorff. But his words transcend both the historical discipline and the speaker's era. Then again, peasant-fancying by imaginative writers, that marked feature of late-nineteenth-century Russian literature, has re-emerged in similar form in neo-populist stories and novels treating the collective farm of the 1960s and 1970s.

Many other features might be quoted to reinforce the aspect of immutability presented by the Russian mentality throughout the ages. They include the love-hate neurosis about the West; the suppression of a Hungarian revolution by both Nicholas I (in 1849) and Nikita Khrushchev (in 1956); the close parallels in peasant life between nineteenth-century enserfment and twentieth-century collectivisation; the tendency for Russians to harangue the world on their country's mission to liberate humanity—a tendency which seems to flourish most in eras of acutest domestic self-enslavement and aggressiveness towards other peoples. There is also the tendency for Russian society to resemble some enormous, badly organised school which never has an end of term, or comically inefficient military formation from which there is no discharge. In the British army troops have notoriously been required, within living memory, to whitewash dumps of coal in preparation for a general's inspection. But in Russia civilians, too, seem subject to such grotesque manifestations of martial law. When the Crown Prince (the future Alexander II) was about to inspect the provincial town of Vyatka in 1837, all the fences had to be hurriedly painted, the muzhiks were put into special festive caftans, and one destitute widow of the locality was compelled to pull up the floorboards in her house as material for refurbishing the wooden pavement in front of it.[2] A similar position is that of Moscow apartmentdwellers doomed to weeks of near-darkness during World Youth Festivals and similar celebrations of the 1970s because their windows are compulsorily blocked out by red bunting as part of the city's decoration plan for the occasion.

Yet I am suspicious of attempts to press too hard on the parallels between the pre-1917 and post-1917 Russian collective mind, for many differences may also be observed. The latter has, for instance, responded to political developments by becoming more cautious, calculating, and apprehensive—less volatile and reckless—than its Tsarist counterpart. Now less likely to perish in infancy of cholera, smallpox or famine, the Russian is far more exposed to bureaucrats and other human vermin than previously, and his life is accordingly safer (but only since Stalin's departure) and duller. He carries a watch. He has learned to tell the time and be punctual. He can also read and write, which renders him still more controllable by officials, but also gives him access to his country's treasury of imaginative literature, previously unavailable through illiteracy to a majority of the population. Then again, the age-old practice of wife-beating has surely become less common even in the backwoods, though no statistics are available on the incidence of this evil. Furthermore, in the key area of penal procedure, the traditional privileges extended to political prisoners under the Tsars have been abolished. Under Stalin, indeed, ordinary non-political criminals were granted a franchise to murder, terrorise and bully their 'political' cell-mates. Now relieved from such gross abuses, the latter still suffer the indignity of living under laws specially worded to delude simpletons into believing that incarceration for political reasons is no longer practised.

For these and other reasons—some creditable, some discreditable to the new dispensation—many reputable observers have claimed change as a factor more significant than continuity in post-1917 Russia. Mehnert states outright that 'Soviet man is not the Russian our fathers knew and often saw in a romantic light.' He speaks of a decline in spontaneity and an increase in personal discipline together with 'a firm determination to succeed and a strong faith in technological progress'.[3] Another authority—Frederick C. Barghoorn—takes issue with two notable Russian *émigré* philosophers, Berdyayev and Fedotov, for over-emphasising the continuity between pre-1917 and post-1917 traits. 'There is certainly,' Barghoorn claims, 'no such cultural gulf between elite and masses in Soviet Russia as existed in pre-revolutionary Russia, divided, as Lenin put it, into "two nations".' Discussing the Kremlin's assertion that socialism has produced a new and superior type of human being, the same observer well adds that 'The Russian and Soviet elements in this pattern stand in an uneasy relationship to one another.'[4]

With this creatively blurred formula one may perhaps leave the vexed problem of Russian-Soviet continuity, for here above all is an aspect of national psychology where a craving for precise outlines risks becoming unhelpful and counter-productive.

So much for the Russian as traditionalist and innovator in his domestic context. What of changes in the outlook of the world at large as influenced by the Russian psyche? Here too the special achievements of Russian authoritarianism spring to mind. Two worldwide institutions—military conscription and political policing—were, as stated above, introduced by Peter the Great long before countries deemed more civilised had dreamed of evolving these crucial adjuncts to modern life. More significant still was the creation, for the Russians by Stalin, of the control system known as totalitarianism—another notable innovation which has since been extensively imitated by nations less administratively adventurous.

Ingenious in evolving official controls, the Russian mind has proved no less successful in evolving techniques of subverting those

controls. From the 1860s onwards some uncanny process of anticipation was inspiring the country's oppositionists to develop a
special style and *modus operandi* which, though it might well seem
bizarre and even primitive at that time to peoples reputedly more
sophisticated, has since been adopted throughout the world by
many who are blissfully unconscious, in the 1970s, of retreading a
path beaten out so long ago by Chernyshevsky and his Russian
contemporaries. Militantly trumpeted sexual egalitarianism and
permissiveness; the deference complacently paid by spineless,
popularity-craving middle-aged men to noisy, rude, hirsute, ignorant, slogan-mumbling adolescents; contempt for money, property
and professional competence high-mindedly voiced by the idle,
pampered, professionally unqualified sons and daughters of the
rich; campus revolutions and the hounding of professors derided as
fuddy-duddies because they seek to maintain academic standards;
the advocacy of destructiveness and revolutionary violence for their
own sake; political idealism and utopistic utterance mindlessly
babbled forth by bomb-throwing juvenile gangsters; the thesis that
more mundane forms of crime are the fault of 'society' for which
responsibility must be taken by a mysterious body defined as 'all
of us'; supreme contempt, pompously preached by a harshly
intolerant semi-educated 'intelligentsia', for the rights of individuals; the whole dismal apparatus of twentieth-century psychopatholitics—before the second half of the present century such
manifestations could have been dismissed as the transitory, quaint
and barbarous eccentricities of a backward nineteenth-century
people. Since then, however, these and allied notions have moved
into the very forefront of modernity. They have become remarkably fashionable and respected everywhere: everywhere, that is,
with the spectacular exception of their country of origin. The new
Russia may be envied or despised, according to taste, for its
effectiveness in suppressing many of the above features—not least
that of juvenile political delinquency—which the old Russia
invented, or at least extensively pioneered, in the first place.

For such reasons history-conscious Russian visitors to the West
can easily receive the impression of seeing their own past reenacted before their eyes. The point has been well made by
Solzhenitsyn, who instances 'adults deferring to the opinion of their
children; . . . professors scared of being unfashionable; journalists

(218)

refusing to take responsibility for the words they squander so pro-
fusely; universal sympathy for revolutionary extremists; people
with serious objections unable or unwilling to voice them.' To
these phenomena the Russian sage appends the general Western
sense of doom; feeble government; societies whose defensive reactions have become atrophied and 'spiritual confusion leading to
political upheaval'.[5]

Can it be then that 'we' are all Russians, albeit nineteenth-
century Russians, now? If so, it is a pity that this collective psyche
—a formidable and fascinating but also, like most other national
mentalities, partly regrettable phenomenon—should be flourishing
internationally even as it may be declining in its country of origin.
But how fortunate it is too that, whatever sweeping statements may
be made about a generalised 'Russian mind', there are still individual Russians with minds of their own.

REFERENCE
NOTES

INDEX TO
REFERENCE
NOTES

INDEX

REFERENCE NOTES

There are so many references in this book that it has often been necessary to consolidate them in groups at or near the end of the paragraph to which they apply in order to avoid disfiguring the body of the text with an excess of figures. References are by authors' or editors' names, or by book titles, as listed in alphabetical order in the Index to Reference Notes, pp. 231–5.

I
FOREGROUND AND BACKGROUND
Life-Enhancers or Life-Deniers? (pp. 9–21)

1 Klyuchevsky, 2:190; Karamzin, 9:156–7.
2 Waliszewski, 153.
3 Westwood, 30.
4 Private information.
5 Orlov, 350.
6 Tupper, 200.
7 Hingley, *The Tsars*, 157.
8 Solovyov, 11:140.
9 Hingley, *The Russian Secret Police*, 45–6.
10 Conquest, *The Great Terror*, 95.
11 Olearius, 192.
12 Herling, 59.
13 Conquest, *The Nation Killers*, 102.
14 Khokhlov, 240.
15 F. Dostoyevsky, cited in Hingley, *The Undiscovered Dostoyevsky*, 149 ff.
16 A. de Staël, cited in Wilson, 187; A. de Custine, cited ibid., 224; Mackenzie Wallace, 1: 252–4; Chekhov, 15:67.
17 Paléologue, 431–2.
18 Leacock, 155–61.
19 Herzen, *Byloye i dumy*, 1:170.
20 Woolf, 174.
21 G. Gould, cited in Brewster, 175.

Problems of Perspective (pp. 21–33)

1 Baena, 5, 16.
2 K. Aksakov, in Raeff, *Russian Intellectual History*, 231.
3 Jarintzov, 25–6.
4 Pipes, *Russia under the Old Regime*, 83.
5 Fedotov, 22.

Thesis or Antithesis? (pp. 33–51)

1 Mehnert, 207; Nikitenko, 1:12.
2 F. Barghoorn, in Simmons, 535; Stalin, 6:186.
3 Nikitenko, 1:13.
4 Klyuchevsky, 1:313–14.
5 Mackenzie Wallace, 1:356.

6 Nikitenko, 1:13.
7 Hingley, *The Tsars*, 16.
8 Gorer, 93 ff.
9 Pares, 16.
10 Pitcher, *Understanding the Russians*, 97.
11 Hingley, *The Undiscovered Dostoyevsky*, 20.
12 Hingley, *The Tsars*, 167-8.
13 Ibid., 245; Custine, 109, 114.
14 Shaw, 4; Hitler, 661.
15 Mackenzie Wallace, 2:229.
16 Gorer, 141.
17 Nikitenko, 1:49; 2:270, 548.
18 Solzhenitsyn, 89-90.
19 Paléologue, 447.
20 Miliukov, 1:46.
21 K. Mehnert, in Black, 509; Mehnert, 31-2; Woolf, 179.
22 Pipes, *Russia under the Old Regime*, 157-8; Mehnert, 182; Custine, 343.
23 Gorky, 17, 19, 40.
24 Gorer, 145.
25 Mead, 27.
26 A. Brumberg, in Strong, 2.
27 F. Dostoyevsky, cited in

Hingley, *The Undiscovered Dostoyevsky*, 203-4.
28 Szamuely, 172-3.
29 Pitcher, op. cit., 92.
30 Pipes, op. cit., 187.
31 Mackenzie Wallace, 1:368; Custine, 230.
32 Hingley, *Under Soviet Skins*, 188-9.
33 Aristophanes, *Ach.*, 77-9.
34 Mehnert, 179.
35 Turbervile, in Herberstein, cxlix; Fletcher, 124; Olearius, 179-80.
36 Herberstein, cxxvii.
37 Olearius, 183.
38 *Trud* (Moscow), 21 Sept. 1973.
39 Schlesinger, 14; Bruford, 46-7.
40 Mackenzie Wallace, 1:379.
41 Lermontov, 4:28-9.
42 Dostoyevsky, 11:455-71.
43 Wilson, 208; J. Kohl, cited ibid., 240.
44 Pitcher, op. cit., 99; Miller, W., 184; Mackenzie Wallace, 2:231.

II

COMMUNICATION SYSTEMS

Signalling Devices (pp. 52-61)

1 R. Hingley, in *Problems of Communism* (Washington, D.C.), Nov.-Dec. 1972.
2 Tolstoy, 13:12.
3 Jarintzov, 46-7.
4 Ibid., 51-2.
5 Mehnert, 68.
6 Forbes, 56-7.
7 Walshe, 26-7.
8 Harrison, 3, 11.
9 Ibid., 11-13; Josselson, 20.

10 *The New Statesman* (London), 11 Dec. 1915.
11 Fedotov, 28.
12 F. Barghoorn, in Simmons, 548.
13 Jarintzov, 4-8.
14 V. Nabokov, cited in 'Profferings', *The Times Literary Supplement* (London), 10 Oct. 1968.

Display Postures (pp. 61–77)

1 Jarintzov, 148; Pitcher, *Understanding the Russians*, 189; Pares, 11; Woolf, 176; Belfrage, 185; Mehnert, 133.
2 Jarintzov, 11, 100–1, 204.
3 Josselson, 50; Brewster, 170; Woolf, 177, 179; Jarintzov, 138–9.
4 Ibid., 59, 94.
5 Coulson, vii.
6 Custine, 351.
7 *Oxford Chekhov*, 3:x.
8 Knipper, 1:432; Chekhov, 19:122.
9 Ibid., 16:32.
10 *Oxford Chekhov*, 6:12–13.
11 E. Garnett, cited in Brewster, 145.
12 I. Bunin, in Golubov, 520.
13 Nabokov, *Speak Memory*, 285–6.
14 Nikitenko, 1:116, 2:453.
15 Jarintzov, 60.
16 Ibid., 12–14.
17 Miller, W., 85; Woolf, 174. Emphasis added.
18 Hingley, *Chekhov* (1950), 232.
19 R. Lyall, cited in Wilson, 194.
20 Pares, 11.
21 Mehnert, 180.
22 Tr. by C. Garnett, cited in *Oxford Chekhov*, 8:xii.
23 Pitcher, op. cit., 106. Emphasis added.
24 F. Dostoyevsky, cited in Hingley, *The Undiscovered Dostoyevsky*, 56. Emphasis added.
25 Hingley, *Under Soviet Skins*, 203.
26 Custine, 152; Nikitenko, 2:299; idem, cited in Szamuely, 155; A. de Custine, cited in Kennan, George F., 81.
27 Hingley, *Under Soviet Skins*, 160.
28 Pitcher, op. cit., 22; Davidson-Houston, 41–2.
29 Pitcher, op. cit., 61.
30 Miller, W., 85.
31 Chekhov, 14:184.
32 Custine, 197.

Camouflage Drill (pp. 77–88)

1 Andreyev, L., 6:225–6.
2 Turgenev, 4:95–6.
3 Andreyev, L., loc. cit., 226.
4 Ibid. Emphasis added.
5 O. Wormser-Migot, in Gaxotte, 204.
6 M. Speransky, cited in Szamuely, 131.
7 Custine, 197.
8 Dostoyevsky, 9:321.
9 Ibid. Emphasis added.
10 Idem, 9:322.
11 R. Tucker, in Black, 604.

Deception Tactics (pp. 88–93)

1 A. Jenkinson, cited in Wilson, 38.
2 G. Fletcher, cited in Wilson, 59; Fletcher, 129.
3 Mackenzie Wallace, 2:72–3; Olearius, 172; Dostoyevsky, 9:320.
4 Custine, 192; Mackenzie

Wallace, 1:275; Belfrage, 185-6.
5 Jarintzov, 148; Woolf, 173.
6 Gorer, 185.
7 Nikitenko, 3:329.
8 Herzen, *Polnoye sobraniye*
sochineniy, 6:445.
9 Mackenzie Wallace, 2:33-4.
10 Kennan, George F., 80.
11 Redlikh, 67-101; Hingley, *Joseph Stalin*, 435-6.

Sealed Lips (pp. 93-101)

1 Herberstein, cvii-cviii.
2 Miliukov, 1:31-2. Emphasis added.
3 W. Richardson, cited in Wilson, 146; A. de Staël, cited ibid., 189.
4 Wilson, 215.
5 Custine, 201
6 *Soviet Analyst* (London), 2:19.
7 Hingley, *Joseph Stalin*, 311.
8 Pipes, *Russia under the Old Regime*, 95; Custine, 119
9 Szamuely 185; Conquest, *The Nation Killers*, 48-9.
10 A. de Custine, cited in Szamuely, 4.
11 Pipes, op. cit., 289.
12 Keenan, passim; V. Avtokratov, cited in Andreyev, N.,
592-8.
13 Khrushchev (1971 and 1974), passim; Rigby.
14 Raeff, *Michael Speransky*, 190-1.
15 Nikitenko, 1:336.
16 L. Vladimirov, cited in *Soviet Analyst* (London), 2:19.
17 R. Hingley, 'Emergency Encyclopaedia', *Punch* (London), 2 June 1954.
18 Rush, 21-2.
19 R. Littledale, cited in Brewster, 139.
20 Nove, 12-13.
21 Gardiner, 61.
22 Hingley, *A Concise History of Russia*, 9.

III
GROUP CONSCIOUSNESS

Togetherness (pp. 102-107)

1 Yu. Samarin, cited in Pipes, *Struve*, 36.
2 Mehnert, 183.
3 Miller, W., 67, 106, 112-13.
4 Gorer, 135.
5 Gorky, 18.
6 Miller, W., 110.
7 F. Dostoyevsky, cited in Szamuely, 72.
8 A. Solzhenitsyn, cited in *Soviet*
Analyst (London), 3:7.
9 Pitcher, *Understanding the Russians*, 129.
10 Miller, W., 67-8.
11 Nikitenko, 1:408.
12 Pipes, *Russia under the Old Regime*, 180.
13 Churchward, 63.
14 Pitcher, *The Chekhov Play*, 10.

Supranationalist (pp. 107–113)

1 V. Tarsis, cited by R. Hingley, *Spectator* (London), 28 Feb. 1970.
2 V. Belinsky, cited in Pipes, *Russia under the Old Regime*, 160–1.
3 Gorky, 28–9.
4 H. Liddon, cited in Wilson, 157.
5 Kennan, George F., 127–8.
6 Mackenzie Wallace, 2:193.

World Citizen (pp. 114–130)

1 Pipes, *Russia under the Old Regime*, 182.
2 Herzen, *Byloye i dumy*, 1:59.
3 Szamuely, 53; Seton-Watson, 407; Wilson, 161, 197.
4 J. Reshetar, in Black, 572.
5 M. Zankovetskaya, in *Literaturnoye nasledstvo: Chekhov*, 593.
6 V. Lenin, cited in Black, 568.
7 Wittram, 7.
8 A. Pushkin, cited in Szamuely, 81; Custine, 148, 176.
9 P. Chaadayev, in Raeff, *Russian Intellectual History*, 162.
10 F. Dostoyevsky, cited in Hingley, *The Undiscovered Dostoyevsky*, 63; Peter I, cited in Pipes, op. cit., 113.
11 Gide, 49.
12 Mehnert, 206.
13 Kiparsky, 11.
14 G. Curzon, cited in Wilson, 214.
15 Nikitenko, 1:153.
16 Mackenzie Wallace, 2:98.
17 Custine, 132.
18 Herzen, *Byloye i dumy*, 1:60.
19 Jarintzov, 29.
20 Kiparsky, 18, 23, 35; F. Dostoyevsky, cited in Hingley, *The Undiscovered Dostoyevsky*, 177.
21 Jarintzov, 13 ff.
22 Mackenzie Wallace, 1:149.
23 Miller, W., 97.
24 Mehnert, 193.
25 V. Dean, cited in Pares, 21.
26 Kiparsky, 107 ff.

Patriot (pp. 130–136)

1 Szamuely, 59–60.
2 F. Dostoyevsky, cited in Hingley, *The Undiscovered Dostoyevsky*, 182; and by J. Reshetar, in Black, 564–5.
3 Idem, cited in Hingley, op. cit., 62; Jarintzov, 74.
4 Tyutchev, 195.
5 Pushkin, 10:598.
6 H. Dicks, in Black, 643.
7 Ivan IV, 142.
8 Stalin, 13:305.
9 J. Reshetar, in Black, 561–3; Pushkin, 3:222–3; Pitcher, *Understanding the Russians*, 56.
10 Pipes, *Russia under the Old Regime*, 33; F. Barghoorn, in Simmons, 532.
11 Szamuely, 332.
12 Herzen, *Polnoye sobraniye sochineniy*, 5:391.
13 Blok, 1:453; Klyuchevsky, 2:398.

14 Stalin, 15:150; F. Barghoorn, in Simmons, 541.
15 R. Chancellor, cited in Wilson, 33; A. de Custine, cited in Kennan, George F., 87; V.

Odoyevsky, cited in Kohn, 16; M. Pogodin, cited ibid., 67–8.
16 F. Barghoorn, in Simmons, 531.

Domestic Pet (pp. 137–140)

1 Dallin, xiii.
2 Baring, xxv.
3 I. Berlin, in Raeff, *Russian*

Intellectual History, 6.
4 H. Salisbury, in Sakharov, 8.
5 Wilson, 30, 59. 157, 261.

The Class Struggle (pp. 140–152)

1 Kiparksy, 97.
2 Woolf, 179.
3 Mackenzie Wallace, 1:437.
4 Brown, 23.
5 Herzen, *Polnoye sobraniye sochineniy*, 6:454.
6 Mackenzie Wallace, 1:442.
7 Nechkina, 2:419.
8 Gogol, 5:51.
9 Churchward, 3–4.
10 Fedotov, 157.
11 Nikitenko, 1:126; Tourguéneff, 2:17.
12 Mackenzie Wallace, 1:297.
13 Starr, 48–9.
14 Custine, 100–01; idem, cited in Kennan, George F., 55.

15 Jarintzov, 88; Mackenzie Wallace, 2:227; Nikitenko, 2:204.
16 Churchward, 112.
17 Miller, W., 167.
18 Mackenzie Wallace, 2:264.
19 H. Dicks, in Black, 636.
20 Gorky, 34, 37.
21 A. Chekhov, cited in Hingley, *A New Life of Anton Chekhov*, 59–60.
22 Chekhov, 12:335.
23 V. Tissot, cited in Wilson, 279; Custine, 129; Nikitenko, 3:329; Pushkin, 7:291.
24 Mehnert, 81.

Intimacy (pp. 152–159)

1 Mackenzie Wallace, 1:154.
2 A. Jenkinson, cited in Wilson, 39; C. d'Auteroche, cited ibid., 139; Gorky, 19–10; Dal, 369–70; Mackenzie Wallace, 1:197.
3 F. Dostoyevsky, cited in Hingley, *The Undiscovered Dostoyevsky*, 139–40.
4 Jarintzov, 127.

5 V. Dunham, in Black, 459 ff.; Kohn, 14.
6 Churchward, 27–8.
7 Miller, J., 139; private information; A. Belyavsky, cited in *The Daily Telegraph* (London), 21 March 1976.
8 Feifer, 167–8.
9 Cross, 225.

IV
REGIMENTATION AND RESISTANCE

Authority and Submission (pp. 160–169)

1 Olearius, 184; Herberstein, 95; A. Jenkinson, cited in Wilson, 60.
2 M. Smith, cited in Wilson, 260; Custine, 114, 172 ff.
3 Mehnert, 111; Bauer, 122.
4 Belinsky, 621.
5 Fedotov, 152.
6 K. Marx, cited in Szamuely, 19; Vernadsky, *A History of Russia*, 56; V. Belinsky, in Kohn, 126.
7 Herberstein, 32.
8 S. von Herberstein, G. Fletcher and A. Olearius, cited in Szamuely, 7.
9 Vernadsky, *The Mongols and Russia*, 367; Berdyaev, 10.
10 N. Cherkasov, cited in Conquest, *The Great Terror*, 75–6.
11 Custine, 170.
12 R. Daniels, in Strong, 22.

Tsarism and Anti-Tsarism (pp. 169–176)

1 Nikitenko, 2:376; Jarintzov, 12; Belfrage, 186.
2 Gorer, 177.
3 N. Kostomarov, cited in Gorky, 7.
4 Longworth, 4.
5 P. Struve, in *Vekhi*, 164–5.

Psychopatholitics (pp. 176–185)

1 M. Karpovich, in Simmons, 129; Pipes, *Struve*, 283.
2 Gernet, 2:156.
3 Hingley, *The Russian Secret Police*, 90.
4 Steklov, 2:85.
5 Nikitenko, 2:80.
6 F. Dostoyevsky, cited in Hingley, *The Undiscovered Dostoyevsky*, 144.

The Intelligentsia (pp. 185–198)

1 Churchward, 3–7.
2 Mirsky, 321–2.
3 Fedotov, 11; Szamuely, 144.
4 Fedotov, 13.
5 S. Bulgakov, in *Vekhi*, 43.
6 Mirsky, 322; Fedotov, 13; Berdyayev, 19.
7 Gorer, 118.
8 Chekhov, 18:88–9.
9 A. Parry, in Kirk, 53.
10 P. Struve, in *Vekhi*, 163–4; Fedotov, 16.
11 Nikitenko, 1:432; S. Bulgakov, in *Vekhi*, 37.
12 N. Berdyayev, in *Vekhi*, 3.
13 Turgenev, 4:325.
14 Feyder, 97–101.
15 Herzen, *Polnoye sobraniye sochineniy*, 5:383; N. Berdyayev, in *Vekhi*, 11; S. Frank, ibid., 180.
16 Dostoyevsky, 10:197.

17 A. Chekhov, cited in Jarintzov, 97.
18 Jarintzov, 124.
19 Szamuely, 178.
20 S. Bulgakov, in *Vekhi*, 30, 37–8.
21 S. Frank, in *Vekhi*, 194; S. Bulgakov, ibid., 24; D. Pisarev, cited in Kohn, 140.
22 Szamuely, 161.
23 S. Frank, in *Vekhi*, 193.
24 Ibid., 207.
25 Szamuely, 194; Chernyshevsky, 6:491.
26 Szamuely, 156.
27 Mackenzie Wallace, 2:226; Nikitenko, 1:462; Herzen, in Kohn, 163.
28 I. Leontyev (Shcheglov), in Feyder, 121.
29 Chekhov, 14:154; P. Struve, in *Vekhi*, 167.
30 Miller, W., 123; H. Salisbury, in Sakharov, 8; Kohn, 13; I. Berlin, in Venturi, xxvii.

Totalitarianism and Anti-Totalitarianism (pp. 198–212)

1 Mandelstam, 126.
2 Katkov, 273.
3 M. Dewhirst, in *Soviet Analyst* (London), 3:2.
4 Pasternak, 294.
5 R. Conquest, in *Soviet Analyst* (London), 4:4.
6 H. Salisbury, in Sakharov, 7–8.
7 Sakharov, 173.

V
CONTINUITY AND CHANGE

(pp. 213–219)

1 J. Kohn, cited in Wilson, 233; Hingley, *Under Soviet Skins*, 156–7.
2 Herzen, *Byloye i dumy*, 1:204.
3 Mehnert, 284.
4 F. Barghoorn, in Simmons, 534, 539.
5 A. Solzhenitsyn, cited in *The Daily Telegraph* (London), 24 March 1976.

INDEX TO REFERENCE NOTES

The following list of works is not offered as a systematic bibliography of the Russian mind, but consists exclusively of titles invoked in the Reference Notes because they are cited in the text or otherwise used as evidence.

Andreyev, Leonid, 'Vserossiyskoye vranyo', in *Polnoye sobraniye sochineniy*, 8 vols (St Petersburg, 1913).

Andreyev, Nikolay, 'The Authenticity of the Correspondence between Ivan IV and Prince Andrey Kurbsky', *Slavonic and East European Review* (London), vol. liii, no. 133, Oct. 1975.

Baena, Duke de, *The Dutch Puzzle* (The Hague, 1975).

Baring, Maurice, Introduction to *The Oxford Book of Russian Verse* (Oxford, 1948).

Bauer, Raymond A., *How the Soviet System Works* (Cambridge, Mass., 1957).

Belfrage, Sally, *A Room in Moscow* (London, 1958).

Belinsky, V. G., *Izbrannyye sochineniya*, ed. F. M. Golovenchenko (Moscow, 1947).

Berdyaev, Nicolas, *The Origin of Russian Communism*, tr. by R. M. French (London, 1948).

Black, Cyril E., ed., *The Transformation of Russian Society: Aspects of Social Change Since 1861* (Cambridge, Mass., 1967).

Blok, Aleksandr, *Sochineniya*, 2 vols (Moscow, 1955).

Brewster, Dorothy, *East-West Passage: A Study in Literary Relationships* (London, 1954).

Brown, Douglas, *Doomsday 1917: The Destruction of Russia's Ruling Class* (London, 1975).

Bruford, W. H., *Chekhov and His Russia: A Sociological Study* (London, 1947).

Chekhov, Anton, *Polnoye sobraniye sochineniy i pisem*, 20 vols (Moscow, 1944–51).

Chernyshevsky, N. G., *Polnoye sobraniye sochineniy*, 10 vols (St Petersburg, 1906).

Churchward, L. G., *The Soviet Intelligentsia: An Essay on the Social Structure and Roles of Soviet Intellectuals During the 1960s* (London, 1973).

Conquest, Robert, *The Great Terror: Stalin's Purge of the Thirties* (London, 1968).

——, *The Nation Killers: The Soviet Deportation of Nationalities* (London, 1970).

Coulson, Jessie, ed. and tr., *Anton Chekhov: Selected Stories* (London, 1963).

Cross, Anthony, 'Pushkin's Bawdy; or, Notes from the Literary Underground', *Russian Literary Triquarterly* (Ann Arbor, Michigan) no. 10, Fall 1974.

Custine, Marquis A. de, *Lettres de Russie* (Paris, 1951).

Dal, V., *Poslovitsy russkago naroda* (Moscow, 1862).

Dallin, David J., and Nicolaevsky, Boris I., *Forced Labour in Soviet Russia* (London, 1947).

Davidson-Houston, J. V., *Armed Diplomat: A Military Attaché in Russia* (London, 1959).

Dostoyevsky, F. M., *Polnoye sobraniye sochineniy*, 12 vols (St Petersburg, 1895).

Fedotov, G. P., *Novy grad: sbornik statey* (New York, 1952).

Feifer, George, *Moscow Farewell* (New York, 1976).

Feyder, V., ed., *A. P. Chekhov: literaturny byt i tvorchestvo po memuarnym materialam* (Leningrad, 1928).

Fischer, George, *Russian Liberalism: From Gentry to Intelligentsia* (Cambridge, Mass., 1958).

Fletcher, Giles, *O gosudarstve russkom*, tr. from English, 3rd ed. (St Petersburg, 1906).

Forbes, Nevill, *Russian Grammar*, 2nd ed. (Oxford, 1916).

Gardiner, Alan, *Egypt of the Pharaohs: An Introduction* (London, 1961).

Gaxotte, Pierre, and others, *Catherine de Russie* (Paris, 1966).

Gernet, M. N., *Istoriya tsarskoy tyurmy*, 3rd edn, 5 vols (Moscow, 1960–3).

Gide, André, *Back from the USSR* (London, 1937).

Gogol, N. V., *Sobraniye sochineniy*, 6 vols (Moscow, 1952–3).

Golubov, S. N., and others, ed., *A. P. Chekhov v vospominaniyakh sovremennikov* (Moscow, 1960).

Gorer, Geoffrey, and Rickman, John, *The People of Great Russia: A Psychological Study* (London, 1949).

Gorky, Maksim, *O russkom krestyanstve* (Berlin, 1922).

Harrison, Jane Ellen, *Russia and the Russian Verb: A Contribution to the Psychology of the Russian People* (Cambridge, England, 1915).

Herberstein, Sigismund von, *Notes upon Russia* tr. and ed. R. H. Major, vol. i (London, 1851).

Herling, Gustav, *A World Apart*, tr. by Joseph Marek (London, 1951).

Herzen, A. I., *Polnoye sobraniye sochineniy i pisem*, 22 vols, ed. M. K. Lemke (Petrograd-Leningrad, 1919–25).

——, *Byloye i dumy*, 2 vols (Minsk, 1957).

Hingley, Ronald, *Chekhov: A Biographical and Critical Study* (London, 1950).

——, *Under Soviet Skins: An Untourist's Report* (London, 1961).

——, *The Undiscovered Dostoyevsky* (London, 1962).

——, *The Tsars: Russian Autocrats, 1533–1917* (London, 1968).

——, *The Russian Secret Police: Muscovite, Imperial Russian and Soviet Political Security Operations, 1565–1970* (London, 1970).

——, *A Concise History of Russia* (London, 1972).

——, *Joseph Stalin: Man and Legend* (London, 1974).

——, *A New Life of Anton Chekhov* (London, 1976).

Hitler, Adolf, *Hitler's Table Talk, 1941–1944*, tr. by Norman Cameron and R. H. Stevens (London, 1953).

Ivan IV [the Terrible], Tsar, *Poslaniya Ivana Groznogo*, ed. V. P. Adrianova-Peretts (Moscow and Leningrad, 1951).

Jarintzov, N., *The Russians and Their Language* (Oxford, 1916).

Josselson, Harry H., *The Russian Word Count and Frequency Analysis of Grammatical Categories of Standard Literary Russian* (Detroit, 1953).

Karamzin, N. M., *Istoriya gosudarstva rossiyskago*, 12 vols (St Petersburg, 1852–3).

Katkov, George, *Russia 1917: The February Revolution* (London, 1967).

Keenan, Edward L., *The Kurbskii-Groznyi Apocrypha: The Seventeenth-Century Genesis of the 'Correspondence' Attributed to Prince A. M. Kurbskii and Tsar Ivan IV* (Cambridge, Mass., 1971).

Kennan, George, *Siberia and the Exile System*, 2 vols (London, 1891).

Kennan, George F., *The Marquis de Custine and His Russia in 1839* (London, 1972).

Khokhlov, Nikolai, *In the Name of Conscience*, tr. by Emily Kingsbury (London, 1960).

Khrushchev, Nikita S., *Khrushchev Remembers*, tr. and ed. Strobe Talbott (London, 1971).

——, *Khrushchev Remembers: The Last Testament*, tr. and ed. Strobe Talbott (Boston, 1974).

Kiparsky, Valentin, *English and American Characters in Russian Fiction* (Berlin, 1964).

Kirk, G. S., ed., *The Language and Background of Homer* (Cambridge, 1964).

Klyuchevsky, V. O., *Sochineniya*, 8 vols (Moscow, 1956–9).

Knipper, O. L., *Perepiska A. P. Chekhova i O. L. Knipper*, 2 vols, ed. A. B. Derman (Moscow, 1934, 1936).

Kohn, Hans, ed., *The Mind of Modern Russia: Historical and Political Thought of Russia's Great Age* (New Brunswick, 1955).

Leacock, Stephen, *Over the Footlights and Other Fancies* (London, 1923).

Lermontov, M. Yu., *Sobraniye sochineniy*, 4 vols (Moscow, 1957–8).

Leskov, N. S., *Sobraniye sochineniy*, 11 vols (Moscow, 1956–8).

Literaturnoye nasledstvo: Chekhov, ed. V. V. Vinogradov and others (Moscow, 1960).

Longworth, Philip, *The Cossacks* (London, 1971).

Mackenzie Wallace, D., *Russia*, 2 vols (London, 1877).

Mandelstam, Nadezhda, *Hope Against Hope* (New York, 1970).

Mead, Margaret, *Soviet Attitudes Towards Authority* (London, 1955).

Mehnert, Klaus, *The Anatomy of Soviet Man*, tr. by Maurice Rosenbaum (London, 1961).

Miliukov, Paul, *Outlines of Russian Culture, Part I: Religion and the Church*, ed. Michael Karpovich, tr. by Valentine Ughet and Eleanor Davis (Philadelphia, 1942).

Miller, Jack, *Life in Russia Today* (London, 1969).

Miller, Wright, *Russians as People* (London, 1960).

Mirsky, D. S., *A History of Russian Literature*, ed. Francis J. Whitfield (London, 1949).

Nabokov, Vladimir, *Speak Memory: An Autobiography Revised* (New York, 1966).

——, *Lolita: roman*, tr. into Russian by the author (New York, 1968).

Nechkina, M. V., *Dvizheniye dekabristov*, 2 vols (Moscow, 1955).

Nikitenko, A. V., *Dnevnik*, 3 vols (Moscow, 1955–6).

Nove, Alec, *Was Stalin Really Necessary? Some Problems of Soviet Political Economy* (London, 1964).

Olearius, Adam, *Podrobnoye opisaniye puteshestviya golshtinskogo posolstva v Moskoviyu i Persiyu v 1633, 1636 i 1639 godakh*, tr. by Pavel Barsov (Moscow, (1870).

Orlov, Alexander, *The Secret History of Stalin's Crimes* (London, 1954).

Oxford Chekhov, The, Chekhov's complete plays, and his fiction from 1888 onwards; tr. and ed. Ronald Hingley, to be completed in nine or more vols (London, 1964–   ), eight of which (1–3 and 5–9) have now (1977) been published.

Paléologue, Maurice, *An Ambassador's Memoirs, 1914–1917*, tr. by Frederick A. Holt (London, 1973).

Pares, Bernard, *Russia* (New York, 1943).

Pasternak, Boris, *Doktor Zhivago* (Milan, 1957).

Pipes, Richard, *Struve: Liberal on the Left* (Cambridge, Mass., 1970).

——, *Russia under the Old Regime* (London, 1974).

Pitcher, Harvey J., *Understanding the Russians* (London, 1964).

——, *The Chekhov Play: a New Interpretation* (London, 1973).

Pushkin, A. S., *Polnoye sobraniye sochineniy*, 10 vols (Moscow, 1956–8).

Raeff, Marc, *Michael Speransky: Statesman of Imperial Russia, 1772–1839* (The Hague, 1957).

—— (ed.), *Russian Intellectual History: An Anthology* (New York, 1966).

Redlikh, Roman, *Stalinshchina kak dukhovny fenomen* (Frankfurt-am-Main, 1971).

Rigby, T. H., Review of *Khrushchev Remembers* (1974), *Slavic Review* (Urbana, Illinois), vol. 34, no. 3, Sept. 1975.

Rush, Myron, *The Rise of Khrushchev* (Washington, D.C., 1958).

Sakharov, Andrei D., *Sakharov Speaks*, ed. and with a foreword by Harrison E. Salisbury (London, 1974).

Schlesinger, M. L., *Land und Leute in Russland*, 2nd ed. (Berlin, 1909).

Seton-Watson, Hugh, *The Russian Empire, 1801–1917* (Oxford, 1967).

Shaw, George Bernard, *Shaw on Stalin: A Russia Today Pamphlet* (London, 1941).

Simmons, Ernest J., ed., *Continuity and Change in Russian and Soviet Thought* (Cambridge, Mass., 1955).

Solovyov, S. M., *Istoriya Rossii s drevneyshikh vremyon*, 15 vols (Moscow, 1959–66).

Solzhenitsyn, Alexander, *Lenin in Zürich: Chapters*, tr. by H. T. Willetts (London, 1976).

Stalin, I. V., *Sochineniya*, vols 1–13 (Moscow, 1946–51); vols 14–16 (Stanford, 1967).

Starr, S. Frederick, *Decentralization and Self-Government in Russia, 1830–1870* (Princeton, 1972).

Steklov, Yu. M., *N. G. Chernyshevsky* (Moscow and Leningrad, 1928).

Strong, John W., ed., *The Soviet Union under Brezhnev and Kosygin* (New York, 1971).

Szamuely, Tibor, *The Russian Tradition* (London, 1974).

Tolstoy, L. N., *Sobraniye sochineniy*, 20 vols (Moscow, 1960–5).

Tourguéneff, N., *La Russie et les Russes*, 3 vols (Paris, 1847).

Tupper, Harmon, *To the Great Ocean: Siberia and the Trans-Siberian Railway* (London, 1965).

Turgenev, I. S., *Sobraniye sochineniy*, 12 vols (Moscow, 1954–8).

Tyutchev, F. I., *Stikhotvoreniya* (Berlin, 1921).

Vakar, Nicholas, *The Taproot of Soviet Society* (New York, 1961).

Vekhi: sbornik statey o ruskoy intelligentsii, 2nd ed. (Moscow, 1909).

Venturi, Franco, *Roots of Revolution: A History of the Populist and Socialist Movements in Nineteenth-Century Russia*, tr. by Francis Haskell (London, 1960).

Vernadsky, George, *A History of Russia* (New Haven, 1944).

——, *The Mongols and Russia* (New Haven, 1953).

Waliszewski, K., *Autour d'un trône: Catherine II de Russie* (Paris, 1913).

Walshe, M. O'C., *A Concise Russian Course* (London, 1949).

Westwood, J. N., *A History of Russian Railways* (London, 1964).

Wilson, Francesca, *Muscovy: Russia through Foreign Eyes, 1553–1900* (London, 1970).

Wittram, Reinhard, *Russia and Europe*, tr. by Patrick and Hanneluise Doran (London, 1973).

Woolf, Virginia, *The Common Reader*, 1st series (London, 1938).

INDEX

abortion, 153, 157

absolutism *see* autocracy

Academy of Sciences, 125

Aeschylus, 32

agriculture, 29, 38, 100, 149–50;
  see also peasant

alcohol, alcoholism, 45, 46–8, 71–2

Alexander I, Tsar, 80, 95, 98, 126,
  166, 172

Alexander II, Tsar, 15, 33, 153,
  167, 173, 174, 175, 178–9, 180,
  182, 216

Alexander III, Tsar, 94, 167, 174

Alexis, Tsar, 47, 60, 99, 165

aliens *see* foreigners

Americans *see* USA

anarchy, anarchism, 161, 165,
  169, 172, 176, 177, 198, 199

Andreyev, Leonid: 'Pan-Russian
  Vranyo' by, 77–8, 79; and
  Thought, 84

Anne, Empress, 35, 37, 124

anti-collectivism, 104–5

Archangel, 124

architecture, 38, 116

assassination, political, 15, 95, 166,
  167, 173–4, 175, 178–80, 181,
  182, 195, 204

Astrakhan, 159

atheism, 49, 111, 136, 183

Augustus, Emperor, 79

Auteroche, Abbé Chappe d', 155

authority, authoritarian rule, 14–15,
  32–3, 91–2, 99, 105, 106, 160–9,
  217; the family and, 153–4;
  intelligentsia and, 196–7;
  resistance to, 169–85; *see also*

dissidents; officials;
  totalitarianism

autocracy, 9, 35, 124, 162–9, 197;
  see also authority

Azef, Yevno, 181

aziatchina, 119

Baena, Duke de, *The Dutch Puzzle*
  by, 22–3

Bakunin, M., 177, 189, 203

Baltic states, 26, 116, 117, 118

Baptists, 112

Barghoorn, Frederick C., 217

Baring, Maurice, 137–8

Basil III, Grand Prince, 93, 163

begging, 81

Belfrage, Sally, 89–90

Belinsky, Vissarion, 163, 189, 195;
  open letter to Gogol of, 111

Belorussia, Belorussians, 26, 27

Benckendorff, General Count,
  124, 215

Berdyayev, Nicholas, 164, 188,
  191, 217

Beria, Lavrenty, 95, 100

Berkholz, Friedrich, 100

Berlin crisis, 42

bezalabershchina, 39, 169, 179

Biron, 124

birth control, 156

Black Hundreds, 183

Black Sea, 82

blat, 148

Blok, Alexander, *Scythians* by,
  119, 134

Bloody Sunday (9 January 1905),
  175, 181

(237)

'boards of shame', 74
bodrost, 75
Bogrov, Dmitry, 181
Bolshevik Revolution *see* Revolution (October 1917)
Bolsheviks, 40, 174, 181, 195, 199–201, 203–4
boredom (*ennui*), 17–20
boy-baba, 156
Brezhnev, Leonid, 42, 55, 81, 167, 206
bribery and corruption, 147, 148, 200, 203
British *see* English
Bukharin, Nicholas, 86, 96
Bulgakov, Michael, 10
Bulgakov, Sergey, 186, 187, 188, 192
Bulganin, Marshal, 85
Bunin, Ivan, 66–7, 70
bureaucrats *see* officials
Butler, Samuel, 80

Canada, 29, 30
Catherine I, Empress, 35, 172
Catherine II, 'the Great', Empress, 11, 15, 26, 28, 35, 79–80, 81, 92, 116–17, 124, 172, 175
Catholic Church, 120, 123, 130
Caucasus, Caucasians, 26, 30, 115, 118, 123, 171
censorship, 99–100, 167, 177, 184, 197, 201, 207; *see also* secretiveness
Central Asia, Central Asians, 26, 118, 130, 136
Central Committee of CPSU, 168
Chaadayev, Peter, 87, 120, 214; *First Philosophical Letter* by, 76–7
Chancellor, Richard, 114, 135
Chechens, 14, 16

Cheka, 203, 204
Chekhov, Anton, 17, 18, 24, 59, 64, 65–6, 90, 94, 106–7, 117, 127, 142, 150–1, 188, 189, 192, 197, 207–8, 210; works cited: *An Anonymous Story*, 65–6; *The Butterfly*, 55; *The Cherry Orchard*, 69, 107; *The Duel*, 124; *Fat and Thin*, 143; *Good-for-Nothings*, 150; *A Hard Case*, 50–1, 54; *A Lady with a Dog*, 20; *The Party*, 76; *Peasants*, 71, 151; *The Russian Master*, 54; *The Steppe*, 190–1; *Three Sisters*, 125
Chernyshevsky, Nicholas, 134, 155, 182, 189, 192, 195, 218; *What Is To Be Done?* by, 155, 184–5
Chicherin, G. V., 177
Chigirin, 174
childlike qualities of Russians, 35–6
children, 153, 157
chinopochitaniye, 146
chinovnik, 50, 109, 145, 146–7; *see also* officials
Christianity *see* Russian Orthodox Church
Chronicle of Current Events, 210
Church Slavonic, 88, 112
Churchill, Winston, 62
civil liberties, 96, 160, 210
civil servants *see* officials
Civil War (1918–21), 41, 98, 133, 150, 201, 202
classes, 31, 33, 115, 140–52, 164, 172, 185
clergy (priests), 105, 109, 111, 141
collective and state farming, 29, 38, 81, 88, 91, 102, 110, 151–2, 204
collectivism, 102–7

Pasternak, Boris, 131, 207, 208;
   Dr Zhivago by, 54, 207-8
patronymics, 52-3, 55
patriotism, 130-6, 139
Pauker, K. V., 11
Paul, Tsar, assassination of, 95,
   166, 172
peasants (muzhiks), 31, 34, 35,
   40-1, 67, 77, 81, 91, 102, 103,
   116, 141, 142-3, 166, 215;
   criticisms and tributes, 149-52;
   families, 152-3; German
   immigrant, 124-5; intelligentsia and, 194-6; laws
   concerning, 96; numerical
   importance of, 148-9; Orthodox
   Church and, 109-10, 111;
   relations with officials, 91-2,
   145, 146; and resistance to
   authority, 148, 165, 171, 172,
   173, 174, 175, 192, 193, 204,
   212; women, 154-5, 156
Perm, 57
Perovsky, Sophia, 178-9, 182
Peter I, the Great, Tsar, 12, 29,
   32, 36-7, 40, 47, 60, 96, 99,
   108, 115-16, 120, 141, 145,
   165-6, 167, 168, 217
Peter III, Tsar, 15, 108
Petrograd *see* Leningrad
Petrov *see* Ilf and Petrov
Pipes, Richard, 41, 177, 178
Pisarev, Dmitry, 193
Pisemsky, A. F., 189
Pitcher, Harvey, 36, 50, 72, 75
Pogodin, Michael, 135, 142
pokazukha, 80
Poles, Poland, 28, 114, 115, 123,
   132-3, 134, 136, 164, 165, 171
police agents/spies, 111, 122,
   180-1, 203
Politburo, 95
political demonstrations, 75

political disgrace, 95-6, 98-9, 112
political parties, 174
political police, 96, 122, 165,
   180-1, 203, 204, 211, 217
political prisoners, 94, 216-17
political secret societies, 179
population, 30-1
populists *see narodniki*
pornography, 158, 159
Potemkin, Prince, 11, 14, 80
Powell, Anthony, 61
pravda ('truth'), 90
Pravda, 73, 100
Preobrazhensky Prikaz (political
   police), 96
Presidium (CPSU), 156
press, 166-7, 177, 196-7
prestige projects, 36-8, 39, 105,
   201-2, 213
pretenders to the throne, 171, 172
priests *see* clergy
prisons, imprisonment, 94, 131,
   147, 153, 192-3, 203, 211, 213,
   214, 216-17
privacy, 106
Procurator of the Holy Synod,
   office of, 105, 109
professional associations, 106
proizvol, 16, 210
proletariat, 195-6; *see also*
   workers
propaganda, 133, 202, 203, 211,
   214
prostitution, 81, 159
Provisional Government (1917),
   196, 198, 199
pseudo-priests, 111
psychopatholitics, 176-85
public disgrace, attitude to, 71
Pugachov, Yemelyan, 161, 172,
   175
Pushkin, Alexander, 18, 24, 117,
   119, 124, 126, 131, 134, 137-8,